The Ideology of Max Weber

A Thomist Critique

E. B. F. MIDGLEY
Department of Politics,
University of Aberdeen

BARNES & NOBLE BOOKS
TOTOWA, NEW JERSEY

First published in the USA 1983 by
BARNES & NOBLE BOOKS
81 ADAMS DRIVE
TOTOWA, NEW JERSEY, 07512

ISBN: 0-389-20343-2

Library of Congress Cataloging in Publication Data

Midgley, E.B.F.
    The ideology of Max Weber.

    1. Weber, Max, 1864–1920. I. Title.
B3361.Z7M53 1982   193   82–16445

Printed in Great Britain

Contents

Preface

Shortly before the Second World War, there was published in the
United States an English translation of Simon Deploige's work under
the title *The Conflict between Ethics and Sociology*. The title could
have seemed provocative and have been thought to imply that the
disciplines of ethics and sociology as such were inherently incompatible
with each other. In fact, Deploige's work was a sober evaluation of the
philosophical or quasi-philosophical presuppositions of certain
sociologists — especially Durkheim and Lévy-Bruhl — to determine the
real extent of their disagreements with a philosophy of objective ethics.
Since that time, comparatively little work of this kind has been written
in English. Some writers whose work is not uncontaminated with
ideology have complained because Max Weber's ideology is not their
own. Even when a philosopher — such as my former teacher, Dorothy
Emmet — has chosen to write about Weber, it has been from a position
not uninfluenced by that moral relativism which tends to insinuate
itself, to some extent, almost everywhere. One of the few criticisms of
Weber from a natural law standpoint is the criticism offered in the
second chapter of Leo Strauss's *Natural Right and History*. Unfortunately, the positions of such critics as Strauss and Eric Voegelin are
found to be not free from internal contradictions and so a definitive
critique of Weber's ideology has remained to be undertaken. This book
is an attempt to indicate how such a critique should proceed.

I should like to acknowledge the permission given by Granada
Publishing Limited to reproduce some short passages which originally

appeared in my earlier book *The Natural Law Tradition and the Theory of International Relations*, Elek, London/Barnes and Noble, New York, 1975.

E.B.F.M.
University of Aberdeen
October 1982.

Introduction

If one were asked to cite two traditions apparently most influential amongst contemporary political sociologists, one might well cite the traditions initiated by Karl Marx and by Max Weber. Weber has been described, by one of his disciples, as the 'best-known and most important sociological theorist today'. If the adherents of the contemporary interpretations of Marxism would contest this claim, the disciples of Weber have not found the various formulations of the Marxist critique convincing. Weber's disciples have tended to recognise that Marxist social science is ultimately inseparable from a Marxist ideology which is its necessary complement. In finding themselves unwilling to accept an ideological social science of the Marxist type, Weber's disciples have maintained the superiority of Weber's social science and have built up an immense bibliography of critical studies and commentaries on his particular sociological investigations and on his supposedly scientific methodology. Although Weber's disciples have tended to reject, as prejudiced and unfounded, the Marxist view that Weber's teaching is ideological, these disciples have not failed to recognise that, in association with his specifically sociological teaching, there are not infrequent references to wider issues whose significance extends far beyond the field of 'scientific sociology'. A number of Weberian scholars have even sought to expound, and sometimes to praise, the 'extra-sociological' evaluations which they discern in Weber's works. Some have seen in Weber an exemplar of the defence of the values of the academic life against the attacks of 'radical scepticism and various forms of anti-intellectualism'.[1] Others have claimed to find in Weber a balanced and sober approach to the general problems of responsible political decision-making. Finally, some have come to argue that Weber provides some kind of intellectual basis for upholding the dignity of the human person in the conditions of our modern life.

This book is not directly concerned either with Weber's specific sociological studies or with his sociological methodology. They will only be adverted to the extent that this is helpful in exhibiting Weber's positions on wider 'extra-sociological' issues in a clearer light. No doubt some students of Weber may suggest that one ought not to concentrate upon the 'extra-sociological' elements or aspects of Weber's thought either because these would seem marginal to the main field of his interest and competency or because the task of analysing them is too elusive. Admittedly, there are relatively few passages in which Weber explicitly discusses fundamental 'extra-sociological' issues. Weber is not a profound philosopher: indeed, he is not even a philosopher *tout court*. However, since, as we have seen, Weber is sometimes regarded as an important 'maker of modern thought', the study of his thought on quasi-philosophical questions is undoubtedly worth undertaking. Moreover, it needs to be recognised that Weber's positions on such questions are at least to some extent implicit in many of his writings on a variety of subjects. In so far as Weber's fundamental views on 'value-choice' obscurely pervade so many of his writings, students of Weber will sometimes absorb these views — by a process of intellectual osmosis — in the course of reading his sociology. Certainly, it is desirable to find out what is being absorbed through this process.

In seeking to detect and to analyse Weber's quasi-philosophical positions, Weber's sociological statements which invariably accompany them will obviously be noticed. Consequently, the reader may conclude that this critical evaluation of Weber's 'extra-sociological' positions must have some implications for the evaluation of Weber's sociological methodology. While there is no doubt that this is the case there will be no attempt to give a serious exposition of any such implications in this book. The task of eliminating ideological distortions from sociological studies by redeveloping sociological methodology in a way which is not inconsistent with the philosophical principles which have been employed here can be left to others.

There appear to be at least two related reasons why Weber's fundamental 'extra-sociological' positions are found to be, in some way, inextricably connected with his sociological methodology. One is that Weber does not accept the claim of philosophy to evaluate the place of the special sciences in the entire field of knowledge. The other reason is that, although Weber knows that his 'value-judgements' are logically distinct, in his system, from his sociological statements, he nevertheless proceeds as if the sociologist *qua* sociologist is somehow better equipped than most people [other things being equal] to make an informed judgement on wider quasi-philosophical issues. Nevertheless, when Weber rejects the view that there is such a thing as theoretical or practical wisdom and when he denies that there is a true intellectual harmony between wisdom and the special sciences, he cannot claim to be passing judgement in his specific capacity as a sociologist. When Weber passes his adverse judgements not only against philosophical and theological wisdom but against the bulk of preceding philosophies and against all theology, he is necessarily putting forward either some new philosophy or some kind of substitute or replacement for philosophy. It will be argued in this book that the substitute for philosophy which Weber invents is properly characterised as his ideology.

At this point, it seems fitting to make some preliminary observations in reply to the objection, offered by some commentators, that Weber was not an ideologist. In particular, it is noticed that Talcott Parsons has suggested that there is a sense in which it can be said that 'Weber heralded "the end of ideology" '.[2] Parsons seems to have had in mind that certain supposedly ideological currents — which he characterises politically as 'conservative', 'liberal' and 'socialist' — might be expected to be superseded and that Weber's own positions may have a role in dissolving these alignments to prepare the way, perhaps, for some kind of cultural unification. Whatever may be the case with these reflections on the present and possible future which Parsons here adduces, the question remains: Are the positions of Weber (whether adopted as the ideology of a party or as the postulates of a wider movement of human culture) basically ideological in character? In order to give a definitive answer to this question, it will be necessary to arrive at a definition of ideology and this is done in chapter 2.

Meanwhile, it is interesting to note how Parsons will understand the 'comprehension' of the ideologies of the time which he supposes Weber to have undertaken. He suggests that Weber achieved a position which clearly transcended all of the three ideologically central positions in such a way as to include in relativised form contributions from all of them.[3] It is important to observe that this so-called *transcendence* is understood by Parsons in terms of his own assessment of the constitutive importance which Weber's intellectual orientation may be thought to have in defining the situation for the emerging social world. The main point that should be stressed here is not the fact that Talcott Parsons adopts a particular kind of evolutionary perspective which is not that of Max Weber. The more fundamental point to be recognised is that, when Parsons writes of 'transcendence', he merely means a supposed actual surmounting of certain actual cultural divergences in a particular historical phase. This is not the sense in which a good philosopher would normally speak of 'transcending ideology'. For him, the thought which transcends ideology is a fundamental truth found at an intellectual level superior to that of the conflicting ideologies. Hence it claims to possess a validity which ideology cannot rightly claim. By contrast, Parsons's analysis cannot — and does not — pretend that Weber's enterprise went further than an attempt to assimilate (as it were) certain other ideologies at the intellectually defective level of ideology itself.

Serious studies of those thoughts of Weber which venture upon the domain of philosophy and theology are much less numerous and extensive than exegetical and critical studies of his sociological methodology. Nevertheless, most of the relevant facts about the content of Weber's substitute 'philosophy' have already been noted. Despite certain disagreements about details of interpretation of Weber's 'philosophy', it does not appear to be mere scholarship that is notably lacking in the more penetrating studies of Weber's system. When A.W. Gouldner likens Weberian man to a Minotaur, when W.J. Mommsen observes Weber's antinomies concerning freedom and dominance and when Raymond Aron expounds Weber's perspective upon the irreconcilable conflicts of the gods, they are providing us with the data which scholarship can provide. Yet they fail to provide something which scholarship alone cannot provide. Those scholars who praise Weber's 'philosophy' (and some who do not) do not fail to see that there are basic contradictions in it. They know that it is a philosophy which does not attempt to teach fundamental truth but they are commonly reluctant to concede that such a philosophy must be false. If they sometimes come close to admitting this, they cannot really explain what has gone wrong or what needs to be done to put it right. Since it appears that even the more serious philosophical critics, Eric Voegelin and Leo Strauss, have not adequately accomplished this unfulfilled task, there is an attempt to deal with it in this book.

Let us begin then by making a few introductory observations about the philosophical perspective of this critical evaluation of Weber's teaching. Certainly, there will be an attempt to bring out the defectiveness of Weber's thought by the juxtaposition of incompatible formulations in his own writings as far as possible. However, it is recognised that it is not possible to give an adequate philosophical criticism of the error in the work of any thinker exclusively in terms of that thinker's own statements and admissions. Moreover, since it will be argued that Weber's 'philosophy' is not an unsuccessful search for fundamental truth but is substantially ideological in character, it is necessary to consider those disordered aspirations, desires or 'needs' which lead Weber to fabricate his ideological rationalisations. More particularly, the paradoxes (occasioned by the various distorting factors already mentioned) which comprise the intellectual content of Weber's ideology will be considered. All these will be assessed in the light of permanent philosophical truth.

The paradoxes of Weber will not be regarded (as the Kantians and the Structuralists regard the antinomies with which they are concerned) as if they were inherent in the human mind. There will be an endeavour to show that they are merely quasi-permanent errors in Weber's ideological system. Of course, it may be objected that, since it is both possible and desirable to study Weber's sociological methodologies developmentally,[4] it is not necessarily appropriate to try to characterise quasi-permanent ideological errors in Weber's system since these errors manifest themselves *pari passu* with his sociological development. Again, it may be argued that Weber's ideological formulations might well be considered correlatively with the concrete exigencies of his professional life, the particular circumstances of his involvement in German politics and the unusual character of his domestic life.

Without ignoring these considerations, there will be more concern with those features of the content of Weber's ideology which bring us face to face with basic philosophical or quasi-philosophical problems. It is relevant here to state the conclusion that has been formed that Weber's ideological thinking is not simply a supposedly tenable position or even a series of different supposedly tenable positions but is essentially a continuing *problem* whose solution — given the limits within which his thought moves — can never be a real solution. Accordingly, the general lines of Weber's ideology — whatever tactical shifts and modifications may be found in it — can be defined by certain quasi-permanent parameters in his thought.

It is evident that it will not be enough merely to situate the ideology of Weber in the local context of his own German contemporaries. Moreover, that method of scholarship which would require us to enter into the thought being examined in such a way that to 'understand' everything would be tantamount to being unable to criticise anything will not be adopted. In order to explain what Weber is really doing and to state objectively what is wrong with Weber's ideology, it is necessary to undertake some kind of reconstruction of his thought.[5] The intention in attempting such a reconstruction is to represent authentically the parameters which Weber's ideology presupposes and whose retention renders certain problems or pseudo-problems inevitable and insoluble within his system. The question may be raised as to whether any such representation, however well intentioned, will prove to be a misrepresentation. Certainly, it would serve no reasonable purpose to promote an adverse criticism of Weber's ideology by first reducing it to a caricature of itself. However, to renounce every kind of reconstruction would be to impose upon oneself an arbitrary requirement to keep within the closed circle of Weber's own thought and thus be unable to find the terms (outside that closed circle) which are needed for an objective criticism.

Some might suppose that these considerations give rise to an insoluble dilemma whereby the philosophical critic must choose between two unsatisfactory alternatives: either a scholarly exegesis which succumbs promiscuously to whatever doctrine is being studied or an objective philosophical criticism which can only be attained by forsaking scholarly exegesis. Yet, on examination, this supposed dilemma proves to be unreal. The reconstruction of Weber's ideology, which philosophical objectivity requires, yields not an unjustified caricature but an exposition of what is really involved in Weber's paradoxes which is more intelligible than what is provided in the formulations of Weber himself. Certainly, such a reconstruction may be difficult to accomplish and perhaps such reconstructions are rarely done well. Moreover, it would hardly be worth attempting unless it is to be undertaken in the perspective of perennial philosophical truth.

Let us consider one or two examples to illustrate the principles of philosophical criticism which have been mentioned. Let us consider whether it is legitimate for the philosophical critic to assert that Hegel is an intellectual opponent of logic and of Christianity. Similarly, let us ask whether Nietzsche can properly be called a nihilist or Weber an ideologist. Certainly, the scholar who has been seduced by the fascination of his subjects of study may complain that Hegel did not oppose logic and Christianity but redefined or reinterpreted them. Similarly, he might argue that Nietzsche cannot be called a nihilist because he sought to overcome nihilism and that Weber cannot be called an ideologist because he did not choose to designate himself as an ideologist. The philosophical critic will reject these objections. He will observe that it was precisely in seeking to redefine radically or reinterpret an objective discipline (logic) and an objective revelation (Christianity), which are not susceptible to being so redefined and reinterpreted, that Hegel showed himself to be an opponent of them both. Similarly, the philosophical critic will point out that, since Nietzsche assimilated an erroneous nihilism (instead of refuting it) and then sought to 'overcome' it in a misguided and impossible way, he can be properly said to have remained subject to nihilism. Finally, although Weber did not describe his 'substitute philosophy' of value-choice as an ideology, he did make certain admissions and concessions which enable the philosophical critic to infer rightly that he was an ideologist. Consequently, in the study of Weber — as in the other two cases — there is no real conflict between the task of denying the fundamental validity of the thought under examination and the task of intelligently understanding the reasons — given certain points of departure — why the erroneous doctrine came to be manifested as it did.

Writing of the intellectual situation of our times, Jean Daniélou has observed that:

> at present, there is a perversion of intelligence: it is of a triple order. It consists either in a certain flattening of intelligence to the level of pure scientific positivism, or in the claim of freedom to be self-sufficient and not to recognise anything above it or beyond it, or finally in a scepticism that sees in values the expression of passing cultures and does not recognise any permanent truth.[6]

In ways of his own, Weber participates in all these three forms of intellectual perversion and they are all included — with other elements — in the ideological synthesis which he fabricates. Accordingly, Weber's ideology, once it has been properly understood, will be seen to exemplify perhaps more comprehensively than many of the others, the eventual futility of ideological thinking as such. Certainly, it will be argued that there is a sense in which Weber's ideology is a closed system from which he apparently failed to escape. Nevertheless, this system is surrounded by a penumbra of hesitations, anxieties and ambiguities. There are moments in which Weber's troubled mind could hardly avoid entertaining uneasy suspicions about his ideological commitments. This well-founded anxiety does not seem to have borne good fruit in Weber's own writings but it serves as a signpost for those who come afterwards. For, in refuting Weber's ideology, we do justice to whatever remained healthy in his natural inclination to know fundamental truth which, in its metaphysical root, is indestructible in human nature and indestructible therefore in Max Weber himself.

Notes and references

1   See *Scholarship and Partisanship: Essay on Max Weber*, R. Bendix and G. Roth (eds.), University of California Press, 1971, Introduction, chapters III, V.
2   T. Parsons, 'Value-freedom and Objectivity: "Weber and the Problem of Ideology" ' in *Max Weber and Sociology Today*, O. Stammer (ed.), Oxford, 1971, p.48.
3   Ibid., p.49.
4   See, for example, J. Rex, 'Typology and Objectivity: A Comment on Weber's Four Sociological Methods' in *Max Weber and Modern Sociology*, Sahay (ed.), London, 1971.
5   In what follows, I have sought to indicate implicitly some points of agreement and disagreement with Copleston's observations on the

philosophical historian's reconstruction of the history of philosophy in his book *Philosophers and Philosophies*, London/New York, 1976.

6   Jean Daniélou, 'Crisis of Freedom — Crisis of Intelligence' in *L'Osservatore Romano*, weekly edition in English, 1 June 1972.

1 Philosophical critiques of Weber by Eric Voegelin and Leo Strauss

Although it has already been suggested that the philosophical critiques of Weber advanced by Voegelin[1] and Strauss[2] are neither complete nor fully satisfactory in themselves, it would appear nevertheless that these two critics have done more than most others writing in English to awaken doubts about the reasonableness of Weber's fundamental doctrine. It would not be fitting to make use of their work — and especially that of Strauss — without an acknowledgement of being indebted to them. Accordingly, this study will begin by briefly summarising the basic positions underlying their main criticisms of Weber in order then to distinguish between those of their positions which appear to provide a secure foundation for further evaluation of Weber and those positions which seem to be faulty or incomplete. A fuller discussion of the substantive points at issue will be given in the author's critique of Weber in later chapters.

Voegelin's critique of Weber

Although, as a young man, Voegelin 'was under Weber's spell',[3] this did not prevent him from advancing subsequently a criticism of Weber's failure to uphold politics as a 'science of order'. However, Voegelin does not appear to have wholly freed himself from certain paradoxes which are not entirely unconnected with the paradoxes of Weber's own teaching. Nevertheless, in his search for politics as a 'science of order', Voegelin deprecates the exclusion of the *scientia prima* from the realm of reason.[4] He surmises that 'we may arrive in the course of our endeavours at the theory that the justice of the human order depends on its participation in the Platonic Agathon, or the Aristotelian Nous or the Stoic Logos, or the Thomistic *ratio aeterna*'. Voegelin supposes that 'For one reason or another none of these theories may satisfy us completely, but we know that we are in search for an answer of this type'.[5] Accordingly, Voegelin regards any attempt at the sociological reduction of the politics of Plato, Aristotle or St Thomas to the rank of 'values' amongst others as self-defeating.[6] Voegelin suggests that classic philosophy together with scholastic theology constituted 'the major and certainly the decisive part of Western intellectual culture'.[7] Voegelin apparently recognises in mediaeval Christianity 'the belief in a rational science of human social order and especially of natural law'. He says that 'this science was not simply a belief but was actually elaborated as a work of reason'.[8] However, we find that Voegelin holds positions which are logically incompatible with the Thomistic teaching on both the natural law and the eternal law.

Aristotle, Cicero and Aquinas had taught that the moral virtues are connected and perfected only in the presence of the virtue of prudence or practical wisdom.[9] When Voegelin claims to be defending the 'moral virtues' of '*sophia* or *prudentia*' against subversion by those whom he characterises as gnostics, he does not simply uphold that classical and Christian teaching on prudence which is fundamentally incompatible with Machiavelli's teaching on political prudence. In fact, Voegelin names Machiavelli as a 'great political thinker who recognised the structure of reality' and who was branded with others 'as an immoralist by Gnostic intellectuals'. Voegelin purports to reconcile this Machiavellian element of his thought with an interpretation of '*sophia* or *prudentia*' which he claims to find in classic and Christian ethics.[10] Observing this, we are bound to conclude that Voegelin's 'science of order' is somewhat ambiguous. He says that the 'life of the spirit is the source of order in man and society'.[11] However, he is not only afraid of arrogating 'the quality of a divine command to a human velleity'[12] but is also unable to give a satisfactory account of the relation of the order of human activity in the world to the natural and divine order.[13] Voegelin's failure to expound the natural moral law in relation to its origin from God the Author of human nature is apparently connected with his theory that the temporal sphere of power is a sphere of power that is 'radically de-divinised'.[14] Certainly, Christianity can be said to have 'de-divinised' the temporal order in so far as it rejected the illusions of polytheism and pantheism and thus denied the pagan gods of the city. On the other hand, the Judaeo-Christian doctrine of the

2

transcendence of the one true God does not exclude the presence of that God from the world that He has created.

Voegelin's teaching on 'de-divinisation' apparently comprises a pastiche of Christian and atheistic elements. Since the atheistic element in this pastiche is not unrelated to Max Weber's atheistic doctrine of the so-called 'disenchantment' of the world, we may surmise that Voegelin's critique of Weber's atheistic ideology is incomplete and that he actually participates to some degree in some of the errors of Weber himself. By contrast, according to St Thomas's teaching, political authority as such has its ultimate origin from God as the Author of human nature and the natural law.[15] St Thomas upholds the true harmony of a political morality in accord with a theistic natural law which is itself in harmony with the truth of the Christian faith. In so far as Voegelin implicitly rejects this synthesis, he seems to envisage two possible types of supposedly Christian morality: first, 'a not-too-well-defined Christian "other worldly" morality'[16] (which Voegelin himself rejects) and a worldly Christian/Machiavellian 'morality' (another not-too-well-defined type which Voegelin is disposed to accept). This typology of morality seems roughly to consist in a supposedly non-atheistic or Christian version of Weber's secularistic typology of the 'ethics of intention or ultimate ends' and the 'ethics of responsibility'. Again, it would appear that Voegelin has not distanced himself sufficiently from Weber's atheistic system to be able to under-take an authentically theistic natural law critique of that system.

Voegelin's failure to advance a coherent doctrine of the relation of political philosophy and divine revelation is signalled when he begins his study *The New Science of Politics* with a quotation from Richard Hooker. Logically, it would have been necessary for Hooker to have chosen between the claims of what he had derived from the tradition of St Thomas Aquinas and the claims of what he had derived from the tradition of Marsilius of Padua.[17] To pose the problem in Aristotelian terms, it would have been necessary for Hooker to conclude, without ambiguity, whether political prudence may dictate to theoretical wisdom what it ought to think about the highest things or whether it may not.[18] Voegelin seems to share Hooker's lack of clarity on this point. Although Voegelin opposes the Hobbesian doctrine of the arbitrary authority of the State over the content of faith and morals,[19] he also says that 'a government has a duty to preserve the order as well as the truth which it represents'.[20] The problem, which Voegelin does not quite squarely face, arises from the fact that Hooker's own justification of the Elizabethan religious settlement did not avoid Erastianism. Voegelin would apparently prefer to avoid the difficulty: it might be better, he thinks, if the discussion of divine things were confined to the wise.[21] Nevertheless, he seems to accept that, once the discussion has been taken up by the vulgar, then, if it could not end with agreement by persuasion, it 'would have to be closed by government authority'.[22] Yet suppose that the Elizabethan government closure is operated not only against those puritans whom Voegelin condemns as gnostic revolutionaries but also against the Church instituted by Jesus Christ: what then?

We shall find that Max Weber's ideological rejection of Christianity presupposes that the acceptance of divine revelation involves an 'intellectual sacrifice' of reason. Voegelin does not seem to be in a position to provide an adequate refutation of this Weberian presupposition. Voegelin rightly insists that the natural order is incomplete and that it needs to be open to that which is divine and transcendent. He also rightly insists that divine revelation is a mystery and that the divine truth cannot be fully comprehended or mastered by man in this life. If Voegelin had confined himself to such statements as these, his teaching could have been reconciled with the teaching of St Thomas Aquinas. Departing drastically from Aquinas, however, Voegelin makes the unjustified supposition that the mysteriousness of divine revelation precludes the dogmatic definition by the Church of the articles of faith.[23] Voegelin insists that 'Uncertainty is the very essence of Christianity'.[24] He writes of the constancy of a tension between truth and untruth as if the persevering attempt to find truth and to separate it from untruth would somehow tend to destroy the reality of human existence.[25] Indeed, he even writes of the 'murderous possession of the truth' as if there were something evil in seeking to find it unalloyed with error.

It is true that Voegelin will advance an incisive critique of those 'modern gnostics', especially Nietzsche and Marx, who reject the truth of a transcendent divine principle and who promote a false ideological 'certitude'.[26] However, Voegelin is not content to oppose the false 'certainties' which are advanced in defiance of the divine truth; he also seems to reject the certainty rightly claimed for the divine truth itself. It may be conceded that some of the ideas advanced within the broad ambit of the Christianities, which Voegelin condemns as gnostic errors, are ideas incompatible with the Christian revelation. For example, Voegelin rejects as gnostic errors the deviant teaching of the mediaeval writer Joachim de Flora. Similarly, Voegelin characterises elements of the Protestant Reformation (especially Puritanism) as the undesirable invasion of Western institutions by 'Gnostic movements'.[27] Nevertheless, it would appear that Voegelin's brand of anti-gnostic teaching is in part anti-Christian.

In a balanced appraisal of the theology of R. Bultmann, L. Malevez eventually concludes that Bultmann 'cannot escape the charge of having made an attack upon the very substance of Christianity'.[28] If an appraisal on a similar scale were to be made of the theological presuppositions of Voegelin's new science of politics, it is to be feared that a similar verdict would be unavoidable. Bultmann claims that St Paul and St John advanced in their writings in the New Testament the first attempts at 'demythologising'. At the same time, Bultmann cannot deny that what he calls 'undemythologised' Christianity is still to be found in the works of the two apostles. Malevez very properly concentrates upon Bultmann's claim that St Paul and St John are, as it were, the precursors of Bultmann and demonstrates the absurdity of that claim. That which, in St Paul and St John, is dubbed by Bultmann, as not Christian but of gnostic and Hellenistic origin,[29] is in reality that which has been Christian belief from the beginning. Unfortunately, Voegelin, like Bultmann, presumes to be more Christian than the Apostles themselves when he asserts that 'Gnosis was an accompaniment of Christianity from its very beginnings: its traces are to be found in St Paul and St John'.[30] Voegelin goes further and suggests that 'gnostic influence and terminology are indeed so clearly recognisable in St Paul that they must stem from a powerful movement in existence before his time'.[31]

It would appear therefore that Voegelin's arrows fall somewhat indiscriminately not only upon ancient gnostics, Protestant sectarians and modern atheistic ideologists such as Nietzsche and Marx but also upon the Catholic teaching of the Apostles and their successors up to the present day.[32] Like Bultmann, Voegelin does not avoid rejecting much of the substance of Christianity in the course of a somewhat confused reaction against gnosticism. Voegelin agrees with the Christian revelation in holding that the consummation of the Christian life is to be found in the life after death.[33] But Voegelin seems unwilling to accept Christian teaching on such matters as the real presence of Christ in the sacraments and the special providence of God in upholding the infallibility of the universal Church. Voegelin seems to be unwilling to entertain seriously the possibility that God has provided an ecclesial *magisterium* because he fears that this belief may be only an illusion begotten by an inordinate human desire for 'certainty' whether true or false. He does not consider that the rejection of the possibility of certainty may often derive from an inordinate human fear which does not wish to encounter the unambiguous demands of God Himself.

Voegelin's critique of the relentless atheistic ideologies of Nietzsche and Marx has been influenced in part by writers such as Henri de Lubac and Hans Urs von Balthasar who do not share Voegelin's own idiosyncratic view of Christianity and man's relation to God. Voegelin is not mistaken when he discerns that Nietzsche and Marx proceed as though from an initial prejudice to the effect that human nature is constituted in a way that is fundamentally wrong. Voegelin is also right when he discerns that both Nietzsche and Marx seek presumptuously to achieve the ontological transformation of man into a new kind of being by means which are invented purely by man himself. Accordingly, Voegelin rightly criticises the false 'certitudes' of Nietzsche and Marx as the erroneous substitutes which modern atheism provides in place of God, morality and Christianity itself.[34] On the other hand, Voegelin's own account of man as necessarily subject to a tension between truth and untruth leads us to ask whether or not Voegelin's own system implies that there is an inherent paradox in human nature itself. There appears to be no really adequate response to this question in the writings of Voegelin. Accordingly, however justified may be his attacks on those gnostics, ancient and modern, who seek presumptuously to achieve a human self-deliverance from what they suppose to be wrong with the human essence, Voegelin is not in a position to propose a truly definitive critique of the starting point of gnosticism, namely, the supposition that human nature is inherently paradoxical and disordered. This is the reason why Voegelin is unable to provide a definitive critique of Weber's ambiguous, uncertain and somewhat inconclusive search for a secularistic ideological response to the supposed paradox of human existence. Weber's paradoxical system is, in some respects at least, a kind of secularistic counterpart of the paradoxical philosophical/theological system of Voegelin himself. Any debate between Voegelin and the disciples of Weber would tend to end in a stalemate. Despite the validity of so much of Voegelin's criticism of Weber, Weber's disciples would be in a position to argue, not entirely without reason, that the specific form or type of Voegelin's philosophical and Christian theology is an idiosyncratic type selected subjectively as one private value-choice amongst others.

Leo Strauss's critique of Weber

Strauss's critique of Weber seems to surpass that of Voegelin in two respects. First, Strauss, unlike Voegelin, does recognise that Machiavellianism is an intellectual and moral evil which, in one form or another, is ubiquitous in the erroneous intellectual enterprises of modernity. Secondly, Strauss's critique has the advantage that it is not complicated by the presuppositions of a rather idiosyncratic form of Protestantism. Unfortunately, as we shall see, Strauss's analysis of Weber suffers from certain other disadvantages.

Strauss rejects the various waves of the increasingly radical intellectual enterprise of modernity from Machiavelli, Hobbes and Locke, through Rousseau, Kant and Hegel to its culmination in Nietzsche.[35]

It would therefore seem to follow that Strauss is in a good position to detect and to criticise the Machiavellian, Kantian and Nietzschean themes to be found in Weber's thought. Certainly, Strauss does advance powerful criticisms against these themes in Weber but, at significant points, his attack is blunted. Although Strauss undertakes a profound, subtle and extensive criticism of Machiavelli as a teacher of evil whose positions are deeply incompatible with classical political philosophy, we find that, at a crucial point, Strauss himself fails to reject an important thesis of Machiavelli.

Strauss's fatal concession to Machiavellianism is occasioned by the fact that his thought is troubled by a certain pessimism — albeit a noble pessimism — about the consequences of the rise of modern technology.[36] Of course, it would not be reasonable to assert gratuitously that the enterprise of modern technological development will not, in fact, end in a temporal disaster. If Strauss were inclined merely to emphasise the dangers rather than the opportunities of modern technology, this emphasis would not necessarily bring in its train any basic philosophical problems. Unfortunately, there lurks in Strauss's tendency to pessimism something which is more than a matter of emphasis. In the midst of his learned defence of classical political philosophy against Machiavelli, Strauss's anxiety about technological innovation is seen to have a deeper root.

Having indicated that the classical writers recommended a strict moral-political supervision of inventions, Strauss observes that these writers themselves were forced to make one crucial exception. Strauss suggests that the necessity of encouraging inventions pertaining to the art of war meant that in an important respect the good city had to take its bearings by the practice of bad cities. It is at this crucial point that Strauss fails to make the necessary distinction between those military means which are technologically powerful but not immoral and those military means — either technologically powerful or not — which are immoral. Strauss seems to signal his failure to appreciate this distinction in so far as he eventually concedes to the Machiavellians in the specific field of military technology that: 'Machiavelli's contention that the good cannot be good because there are so many bad ones proves to possess a foundation'.[37]

Although Strauss seems to seek to excuse his concession to Machiavelli by arguing that this concession had already been made by classical authors in antiquity, this excuse does not constitute a valid justification. In truth, the concession to Machiavelli on the subject of war is a symptom of a serious weakness in Strauss's critique of Machiavellianism. Moreover, if Strauss's criticism of Machiavellianism is defective, his criticism of the Machiavellianism of Max Weber will also be correspondingly inadequate.

Strauss is an opponent of the modern theories of individualism and of the social contract advanced by Hobbes, Locke, Rousseau and others. This would seem to indicate that Strauss is well placed to refute Weber's individualism and Weber's rejection of the classical and Christian teaching on the common good of the political society. Certainly Strauss is critical of Weber's political theory but he fails to uphold properly the doctrine of the common good against Weber because his own thought about the common good is in some way ambiguous.[38] This ambiguity seems to arise from the coexistence, in Strauss's thought, of a utopian perspective and a peculiar perspective on practical politics which are severally and jointly not reconcilable with a valid political philosophy founded upon the doctrine of the common good.

Strauss derives his utopianism from a certain reading of Plato and he derives his approach to practical politics from a certain reading of Aristotle. From these readings, Strauss formulates a deep distinction between theory and practice which would appear to be not compatible with either Platonism or Aristotelianism. Strauss's utopianism rests heavily upon Plato's preoccupation with a so-called 'divine madness' which Strauss considers to be a virtue of the intellect. Strauss does not seek to perfect Aristotle's philosophy but rather to diminish the nobility of the Aristotelian teaching. Having thus diminished it, Strauss then has recourse 'to an acceptance *by contract*'[39] of Aristotle's polity which he supposes to be essentially inferior to that of Plato. Strauss explains his teaching on practical politics when he argues that the allegiance we may need to give to the 'essentially inferior polity' is derived from 'a compromise of reason with unreason, of wisdom with folly'.

All this means that Strauss is not in a very strong position to correct Weber on the question of individualism and the common good. It also means that Strauss is at some disadvantage in seeking to refute the views of Machiavelli, Nietzsche and Weber about a supposed political 'realism' and its supposed alternative of ethical 'idealism' which are both, in reality, philosophically unjustified. Strauss is in difficulties in considering the Machiavellian and post-Machiavellian distinctions between 'realism' and 'idealism' because he is not in a position to reject them in the thorough-going way in which they are rejected by Jacques Maritain. Maritain points out rightly that, in order to keep oneself free from the evils of Machiavellianism, it is necessary not only to refute Machiavelli's political 'realism' but also to deny the modernist suggestion that the only alternative to the Machiavellian 'realism' is an ineffectual and even unfounded notion of ethical 'idealism'.[40] Strauss would want to distinguish his utopianism from this bogus ethical 'idealism' and also to distinguish his 'compromise of wisdom with folly' in practical politics from the Machiavellian 'realism'. Nevertheless, his argument on these points could hardly be developed in an entirely satisfactory way.

It is true that Strauss cannot reconcile himself to Weber's neo-Machiavellian 'ethics of responsibility'. Similarly, Strauss is bound to reject the presupposition (namely that ethical convictions are merely subjective value-choices) which underlies Weber's characterisation of the type of 'ethics of conviction'. Nevertheless, Strauss is not in a position to deliver a definitive judgement against Weber's ideological sociology of ethics. Strauss will rightly criticise Weber for his erroneous rejection of the natural law and for his assertion of the heterogeneity of ethics but he will be exposed to criticism in his turn because his own doctrine of natural law is in a certain way elusive and uncertain. Although Strauss is not an atheist, his teaching on natural law is not theistic. Indeed, he seeks to exclude from the sphere of natural law not only the authority of God but even the 'authority' of those norms built into human nature by God. Strauss insists upon taking human nature as a 'standard' apparently in the sense that man is the ultimate measure of the natural law.[41] Since Strauss nevertheless seeks to uphold the reality and the truth of the eternal order against the errors of modernity, it would appear that Strauss's attitude towards the eternal order is hesitant and ambivalent.[42]

Certainly, Strauss has undertaken an extensive critical attack upon Weber's distinction between facts and values. Since Strauss seeks very generally to uphold both nature and truth against the modernist sub-version, he is unwilling to acquiesce in Weber's purported detachment of values from both nature and truth. However, in order to see the relation between facts and values in a true light, it seems necessary to have a correct philosophical understanding of the relation between being and goodness. It might be possible to go further and suggest that the philosophical treatment *par excellence* of this important subject is to be found in St Thomas Aquinas.[43] The conclusion might eventually be reached not only that Strauss does not accept Aquinas's teaching on being and goodness but also that Strauss's perspective on the relation of being and goodness is not fully intelligible.

Strauss is generally committed to opposing the modernist revolt against wisdom and he will wish to criticise Weber's rejection of both theoretical and practical wisdom. This means that Strauss will raise objections against the paradoxes and contradictions which result from this modernist — and, more specifically, Weberian — attack on wisdom. Unfortunately, however, Strauss's own thought about wisdom is beset by paradoxes and contradictions arising from his own readings of certain *pre*-modern formulations of wisdom. His difficulties concerning wisdom are somewhat complex. He holds that wisdom is twofold:

philosophical wisdom (found in his reading of Plato) and revealed wisdom (disclosed in his reading of Judaism). Each is held to be in some ways self-contradictory and each is logically incompatible with the other.[44]

It is evident that Strauss is entangled in what he would regard as *pre*-modern paradoxes and contradictions concerning wisdom. Moreover, these are the defects, supposedly endemic in the ancient wisdoms, which, in his view, give rise to the erroneous intellectual enterprise of modernity. It is true that Strauss takes the view that the paradoxes of pre-modernity are less malignant than the paradoxes of modernity which succeed them. Nevertheless, Strauss is obviously hampered, in his critique of Weber, by the fact that he himself is not in a position to provide a definitive defence against the charge that the concept of wisdom is absurd.

Accordingly, Strauss envisages modernity as a series of vain attempts to reconcile — on a progressively more secularised basis — the supposedly irreconcilable principles of reason and revelation. His difficulties in refuting the diagnoses and pseudo-solutions of this modernist predicament, advanced by writers such as Weber and Nietzsche, derive partly, as we have just seen, from the fact that his general perspective would make it impossible to achieve any solution to the problem of the mutual relations of reason and revelation. In addition, however, Strauss has a particular difficulty about fully entering into the task of criticising the paradoxes of those secular thinkers whose thought proceeds by way of an abandonment but also a transvaluation of Christianity. As a Jew, Strauss is committed to the view that there is no such thing, properly understood, as the Judaeo-Christian tradition. On the other hand, if there really *is* such a thing as the Judaeo-Christian tradition, Strauss is inevitably hampered to some extent in giving a complete account of the real significance of the revolt against — and the transvaluation of — that tradition in the intellectual enterprise of modernity.

One example of Strauss's difficulty in entering into the task of evaluating the rejection or the transvaluation of Christianity is the treatment of Hobbes in his early book on Hobbes's political philosophy. E.J. Roesch observed that, in this early work of Strauss, 'there is a peculiar point of view from which this modern revolt appears as a movement against the classical tradition rather than against the Christian tradition ...'.[45] (Roesch himself takes the view that Hobbes reacts primarily against the Christian tradition and only secondarily against the classical tradition.) A later illustration of a certain diffidence on the part of Strauss in fully entering into the understanding of the revolt of modernity against Christianity is perhaps to be found in his elegant and perceptive paper on Nietzsche's *Beyond Good and*

Evil.[46] Strauss knows that there is something impure in Nietzsche which may be given the courtesy title of Nietzsche's 'theology'. Strauss seems somewhat unwilling or unable to analyse it, perhaps because Nietzsche's teaching pertains to the quasi-Satanic revolt not merely against Platonism and Judaism but more specifically against the Christian revelation. Of course, this partial reluctance or incapacity of Strauss should not be exaggerated. There are many issues internal to Christianity on which Strauss has made relevant and valid observations. One example would be his appreciation of the distinction between Catholic and Protestant concepts of charisma which we shall discuss in chapter 4.

It would appear that, if the modernist treatment of reason and revelation is to be definitively corrected, this can only be done in terms of right reason and right faith. We have seen that Strauss does not think it possible to produce a synthesis of the philosophy that he prefers (namely, Plato's) with the theology of Judaism to which he has a certain commitment. Strauss seems sometimes to recognise, from afar, a certain intellectual superiority in Thomism. He writes, for example, as follows:

> The Thomistic doctrine ... of natural law is free from the hesitations and ambiguities which are characteristic of the teachings, not only of Plato and Cicero, but of Aristotle as well. In definiteness and noble simplicity it even surpasses the mitigated Stoic natural law teaching ...[47]

It would seem to follow from this affirmation that Strauss was not in a position to reject the Thomist synthesis merely because Aristotle's teaching was, in some ways, inadequate and incomplete. Strauss knows that St Thomas sought to correct and perfect the Aristotelian teaching especially on the relation between the temporal and eternal good of man and on the relation between the practical and the contemplative life.

Strauss appears to reject the Thomist synthesis on the grounds that any synthesis of reason and revelation is theoretically impossible. Evidently, divine revelation concerning mysteries which are simply inaccessible to unaided human reason cannot be made subject to human reasonings as if it were inferior to human reasonings. However, Strauss considers that in so far as divine revelation is held to be superior to human reasonings, any synthesis of reason and revelation will necessarily involve the *absorption* of philosophy by revealed theology in a way which is incompatible with the independent validity of human reasoning about philosophy generally and about natural law in particular. Strauss seems to take the view that the only way of avoiding such a supposedly improper 'absorption' of philosophy into

11

revealed theology would be to have recourse to a principle higher than either reason or revelation but that no such principle is available.

Certainly, St Thomas would respond to Strauss's difficulty by pointing out that the truths of both philosophy and revelation have their ultimate origin in God Himself. The eternal law which is comprehended fully only by God Himself is the ultimate source of all law[48] and all human knowledge. Subject to the eternal law, divine revelation is superior to philosophy — not because revealed truth can suppress naturally known truth (for every truth is in harmony with every other truth) — but because revelation brings a certitude which is sometimes lacking in our human reasonings. Since Strauss lacks the certitude of a philosophy substantially free from basic contradictions and since his reading of Judaism leaves him — so many centuries after the last of the prophets of Israel and after the ending of the Sanhedrin — without the certitude of that criterion of faith which the *magisterium* of the Catholic Church has been instituted to provide, he finds himself attempting to defend an apparently paradoxical heritage of reason and revelation against the onslaught of modernity.

Certainly, Strauss's positions are to be preferred to those of Weber. Admittedly, Strauss's love of the ancient wisdoms of Platonism and Judaism is deeper than that apparently ineffectual nostalgia which Weber sometimes shows for Christianity. If Strauss's love of ancient wisdoms seems to be somewhat stronger than even a superior kind of nostalgia, it is nevertheless somewhat lacking in real conviction. Again, we observe that Strauss's view of what is involved in intellectual and moral authenticity is superior to the corresponding views of Weber and Nietzsche.[49] Weber and Nietzsche detach authenticity from both nature and truth. Strauss does not wish to do this. Nevertheless, given Strauss's preoccupation with the intellectual 'virtue' of 'divine madness' (which he derives from Plato) and his unwillingness to accept the Aristotelian teaching that knowledge requires the obedience of the mind to the truth of things, we can conclude that Strauss's own approach to intellectual and moral authenticity is not related to nature and truth in an entirely satisfactory manner.

Although Strauss has rejected the erroneous teachings of modernity precisely because they lead towards (or actually attain to) nihilism, he finds himself unable to dispose of the germ of the trend towards nihilism which is present even in his own thought.[50] Since Strauss cannot provide the definitive refutation of nihilism, and given that he is unwilling to conclude to nihilism, his thought inevitably remains in a state of arrested development. Accordingly, despite the brilliance of Strauss's critique of Weber (and of Machiavelli and Nietzsche), the contest between the theses of Strauss and the modernist ideology of Weber results in a kind of stalemate.

Certainly Raymond Aron, a disciple of both Machiavelli and Weber, has expressed the view that Strauss's own position is eventually not proof against the very difficulties which Strauss raises in his criticisms of Machiavelli and Weber. Aron does not deny that there is an element of nihilism present in Weber's thought. He freely admits this difficulty. The crucial criticism which Aron levels against Strauss is in the form of a *tu quoque*. He implies that, if Weber's thought does not exclude nihilism, Strauss's own thought is also eventually vulnerable to nihilism. Aron has advanced this criticism of Strauss by presenting examples of the so-called moral paradoxes of practical (and especially political) life and he finally concludes: 'I do not think that Mr Leo Strauss would deny these evidences'.[51] Clearly, Aron regards his 'evidences' not merely as evidences of actual conflicts but as evidences of necessary and unavoidable moral conflicts which arise from basic paradoxes inherent in human existence. Indeed, Aron takes these alleged paradoxes so much for granted that he suggests that the question is simply to determine the place that one assigns to such 'inevitable antinomies of action' in one's political philosophy.

Naturally, when an advocate of Weber's teaching advances the type of argument which Aron advances against Strauss, he does not thereby establish the validity of Weber's position. It is, after all, a desperate kind of argument in which the Weberian controversialist can succeed in exposing a defect in Strauss's teaching only by first admitting that there is in Weber himself an intellectual defect of a more evidently fatal kind.

Towards a definitive critique

The criticisms of Voegelin and Strauss can lead the perceptive reader to recognise that there is a doctrine implicit in Weber's writings which is not really true and not really harmless. However, the brief analyses, in this chapter, of various intellectual presuppositions of Voegelin and Strauss may suffice to indicate that their critiques of Weber are not complete and not entirely satisfactory as they stand. Whilst each of them disagrees with Weber's modernist rejection of the classical and Judaeo-Christian traditions, neither of them has remained entirely unaffected by that modernist revolt which they variously repudiate. It is not insignificant that Voegelin and Strauss have both directed their readers' attention, beyond their own intellectual positions, to the special achievement of the philosophical/theological synthesis of Thomism. It is to the fundamental guidelines of that synthesis that we shall have recourse in seeking to develop a more definitive critique of Weber's ideology in the following chapters.

Notes and references

1   See especially E. Voegelin, *The New Science of Politics*, Chicago, 1952.

2   See especially L. Strauss, *Natural Right and History*, Chicago, 1953, ch.2.

3   See *Scholarship and Partisanship: Essays on Max Weber*, R. Bendix and G. Roth (eds.), p.63, footnote 21.

4   Voegelin, *The New Science of Politics*, p.23.

5   Ibid., p.6.

6   Ibid., p.20.

7   Ibid., pp.140–1.

8   Ibid., p.20.

9   See St Thomas Aquinas, *Commentary on the Nicomachean Ethics*, Chicago, 1964, Book VI, lect. XI, para.1287; and *Summa Theologiae*, I–II, q.65, art.1.

10 Voegelin, *The New Science of Politics*, pp.169–70.

11 Ibid., p.131.

12 Ibid., p.17.

13 When Voegelin distinguishes between the 'cosmic order' and the 'truth of the soul' (ibid., p.162), he fails to explain that, properly understood, these two are both in harmony with the divine truth.

14 Ibid., pp.106, 107 and elsewhere.

15 For detailed discussion of this matter, see G. Bowe, *The Origin of Political Authority*, Dublin, 1955.

16 Voegelin, *The New Science of Politics*, p.17.

17 See discussion of these disparate elements in Hooker in P. Munz, *The Place of Hooker in the History of Thought*, London, 1952.

18 See Aristotle, *Nicomachean Ethics*, Book VI and the *Commentary* of St Thomas Aquinas, Book VI, lect. XI. See also Aquinas, *Summa Theologiae*, I–II, q.57, art.2, reply to obj.1 and q.66, art.5, reply to obj.2.

19 Voegelin, *The New Science of Politics*, pp.152–61, 178–84.

20 Ibid., p.144.

21 Ibid., pp.142–3.

22 Ibid., p.143.

23 In summarising Voegelin's various statements on the preceding points, J.L. Wiser correctly infers that Voegelin's position postulates 'the inevitable failure of all dogma', see Wiser, 'From Cultural Analysis to Philosophical Anthropology: An Examination of Voegelin's Concept of Gnosticism', *Review of Politics*, vol.42, no. 1, 1980, pp.92–104.

24 Voegelin, *The New Science of Politics*, p.122. (In footnote 24 to that page, Voegelin attributes his view of the uncertainty of faith to a psychology of experience. Although he refers to St Thomas, Voegelin's

view of faith is manifestly incompatible with St Thomas's teachings.)

25   This point is made in a significant passage quoted by J.H. Hallowell from Voegelin's then unpublished MS. 'Equivalences of Experience and Symbolization in History'. See Hallowell's *Introduction to Voegelin: From Enlightenment to Revolution*, Durham, North Carolina, 1975, p.viii.

26   See especially E. Voegelin, *Science, Politics and Gnosticism*, Chicago, 1968.

27   Voegelin, *The New Science of Politics*, p.134.

28   L. Malevez, *The Christian Message and Myth*, London, 1958, p.125.

29   Ibid., p.125. (On page 59, Malevez points out that Bultmann rejects as mythology both the gnostic and the Catholic doctrines of a supernatural order.)

30   Voegelin, *The New Science of Politics*, p.126. (In his footnote 29, Voegelin specifically refers to Bultmann's work.)

31   Voegelin, *Science, Politics and Gnosticism*, p.86.

32   Voegelin objects to a variety of types or elements of what he regards as 'Christian gnosticism' involving what he characterises as erroneous attempts to 'draw the spirit of God into man' or as erroneously 'massive' purported modes of participation in divinity by those who nevertheless retain the doctrine of a transcendent God. (See *The New Science of Politics*, pp.124–5 and also p.12.)

33   Voegelin, *Science, Politics and Gnosticism*, p.87.

34   See Voegelin, *Science, Politics and Gnosticism* and also Voegelin's article 'The Formation of the Marxian Revolutionary Idea', *Review of Politics*, XIII, 1950, pp.275–302.

35   L. Strauss, 'The Three Waves of Modernity' in *Political Philosophy: Six Essays by Leo Strauss*, H. Gildin (ed.), Indianapolis, 1975, pp.81–98.

36   L. Strauss, *What is Political Philosophy?*, New York, 1959, pp.306–11.

37   L. Strauss, *Thoughts on Machiavelli*, repr. University of Washington Press, 1969, pp.298–9.

38   Strauss's failure to uphold the doctrine of the common good of world society is manifested in his *Natural Right and History*, pp.148–50 and in his 'Jerusalem and Athens: Some Introductory Reflections', *Commentary*, XLIII (1967), pp.51, 57.

39   On this and many related points, see C.N.R. McCoy: 'On the Revival of Classical Political Philosophy', *Review of Politics*, vol.35, April 1973, pp.161–79.

40   J. Maritain: 'The End of Machiavellianism', repub. in *The Social and Political Philosophy of Jacques Maritain*, Evans and Ward (eds.), London, 1956, p.323.

41   For a critical analysis of Strauss's preference for nature 'as standard' instead of nature 'as authority', see C.N.R. McCoy, *On the Revival of Classical Political Philosophy*.

42   Strauss's ambivalencies on this and many other points are analysed in V. Gourevitch, 'Philosophy and Politics', *Review of Metaphysics*, XXII (1968–9), pp.58–84, 281–328.

43   Aquinas, *Summa theologiae*, I, q.5, art.1.

44   L. Strauss, 'Jerusalem and Athens: Some Introductory Reflections'.

45   E.J. Roesch, *The Totalitarian Threat: The Fruition of Modern Individualism as seen in Hobbes and Rousseau*, New York, 1963, p.94.

46   L. Strauss, 'A Note on the Plan of Nietzsche's *Beyond Good and Evil*', *Interpretation: A Journal of Political Philosophy*, vol.III, Winter, 1973.

47   Strauss, *Natural Right and History*, p.163.

48   Aquinas, *Summa theologiae*, Ia, IIae, q.90–q.97. (The problem of the relation of the natural to the supernatural is discussed under particular aspects in other chapters of this book. For a more general treatment, see E.B.F. Midgley, *The Natural Law Tradition and the Theory of International Relations*, London/New York, 1975, especially chapter 1.IV.)

49   Strauss, 'A Note on the Plan of Nietzsche's *Beyond Good and Evil*'.

50   See discussion of Strauss's perspective in my articles: 'Concerning the Modernist Subversion of Political Philosophy', *New Scholasticism*, LIII, 2, Spring 1979, pp.168–90 and 'The Crisis of Modernity in the Theory of International Relations', *Year Book of World Affairs*, 1981, pp.235–47.

51   R. Aron's Introduction to *Max Weber: Le Savant et le Politique*, Paris, 1959, p.45.

2 Scientism and the genesis of ideology

The nature of ideology

Since writers with widely differing points of view have made use of the word 'ideology', it is not surprising that it has been employed in a variety of different senses. Often it has been used pejoratively; sometimes not. Yet even when the word 'ideology' has not been uttered as a reproach, its usage has usually involved the makings of a reproach. It is true that Marx regards what *he* calls the ideological standpoint as inevitable in the historical periods prior to the decisive changes which are supposed to usher in the era of 'socialised humanity'. It might be argued therefore that Marx, from his allegedly 'scientific' point of view, does not reproach that ideological thinking which he supposes to have occurred inevitably just as it is destined (in his view) to be inevitably superseded by 'practical-critical activity' and 'socialised humanity'. Nevertheless, Marx would not deny that his analysis of 'ideology' is pejorative at least in this sense: that all thought which has claimed to have sought — or to have found — fundamental intellectual truth in philosophy is to be designated as having a significance very different from the significance which it actually claims to have.

Some Marxist-Leninists will no doubt be willing (as Lenin[1] was willing) to characterise their own thought as 'revolutionary ideology'. This might be supposed to imply that ideology *per se* is not regarded by them as invariably perverse. Yet, since these Marxist-Leninists not only fail but do not even attempt to find fundamental philosophical truth, then perhaps their underlying ideology is more evidently false than are some of the liberal ideologies which they criticise. The fact that these Marxist-Leninists do not reproach themselves for their own resort to ideology does not mean that their resort to ideology is irreproachable.

If some thinkers wrongly suppose that all purported philosophical thinking is properly called ideological thinking and that the designation 'ideological' does not, of itself, bear any reproach, there must be some explanation of this apparently strange state of affairs. For some minds, the desire for fundamental truth has become so atrophied by evil custom and evil habit that a mentality is formed which does not commonly advert to the question of fundamental truth but prefers to feed upon more or less irrational ideological aspirations. In the case of intellects less deformed than this, the explanation for the curious misunderstanding of the nature of fundamentally ideological thinking may rest in part upon the fact that ideology presents itself not only in the form of substantive ideologies but also in the form of accidental ideological elements which may only partially distort thinking which remains in some sense philosophical. It needs to be borne in mind that there is a permanent danger of ideological distortion — a recurring threat to the integrity of philosophical thinking — in the actual conditions of our human life. Accordingly, it is possible to speak of a certain ideological weight which presses upon us (even when we entertain true propositions) and which tempts us to introduce inordinate emphases and even actual error into our thinking.

Yves Simon seems to have considered 'ideological statements' in a broad sense to include not only what are called here substantively and partially ideological statements but even the kind of statement which merely bears a certain ideological weight and which is therefore in danger of giving rise to ideological distortion. Simon defines ideology as a body of statements (about facts or essences) which refers to the aspirations of a given society at a certain time.[2] Accordingly, for Simon, the term 'ideology' is preferably used in a sense which is not absolutely inherently pejorative. The fact that a statement belongs to an ideology, in Simon's sense of the word, does not necessarily mean that it is an erroneous statement but it does mean that the statement is being put forward in a context in which it may frequently happen that error will arise. Accordingly, even a true proposition can be subject to some distortion of emphasis if it happens to be a peculiarly 'timely' or 'relevant' truth for some society or group or even for some interested individual. Simon holds very generally that human thought — which, after all, is always entertained by human beings who have practical problems and difficulties which they aspire to overcome — is subject to ideological weight which, to a greater or lesser extent, is liable to occasion distortion.

Without denying in any way the value of Simon's important discussion of the concept of ideological weight, it is nevertheless legitimate to insist upon the distinction between the philosophers and the ideologists. For, if all men are tempted to admit ideological distortion into their thinking, all men do not equally succumb to this kind of temptation. Moreover, even amongst those who succumb in varying degrees, certain distinctions can be made. There is a vast difference between a thinker who explicitly intends to seek fundamental truth (even if he is not very successful and even if his failure involves a failure to resist adequately the ideological pressures of the time) and a thinker who does not even intend to use his intellect to seek fundamental truth because he prefers to use his will to choose or impose certain 'values' irrespective of their truth or falsity.

It is on the foundation of this basic distinction between two types of human intention in relation to intellectual truth in philosophy that we are entitled to agree with W.O. Martin that philosophy and ideology ought to be clearly distinguished. Martin rightly points out that:

> since metaphysics and ideology are, intellectually and
> otherwise, absolutely incompatible, it would be well for
> metaphysicians to avoid using the terms interchangeably
> and to recognise the distinction which the ideologist dare
> not admit.[3]

We should do well to follow Martin's advice in analysing the ideology of Max Weber because, as we shall see, Weber's ideology is not merely a case of ideological temptation nor merely a case of a substantive philosophy distorted by ideological influences; it is rather a case of thought fabricating 'values' in a system which is substantially ideological in character.

Of course, the foundations of ideological thinking were laid long before the birth of Max Weber. Weber himself knows that his thought has an historical context but he misunderstands its import. He surmises that that part of his thought which we shall properly designate as his ideology is some kind of side effect of the progress of the special sciences. It is true that Weber does not bluntly assert that all religious thought and belief is permanently excluded from the human mind by strict logical necessity as the result of the progress of the special sciences. Nevertheless, he holds that there is some sort of connection between the progress of the sciences and the decline of religion and this is the principal context — as Weber understands it — for the deployment of that part of his thought which we shall have reason to designate as his ideology.

We shall argue not merely that Weber's ideology is not a necessary consequence of the progress of the special sciences but also that the Weberian ideology presents a real, though ambiguous, threat to the very existence of the special sciences themselves. In noting this, we must be careful not to forget that the most fundamental objection to Weber's ideology arises from the fact that it is incompatible with true philosophy and, indeed, with the philosophical quest as such.

Wherein lies the temptation which ultimately leads to the employment of ideology where philosophy is in point? Certainly, the temptations are legion. In modern times, this inadvertence to philosophical truth and this groping for an ideological substitute is the outcome of an intellectual amnesia endemic in the post-Renaissance/post-Reformation intellectual enterprise (and having even earlier origins) which gives rise to a whole spectrum of errors. G.M. Garrone has noted that 'It is a psychological law that we forget what we do not repeat, even things that are most certain, things least open to question'. Certainly, one of those things which Garrone would regard as least open to question, but which Weber did not retain, was the truth that the entire universe is, in a profound sense, intelligible since it owes its contingent existence to the necessary existence of the prime intellect which is God. Yet, even such truths as these — concerning the prime intellect and the intelligibility of the universe — will sometimes be not only denied but, at the same time, misconceived so that, through human error, they become the occasion not of harmony but of contradictions between propositions held to be true in different fields of knowledge. Of course, objectively, there can be no real conflicts among propositions which are really true — whether these are truths of faith, truths in the philosophical sciences or truths in those special sciences which do not belong to philosophy.

However, in practice, men sometimes fail to retain the truths of faith; they are sometimes ignorant of important philosophical truths and they sometimes misunderstand the weight and import of results in the non-philosophical special sciences in relation to faith and philosophy. Accordingly, the fact that there is a basis for a valid synthesis of the various distinct but compatible orders of truth does not prevent that synthesis from being rejected in practice (and even denied in theory) by many people since men retain fundamental truth in its integrity, if at all, only with difficulty. Indeed, it is particularly striking to observe that the basic principles of the Thomist synthesis were rejected even in the thirteenth century by exponents of the double truth theory who held that a proposition could be deemed true in philosophy even when it is deemed false in theology. Against the remote preparation afforded by the decadent phases of scholasticism, however, the proximate preparation for the denial of any intellectual synthesis by Max Weber is provided by the denial of any scholastic synthesis by the post-Renaissance/post-Reformation teachings in the Protestant, rationalist, voluntarist and other traditions.

A.W. Gouldner's critique of Weber

At this point, it seems appropriate to refer to the article in which A.W. Gouldner attempts to envisage the central problem which Weber faces and the solution which he proposes not merely in the context of modern thought but even against the background of the intellectual life of the Middle Ages. Gouldner's analysis is based upon his view that there is a close analogy between the problem of the relations between reason and faith in the Middle Ages and the problem of the relations between science and values in modern sociological thinking. In pursuing the implications of this supposed analogy, Gouldner seems to begin with an error of perspective in presupposing that, in mediaeval thought generally, there is 'a conflict between faith and reason' and that the task of the mediaeval theologian was one of 'keeping the peace between them'. This is an unjustified presupposition because it is evident in many cases — and especially in the case of St Thomas Aquinas — that mediaeval theologians explicitly denied that there could be any real conflict between the truths of faith and the truths of reason.

Certainly, Gouldner is aware that there is a difference between the 'double truth theory' and the teaching of St Thomas. Commenting on the double truth theorists, Gouldner writes: 'They ... built a water-tight compartment between philosophy and faith, a separation which St Thomas Aquinas continued and yet sought to transcend'.[4] This formulation is obscure and unsatisfactory. The general impression which is received from Gouldner's article as a whole is that he wrongly supposes that the difference between the double truth theorists and St Thomas is a difference of degree and not a difference of kind.

If we are to compare Weber's doctrine with mediaeval thought, it does seem necessary to remember that, unlike the mediaeval thinkers, Weber does not assent either to the truths of faith or even to the truths of philosophy. Of course, it might be said that the mediaeval double truth theory leads logically to scepticism. (This is so whatever the double truth theorists themselves might have supposed.) Accordingly, the double truth theory and the Weberian doctrine have this in common: they both lead logically to philosophical and theological scepticism.

Gouldner admits that 'Like Freud, Weber never really believed in an enduring peace or in a final resolution' of the conflict between science and values.[5] Gouldner seems to assume that in reality the various 'accommodations' between religion (more specifically, Christianity, whether Catholic or Protestant) and science are compromises more or less unsatisfactory to the intellect as Freud's treatment of science and values is intellectually unsatisfactory. It is only on this assumption that Gouldner can argue at all plausibly that Weber's doctrine 'which creates a gulf between science and values' is in the general tradition of attempts to 'accommodate' Christianity and modern science. More specifically, Gouldner seems to imply (wrongly) that even a Thomist perspective upon the relations between faith and the special sciences would be more or less intellectually unsatisfactory. Indeed, it is only on the basis of such an erroneous assumption that Gouldner could even begin to argue his untenable thesis that Weber produces 'a Protestant version of the Thomist effort at harmonising' the relations between science and values.

Latin Averroism and the teachings of certain 'would-be disciples' of Weber (whom Gouldner regards as too little concerned with real problems and too much concerned with a certain professional status narrowly conceived) are no doubt alike — at least, in the minimal sense that these two types of teaching are both intellectually unsound. To this extent, Gouldner might be in a position to justify his opinion that Weber's 'would-be' followers tend to be in some way akin to the Latin Averroists. Certainly, these people are very far from either the letter or the spirit of St Thomas Aquinas. It is when Gouldner argues that the doctrinal separation of fact and value in the thought of Weber himself is 'nearer to St Thomas' that it is necessary to register one's dissent. Gouldner's supposition of a similarity between Weber's doctrinal separation of fact and value and St Thomas's careful distinctions and syntheses relating to theology, philosophy and the special sciences could only be justified if the Thomist distinctions and syntheses were fraudulent or radically faulty. Indeed, Gouldner provides evidence against his own thesis when, for example, he admits that Weber's supposed 'personal synthesis' is nothing more than a search for a 'truce' [not a true peace] between [opposed] 'contenders'. This correct admission means that Weber's supposed 'synthesis' is not really a synthesis at all.

Gouldner does not offer a properly developed perspective upon the intellectual history of the relations between reason and revelation and between science and values. Indeed, he admits this and more when he says, in the third paragraph of his article, that he does not wish to enter into the *logical* arguments involved in the debate about value-free sociology. Nevertheless, there is a somewhat rough and ready perspective upon the intellectual history of reason *vis-à-vis* revelation and of fact *vis-à-vis* value in Gouldner's article. If, *per impossibilia*, this perspective were acceptable and accepted, certain untoward conclusions would follow. Certainly, it seems to be one of the exigencies of Gouldner's perspective that no objective values can be justified on the basis of true theology, true philosophy, true natural science or true sociology. Accordingly, it is implicit in this perspective that any statement outside the special sciences on the subject of values (or faith or philosophy) would be necessarily ideological in the sense in which ideology has been defined here. At the same time, Gouldner's approach suggests to him that although the historical distinctions between science and values — especially in the work of Weber — may have served certain personal, social or institutional purposes, these distinctions are eventually unfruitful. For this reason, Gouldner believes that values (that is, for him, subjective value-judgements) ought not to be excluded from science. Thus he seems to hold that science — or, at least, sociology — may properly and explicitly accept something which is here properly called ideological scientism and which, Gouldner implies, is not only acceptable but even unavoidable in practice in the pursuit of the social sciences.

In other words, we conclude that Gouldner's critique of Weber's approach does not tend towards the elimination of scientism and ideology from our intellectual life. On the contrary, Gouldner's own position seems explicitly to posit the propriety and the inevitability of both scientism and ideology. Gouldner merely removes from Weber's approach a certain intellectual tortuousness whereby Weber (for reasons of his own) complicates and obscures his own resort to ideology. It is right to conclude, over against both Weber and Gouldner, that ideology and scientism are unjustified intellectual aberrations which cannot be regarded as legitimate or necessary concomitants of true developments either in philosophy or in the special sciences themselves.

In the actual history of thought, we find that ideology is not infrequently parasitic upon philosophy and that it may even come to replace philosophy in the minds of certain thinkers. Similarly, we learn from history that scientism is not infrequently parasitic upon the special sciences. Moreover, these two parasites are not infrequently found together and this joint incidence is not a mere accident. For, since wisdom and the special sciences, rightly distinguished, are seen to postulate each other, it is only to be expected that, when these disciplines are perverted into ideology and scientism, the two perversions will also, in a sense, postulate each other within an erroneous system of doctrine.[6]

So far as the relation of science to religion is concerned, a reply to Gouldner might begin by quoting the following passage from W.J. Ong:

Alfred North Whitehead and others long ago made the suggestion that the patience to attack a problem scientifically implies an act of faith in the intelligibility of the universe, and that historically the great impetus to this act of faith has been Christianity, with its unequivocal belief in a personal God and in a universe created by Him in time and with a determined purpose ... . This explanation is undoubtedly true in the large ... .[7]

This general position which Ong accepts from Whitehead needs perhaps to be expounded a little more precisely. Although Christian faith is undoubtedly helpful in engendering a belief in the intelligibility of the universe (a belief appropriate for both the philosopher and the scientist), this belief does not inherently depend upon supernatural faith. The intelligibility of the universe is something which can be rationally known by the philosopher and confidently explored in various special aspects by the scientist.

At this point in the argument, we need to take account of a further point which Ong makes, namely, that Whitehead's general explanation was inadequate for the understanding of the complexity of the framework in which the scientific mentality took shape. Ong is here adverting to the fact that the scientist has a certain justified confidence in the *segmented* explanation of reality which is undertaken by the special sciences. Certainly, in the seventeenth century, there arose an increasing preoccupation with the segmented intelligibility to be found by the special sciences. We shall therefore consider in the next section of this chapter how this segmented intelligibility came to be commonly misrepresented in the general climate of the post-Renaissance and post-Reformation intellectual enterprise.

The intellectual origins of scientism

In support of our thesis that there is no inherent relationship between either ideology or scientism on the one hand and the valid development of the special sciences on the other hand, let us first consider the following passage from J. Wellmuth's lecture on *The Nature and Origins of Scientism*:

> The movement called scientism needed no Renaissance to give it life, nor any fullgrown scientific method to foster its development. It was the natural outcome of a trend of thought which began in the early Middle Ages, which was strongly opposed by St Thomas during his lifetime, and which ultimately led to the breakdown of mediaeval philosophy before the end of the fourteenth century, at a time when the traditional fathers of modern science had still about two centuries to wait before being born.[8]

As a matter of historical fact, then, both ideology and scientism can be seen to have found in nominalism a congenial habitat. Since nominalism is an ancient philosophical error which began long before the scientific revolution of the seventeenth century, it is not unreasonable to suggest that the key to the understanding of the incidence and the significance of both ideology and scientism consists in a certain misconception about the nature of philosophy.

Scientism — considered very generally — is the inappropriate application of some method of the special sciences to some subject matter for which that method is improper. The characteristic case of scientism is the case in which an attempt is made to apply to philosophy itself a method proper to some special science or other. The error is not confined, however, to scientism in philosophy; there is also scientism in the field of the special sciences themselves in so far as the method of one comes to be inappropriately applied to another and different one. Very generally, one can say that scientism in all its manifestations involves a misconception and a denigration of what are in fact the true principles of philosophy. This rejection of the true principles of philosophy will be generally connected with the disordered pursuit of some practical purpose or purposes. So we find a mentality in which a tendency to scientism is conjoined with a tendency to ideological thinking.

It is true that the valid distinctions between philosophy and the special sciences were set out, at least in a general way, as early as the thirteenth century when St Thomas dealt with the matter in his Commentary on the *De Trinitate* of Boethius.[9] But although St Thomas had provided a broad intellectual basis for the distinctions among the various intellectual disciplines, later scholasticism receded from this foundation and it tended towards a division of the disciplines which was determined to an excessive extent by pedagogical considerations. When later methodologists — outside of scholasticism — gave a segmented analysis of the disciplines of an apparently new type, it might easily be assumed that these methodologies were authentic approaches properly apt to provide for the valid scientific developments which were to come and that they might also be presumed to be more in accord with philosophical truth. We shall see, however, that both these assumptions are generally unjustified.

In reality, the various actual methods of segmenting the disciplines which were employed by the logicians, philosophers and educationists of the sixteenth and seventeenth centuries cannot be correlated very well with strictly scientific advances. Indeed, it might be reasonably concluded that the pressures of a certain educational ideology were of greater importance in the determination of methodologies than truly scientific requirements. N.W. Gilbert has observed, in the case of the sixteenth century logician Peter Ramus, that there was a kind of 'democratic motivation' which led him to desire to make education more accessible to all.[10] Ong has shown how Ramus's preoccupation with teaching methods, rather than with strictly scientific and philosophical considerations, could lead to misconceptions. He illustrates the pedagogical or didactic approach of Ramus in the following passage:

> What is 'clearer' for pupils is, in practice, simply what one can make 'work' when one is teaching them. Ramus and Ramists, in one way or another, could make their presentation of the arts work. From here one could readily leap to the conclusion that the presentation proceeded from what was 'clearer' *of itself* or 'in the nature of things' and thereby 'more known'. To prove this conclusion was a difficult business and best not attempted. One simply supposed that 'clarity' (more or less measured in the classroom) and intelligibility were one. Thus was the ground being prepared for the Cartesian venture.[11]

Ramist influence or Ramist tendencies can be found in Althusius, in Bodin and, directly or indirectly, in many other writers from the sixteenth century onwards. A variety of ideological purposes could be served by a separation of disciplines which could help to conceal the radical defects of prevalent intellectual positions. This separation of disciplines tended to hinder the mind from noticing the faulty presuppositions of any particular discipline and to prevent it from adverting to the lack of any coherent intellectual synthesis of the philosophical and theological disciplines. The Reformation resulted in forms of Protestant theology which no longer even attempted to envisage for theology an architectonic function. Similarly, the tendency, in Althusius, Grotius and so many others, to treat the philosophical disciplines separately without an adequate philosophical exposition of their interconnections was related to the deficiencies of Protestant, rationalist and voluntarist tendencies in natural law theory and to the general decline away from metaphysics as an authentic philosophical science of being.[12]

Accordingly, we conclude that, against the background of nominalism (and philosophies of law based upon an erroneous teaching on the primacy of the will) which manifests itself in the decadent phases of mediaeval thought, an intellectual disintegration is set in train from the sixteenth century onwards in which rationalism and voluntarism both flourish in varied, and sometimes bizarre, combinations. Perhaps one of the most bizarre — and certainly one of the most brilliant — attempts to deal with the problems engendered by this intellectual disintegration was the critical philosophy of Immanuel Kant. We shall therefore consider the role of the Kantian philosophy in preparing the way for modern ideology and for Weber's ideology in particular. In order to do this we shall begin by referring to consequences for modern ideology of the work of the Scottish philosopher who woke Kant from his 'dogmatic slumbers' in the midst of the Wolffian rationalism.

Hume and Kant in the philosophical preparation for Weberian ideology

David Hume's intellectual life is set against the background of the Protestant, rationalist and voluntarist trends which we have mentioned. As we have seen, any scholastic influences upon these trends came from the decadent phase of scholasticism. Certainly, Hume does not enter into any serious and direct dialogue with the theories of metaphysics and natural law which truly belong to the Thomist tradition. Obviously, Hume's positions — if they could be fully sustained — would imply that the Thomist teaching is false. However, it is not correct to conclude that Hume in effect refuted Thomism merely because he succeeded in revealing some of the confusions in the unsatisfactory natural law theories of thinkers such as John Locke.

Hume certainly demonstrated, in effect, that the rationalist, voluntarist and empiricist philosophers had not sustained metaphysics as a philosophical science and that they had not offered any adequate philosophical basis for rational norms of human action. One can conclude from Hume's achievement (such as it was) that once men come to abandon the metaphysics of being and the doctrine of natural law in the tradition which is authentically Thomist, they will hardly avoid being driven along the road to scepticism.

Accordingly, anyone who rashly assumes that Hume has succeeded in demolishing *every* doctrine of metaphysics and natural law (including Thomism) will either be reduced to silence about matters fundamental to our human life or have recourse to an ideological substitute for philosophy. The convinced disciple of Hume who wishes (despite his scepticism) to fabricate an intellectual framework for his practical or political life will only be able to make use of his reason as the slave of his feelings. By this means, a man might 'construct a world in idea to satisfy some practical purpose' (or purposes) but in doing so (as Martin has rightly pointed out) he will become an ideologist and not a philosopher.[13]

Since it is quite evident that Weber rejects all metaphysical truth and since he believes that human reason is not able or competent to establish norms whereby the reasonable man could offer a valid prescription for another man, Weber is certainly a sceptic. For Weber, the reason of an individual man is not able or competent to afford a truly rational prescription even for that individual himself. Obviously, Weber denies that human nature itself contains a norm of right appetite. The conclusion follows that the practical reason of Weberian man is envisaged as prompting him to act only when that reason is acting as the slave of feelings, passions, inclinations and so on which are neither connected together nor justified in terms of any principle of order known to be valid. Accordingly, the 'values' held by Weberian man, and the choices which he makes, are precisely *ideological* 'values' and *ideological* choices.

When Weber suggests, very generally, that one cannot prescribe a moral code to anyone, he takes the opportunity to offer us instead an ultimate antinomy between 'an ethic of ultimate ends' and 'an ethic of responsibility'. Yet, the Weberian man makes an ideological choice whether he chooses to act in accord with 'an ethic of ultimate ends' or whether he adopts 'an ethic of responsibility'. The reason for this is simple: the Weberian man purports to 'know' that 'ultimate ends' have only a subjective meaning and have no ontological status or validity just as he purports to 'know' that responsible action can be responsible only in relation to objectives which are choiceworthy only as subjective preferences (however widely they may be shared) and not in terms of any objective goods.

Of course, Weber did not become the ideologist he was, simply as the result of reading some key passages in the works of David Hume. The Kantian and neo-Kantian background was of crucial importance. Certainly, there is a substantial element of 'scientism' (or 'physicism' as E. Gilson[14] has preferred to call it) in the critical philosophy of Kant. Since Kant, like Hume, denied that the natural finalities of human nature could be found, the basis for a Thomist (or even a Suarezian) doctrine of the natural law was absent from the Kantian teaching.

Kant has something in common with the nominalist and voluntarist scholastics of the late Middle Ages but, even in this scholasticism in decline, the divine will supplies (in theology) for the deficiencies in moral philosophy. Since Kant had not only rejected dogmatic theology but had even denied the proofs for the existence of God, he was unable to provide any plausible basis for moral obligation.[15] To sum up, there is, for Kant, no basis in human nature even for a *lex indicans*; nor is there any basis in the human intellect, in the divine intellect or in the divine will for a *lex obligans*. It follows, given these erroneous assumptions, that any Kantian notion of a *lex obligans* can have no other recourse, for its 'foundation', than to a supposedly autonomous human will.

Despite the fact that Arthur Schopenhauer's own teaching on morality is fundamentally unsatisfactory, one can say that no-one has seen more clearly than Schopenhauer that there is an internal inconsistency between the voluntaristic and the rationalistic elements in Kant's moral and legal philosophy. Indeed, Schopenhauer's relentless exposure of the paradoxes in the Kantian philosophy[16] seems to be his main — perhaps his only — positive contribution to a true philosophical understanding. L. Krieger has commented upon the consequences of Kant's rejection of natural law in its integrative function and has suggested that Kant

> spent the rest of his philosophical career in seeking to rejoin what he had put asunder, for, as he himself recognised, the human mind tends towards unity, and only there does it find peace and satisfaction.[17]

Nevertheless, it must be admitted that any attempts which Kant may have made to seek intellectual unity were quite unsuccessful. Whether we consider his moral philosophy or his legal philosophy, Kant's treatment can be seen to have failed to expound or even to find that unity which Taparelli d'Azeglio summed up in the following sentence, 'There is no reign of law without unity of law; there is no unity of law without the unity of the doctrines which engender it'.[18]

Although Kant held that the moral law is universal, Kantian morality was no longer based upon a real natural moral law but only upon a certain peculiar notion of 'possibility'. Clearly, this attempt to base a universal moral law upon mere 'possibility' could not establish a stable intellectual position capable of effectively resisting subjectivism. Accordingly, L.W. Beck will admit that the Kantian ethics are fundamentally paradoxical. Indeed, it is not surprising to find that, in an effort to defend Kant against his adversaries, Beck finds himself driven *in extremis* to write of the admitted paradoxes in the Kantian ethics in terms which reveal to the reader how the unstable doctrine of Kant tends to decompose into irrationalism.

If Kant distinguishes sharply between the order of phenomena and the noumenal order, we know that his doctrine of the noumenal order has no proper foundation and that it is bound to disintegrate. Many of Kant's successors will come to accept the phenomenal order as the realm of facts but the concept of the noumenal realm will be subjected to a progressive transformation leading to its eventual replacement by a realm of subjective 'values' available for the arbitrary choice of the autonomous will. Accordingly, if we are to enter into the debate about whether Weber is a kind of neo-Kantian or a disciple of Nietzsche, it is necessary always to remember that Kantianism itself is susceptible of decomposition into the Nietzschean doctrine. Indeed, it has been increasingly made clear by modern Kantian scholarship that Nietzsche was mistaken in underestimating his own indebtedness to Kant.

F.P. van de Pitte rightly observes, for example, that the Kantian revolution 'involves a transvaluation of values which in many respects foreshadows that of Nietzsche'.[19]

It is against the background of H. Rickert's 'philosophy of values' — which was itself an impoverished descendant of Kantianism — that Weber comes to distinguish sharply between facts, science and intellect belonging to one realm, and values, commitment and will belonging to another realm. Weber is also quite evidently a disciple of Nietzsche. Since the Kantian and neo-Kantian positions are in fact closer to the Nietzschean position than has sometimes been supposed, it is not surprising to find that Beck (in defence of Kant) and Aron (in defence of his own position which is indebted to Weber and Nietzsche) are found to use almost identical formulations. Whilst Aron writes of the [supposed] 'antinomies inherent in human existence which no philosopher ancient or modern has even been able to resolve',[20] Beck also appeals (in defence of Kant) to the [supposed] 'paradoxical predicament of human life itself'.[21]

If it is necessary to declare oneself on the question as to whether Weber is a neo-Kantian or a Nietzschean, one must agree up to a point with Fleischmann that Weber is, on the more important issues, a Nietzschean.[22] Nevertheless, as has been indicated, the difference between neo-Kantianism and the doctrine of Nietzsche is not so great as has sometimes been supposed. Fleischmann is certainly right in saying that Weber rejected Rickert's 'atemporal system of values' as an absurdity. However, it is perhaps sufficiently clear that Rickert's 'atemporal system of values' is internally flawed by subjectivism and that, since it does not possess objective validity, it has no genuine application with real significance for moral and political life. In insisting upon the more extreme subjectivism of Weber and Nietzsche, let us not overlook the subjectivism of the Kantians and the neo-Kantians. Accordingly, in their derivation from Hume and in their foreshadowing of Nietzsche, the Kantian, neo-Kantian and post-Kantian philosophies prepared for the emergence of modern ideological thinking and of the ideology of Max Weber in particular.

Ideology and sociology in Weber

Against this background, we shall begin our investigation of Weber's ideology by considering, according to his vision of the world, the juxtaposition or confrontation between the vocation of science and the vocation of politics. Are we to envisage the confrontation of these two vocations as a juxtaposition of simple coexistence, of implicit hostility or of friendly alliance? Owing to the ultimate incoherence of Weber's vision, no final definitive answer can be given to this question. A case could be made, out of the diverse elements of Weber's thought, in favour of each of these interpretations. Moreover, this fact would appear to be implicitly conceded — whether consciously or unconsciously — in some of the commentary on Weber which is broadly sympathetic towards his work.

On some interpretations, the most prominent factor in Weber's approaches to science and politics is the factor of coexistence between them. The so-called 'ethical neutrality' of scientific sociology is thus supposed to free science from adulteration with extraneous value-judgements whilst enabling the distinctive character of the vocation of politics to stand forth with greater clarity. J. Freund gives a favourable opinion of Weber's strict separation between value and fact, between will and knowledge, when he suggests that Weber's clear definitions of science and politics enable these two to 'collaborate more successfully because their very separateness will have eliminated confusions that would only have hampered both'.[23] This observation raises the question, which we shall shortly consider, whether or not Weber's thought involves both a separation *and* a collaboration between the spheres of science and value which cannot be simultaneously achieved.

Freund certainly does not deny that there is an 'antinomy' as well as a 'correlation' between 'scientific rigorousness' and 'freedom of choice' in the thought of Weber. Indeed, the scientific method, as Weber expounds it, seems bound to have an incidental corrosive effect upon many existing value-judgements if these value-judgements are lacking in a certain kind of consistency. Since, in politics, Weber does not actually prescribe anything as objective — not even any kind of consistency — to anyone, there seems to be a certain hostility between Weberian science and Weberian politics. Freund seems implicitly to recognise this factor of hostility when he suggests that Weber's theory of science 'attempts to overcome the contradictions' which are 'the lifeblood' of Weber's theory of action.

Whilst recognising the factors of separation and of antagonism between the Weberian value-choice and the Weberian social science, it is also necessary to understand the sense in which it can be said that there is a factor of affinity between them. Writing of what he calls the deep affinity between the two vocations in Weber, Freund observes:

> In a sense, Weber's conception of science is governed by his idea of politics, namely, that the multiplicity and antagonism of values and objectives find their parallel in the multiplicity and antagonism of the points of view from which a phenomenon can be scientifically explained ... .[24]

Is this 'government' of Weber's concept of science by his concept of politics an 'intrinsic' factor or an 'accidental' factor in the structure of Weber's scientific method? Moreover, if it were intrinsic, would it not be illicit according to Weber's other criteria of scientific method?

All commentators agree that it is Weber's doctrine that values will govern the choice of subjects for sociological investigation. They are divided about the interpretation of the role which values play in the genesis of the actual 'scientific' results produced by Weberian sociology – those results for which Weber himself seems to claim value-neutrality. A. Dawe criticises what he considers to be an excessive stress laid by some commentators upon the place of value-neutrality in Weber's thought and he refers to 'Weber's many-sided attempt to bridge the gulf between science and value'.[25] Dawe appeals to a number of texts in Weber in support of his thesis and, particularly, to the text in which Weber suggests that: 'without the investigator's evaluative ideas, there would be no principle of selection of subject-matter and no meaningful knowledge of the concrete reality ...'.[26] The problem turns upon the fact that Weber claims that scientific sociology is value-neutral and yet holds, at the same time, that there is no absolutely scientific analysis of culture.

Ideology and individualism in Weber

We have already seen that there are certain ambiguities in the role played by values in Weber's sociology. Since our primary concern is with Weber's *ideology*, we must consider what lessons the conflict of interpretations of his 'scientific' method may have for our study of his ideology. The principal lesson is this: that *Weber's ideology can live neither with nor without the concept of a value-neutral social science.* The reason why this is so is explicable only if we bear in mind that Weber's ideology is a complex and eclectic pastiche of incompatible elements. Basically, it is a combination of ideological individualism (of a kind which concludes to nihilism) and certain positive ideological 'values' which are posited in spite of – and also because of – Weber's nihilism. The 'values' of Weber's ideology are posited *in spite of* his nihilism in so far as they are not nothing but have a positive content. The 'values' of Weber's ideology are posited *because of* his nihilism in so far as these 'values' are not true but merely ideological.

Now Weber's ideological individualism (concluding to nihilism) is intimately connected with a corresponding methodological individualism (concluding to nihilism) in sociology. Yet, a *complete* methodological individualism (which is, under another formulation, a *complete* value-neutrality) would make sociology impossible. Then the non-existence of sociology would put Weber in a position in which he would find himself facing nihilism naked and unashamed in every department of his intellectual life including the field of science. Very generally, he could not have endured the intellectual disintegration which this would have involved. More specifically, this deeper acceptance of nihilism even in sociology would have made it more psychologically difficult for him to sustain those positive ideological 'values' for which he has no rational justification. (We need to remember, in this context, that the existence of Weberian sociology provides not a justification but only a kind of illicit psychological support for Weber's choices of particular ideological values — for example, in the field of the 'ethics of responsibility').

In order to understand the relations between ideological individualism and the ideological social 'values' in Weber's thought, it is perhaps not irrelevant to refer to some of the preceding ideological exercises in the paradoxical entertainment of individualism and totalitarianism in the history of modern political thought. It can be seen that when radical individualism — as it appears, for example, in Hobbes and Rousseau — is taken to its logical conclusion in the field of politics, it so misconceives the nature of the philosophical problem of sociopolitical cohesion that it makes it appear philosophically absolutely insoluble. Since radical individualism cannot provide a truly rational solution for the problem of political order, it is driven — if the individual happens to want order — to seek a merely ideological solution. In propounding such a 'solution', reason is used only as an instrument of disordered passions.

Such an ideological 'solution' to the problem of achieving political order will be, in a way, contrary to the radical individualism which constitutes the starting point. At the same time, the *ideological* solution for the problem of order can be correlated, in another way, with the *ideological* character of the individualistic starting point itself. This can be illustrated by considering the political thought of Rousseau. Rousseau begins with radical individualism and ends with a solution to the problem of socio-political order which it is not unjust to designate, in a certain sense, as totalitarian. Some writers have been puzzled that the starting point should not hinder Rousseau from reaching his solution. Yet there is a certain sense in which we can say that Rousseau is enabled to end with a totalitarian solution *precisely because* he begins with a doctrine of radical amoral individualism.[27] Radical individualism — entailing, as it does, philosophical scepticism — cannot properly envisage a use of practical reason which is not ideological. In the realm of ideology, reason no longer operates according to the canon of right reason; it simply acts as the slave of passions not controlled by objective standards of right appetite. Accordingly, the ideologist tends to proceed by means of an instrumental use of reason to construct an ideological schema which may include both an individualism which presents a (rationally insoluble) pseudo-problem and a totalitarianism which propounds a (rationally invalid) pseudo-solution.

Returning to Weber, we see that his difficulty is that his ideology — and indeed ideological thinking generally — is not something which can be perfected after its kind. Weber needs to advert, in one moment, to a supposedly intrinsically meaningless universe — a *tabula rasa* — upon which any and every ideological 'meaning' can be equally well imposed but always without any effect. In another moment, Weber needs to advert to the positive ideological 'values' which he himself wishes to impose but not without some effect. This is not only the dilemma of Weber's ideology in the narrow sense, it is the dilemma facing all 'knowledge' in the Weberian perspective. For, if men are confined to the totally 'free' attribution of subjective 'meanings' which are all equally meaningless in so far as they cannot either discover or confer any real meaning upon an intrinsically meaningless universe, then there can be no point in attempting to find any rationale or pseudo-rationale in these 'free' human value attributions.

However, since the Weberians do not really live in a meaningless Weberian universe but do in fact live in a universe subject to a natural (and divine) order, ideological thinking — however deliberately it may be adopted — cannot be undertaken in practice without some reference at least to the non-ideological truth about some things. Even in basically ideological thinking, men are misusing a human reason which is really in its ontological character ordered to the truth in general. 'Weberian man' really possesses the same human nature as other men although 'Weberian man' does not properly recognise it for what it is. Consequently, the Weberian ideologist cannot help proceeding sometimes and to some extent in accord with the rational norms of natural law even though he is committed to ideological thinking. Accordingly, Weber will seek to make some kind of sense of human culture, of man in society and so on despite the fact that his basic individualism would logically result in this being impossible for him. Hence Weber's ambiguous preoccupation with sociology and his perplexed employment of ideology as an irrational substitute for philosophy.

In the following passage, Weber *begins* to appreciate the difficulties there are in attempting to save the significance of his scientific results in terms of his own ideology:

Science further presupposes that what is yielded by scientific work is important in the sense that it is 'worth being known'. In this, obviously, are contained all our problems. For this presupposition cannot be proved by scientific means. It can only be *interpreted* with reference to its ultimate meaning, which we must reject or accept according to our ultimate position towards life.[28]

Yet the difficulties of Weber's position go deeper than he realises in this passage. Certainly, Weber uses — to some extent — the laws of logic in the course of his sociological studies. In addition to the pre-supposed values of logic (presupposed at least when they are convenient for Weber), Weber's sociological understanding of value-positions which he does not share depends upon a certain flawed and adequate (but not entirely illusory) knowledge of man which would not have been available to him if his thinking had been, *per imposs-ibilia*, conducted in terms of an impossibly 'perfected' methodological individualism and value-neutrality.

In conclusion, we should observe that Weber's ambiguous preoccupation with value-neutrality cannot be explained exclusively in terms of the immediate day-to-day practical problems of his professional life in the German society and the German academic circles of his time. We shall refer in chapter 8 to the fact that it is possible to follow the development of some of Weber's positions in relation to value-neutrality by reference to events in his academic and public career. Nevertheless, it should be recognised that a pragmatic assumption of value-neutrality has more basic roots in his thought. Value-neutrality seems, in fact, to be an essential moment, or phase or tendency in Weber's thought in so far as it apparently serves to 'protect' (in a spurious psychological sense) the fragile system of ideology and sociology from dissolution. Accordingly, Weber can live neither with nor without value-neutrality in consequence of certain fundamental tensions within the structure of his system of ideological/sociological thought as a whole.

A note on the relations between sociology and philosophy

In view of the susceptibility of sociology to becoming contaminated by the admixture of errors from erroneous philosophies or ideologies, the question arises as to whether, and in what precise sense, one may properly speak of a legitimate discipline of sociology which may proceed without the explicit and formal employment of the metaphysics of being and the Thomist doctrine of natural law. In reply to this question, it must first be emphasised that it is not the purpose of this book to treat specifically of the methodology of sociology. The purpose, in this section, is merely to say what needs to be said in support of the critique of the ideology which is parasitic upon Weber's sociology. One or two guidelines will be offered in order to indicate why it is necessary to avoid certain extreme positions. It will be suggested that it would be mistaken to imagine that sociology could be properly conducted as if it could be absolutely autonomous in relation to philosophy. However, it would be wrong to imagine that no serious contribution could be made to sociological studies by someone who rejects the Thomist teaching on metaphysics and natural law.

The most usual argument in support of the absolute autonomy of sociology as a social science rests upon a certain comparison with the physical sciences and especially with physics itself. Certainly, the work of modern physicists does not seem to involve the explicit and formal employment of metaphysical principles. Physicists with very different philosophical positions seem to be able to reach agreement about conclusions within their science. The disagreements amongst physicists do not usually arise from philosophical or ideological disagreements amongst the physicists concerned. Accordingly, the question is raised as to whether we may be able to look forward to a period in which there may be an accepted science of sociology which may be able to proceed without the inconvenience of philosophical or ideological conflict.

In replying to this question, it seems necessary to insist that, although the science of physics may proceed without the explicit and formal employment of metaphysical principles, such principles are the *eventual and ultimate* defence of even the science of physics against subversion by erroneous philosophies and ideologies. The dangers to the natural sciences of the philosophical aberrations of certain scientists themselves arise not only in cultures in which totalitarian ideologies are dominant but even in cultures in which liberal ideologies are dominant. E. Gilson has considered why it was that certain intellectuals in a liberal culture could adopt positions which were potentially or actually subversive of the rationality of science. He has observed that 'for want of a rational metaphysics by which the use of science could be regulated, the liberal philosophers had no other choice than to attack science itself and to weaken its absolute rationality'.[29] Pointing out that this was a mistake, Gilson continued: 'Losing science will not give us philosophy. But if we lost philosophy itself we must be prepared to lose science, reason and liberty; in short, we are bound to lose Western culture itself together with its feeling for the eminent dignity of man'.

It has already been argued elsewhere that the non-philosophical special sciences do not seem, at least in our times, to be *equally* exposed to the risk of distortion by the intrusion of erroneous ideological elements.[30] Biology seems to be more vulnerable than physics and sociology seems to be more vulnerable than biology. Certainly, in order to maintain securely the complete intellectual integrity of sociology as an intellectual discipline, a sound philosophical background is at least *practically* necessary.

We have already recognised that the ideologist who denies right reason and who is committed to the instrumental use of reason as the slave of disordered passions, cannot 'perfect' the ideological character of his thought. Consequently, he retains some understanding of man which is not wholly erroneous. Of course, an ideologically orientated sociologist who is mistaken about the nature and content of natural morality will presuppose certain evaluations of social life and culture which involve, in varying ways, an implicit rejection of that objective natural law to which actual social life and culture will fragmentarily conform and from which it will often diverge. This implicit rejection of natural morality will arise, for example, in the course of comparing one more or less deformed type of society or culture with another type of society or culture which is equally deformed in other ways. Without a standard of natural morality, the ideological sociologist will very generally misunderstand the significance of those human social customs and habits which are morally evil. He will be in danger of attributing to man *as such* certain failings which are merely common human failings. Yet, although he will tend to misunderstand the ontological and philosophical, as well as the theological, significance of such evils, he will not wholly misunderstand them in every respect. In particular, even the ideological sociologist will be likely to retain some understanding of patterns of action which are in accord with the 'law' of disorderly concupiscence which St Thomas Aquinas designates as the *lex fomitis*.[31]

The ideological sociologist will not advert to St Thomas's teaching that the *lex fomitis* arises in consequence of original sin. Nor will the ideological thinker properly perceive that the *lex fomitis* is related to a certain precariousness in the balance between man's rational nature and his sensitive nature and *not* from any inherent contradiction in man. Finally, the ideologist will not properly assess private and social actions which flow from the *lex fomitis* as deviations from right reason and practical wisdom. Nevertheless, the ideological sociologist may well grasp, in his own inadequate way, a part of what St Thomas had in mind when he pointed out that the wise who follow the law of reason are less numerous than those who succumb to the assault of sensuality. Every observer — including even the ideological sociologist — will observe the common practice of men who frequently follow desires (such as sexual desire or desire for money or power) that are, in truth, inordinate desires subject to the *lex fomitis*. Accordingly, the *lex fomitis* seems to underlie certain quasi-constants which may enable us broadly to predict the common mediocrity of so much that takes place in private lives and in commercial and political life. A.M. Parent has specifically referred to the fact that rich men commonly tend to be inordinately concerned with increasing their riches and has suggested that this fact is a kind of constant (pertaining to the *lex fomitis*) which is even known, albeit in a perverted ideological system of doctrine, by Karl Marx.[32] Similarly, certain limited and somewhat ideologically distorted kinds of knowledge of sociological quasi-constants are certainly available also to the Weberian sociologist.

To sum up, we may say that, since man's life is the life of a being which cannot be totally subverted ontologically,[33] since his ideological perversion cannot be 'perfected', since his sins are negations and not something positive and, finally, since his essays in nihilism — however depraved — cannot be carried to a logical conclusion, the evil effects of ideological distortion in sociology are limited. However, these absolute limits upon the ideological perversion of man's thinking are terrifyingly wide. In practice, without the protection of some fairly substantive and salutary implicit philosophy — containing some significant measure of fundamental truth — sociological thinking will be commonly damaging both to man's intellectual life and also, to the extent that it has a social influence, upon the life of society.

Accordingly, the distorting effects of Weber's ideology upon his sociology will be, in a number of cases, very limited; in other cases, the distortion may be very grave. However that might be, one could not sufficiently defend Weber against the charge that his sociology is contaminated with ideological error merely by recalling his well-known distinction between the value-judgement (which he claims to exclude from social science) and the value reference.[34] Nor can Weber exonerate himself merely by pointing out that he claims for his sociological explanations only the status of partial explanations which make use of an appreciation or comprehension of the values of the cultures or persons under examination without commitment to those values. Clearly, there will always be, at least, a certain tension between true philosophy (the *philosophia perennis*) and Weberian sociology despite the fact that some of Weber's specific sociological results may not be in substantial contradiction with the principles of true philosophy. The practical tendency of the study of a Weberian sociology of moral, legal, political and religious phenomena can hardly help being far from 'ethically neutral'. The idea that really interesting and important sociological conclusions will be wholly 'neutral' in relation to the fundamental truth about the natural socio-political inclinations belonging to human nature is an idea which is both unrealistic and false.

Finally, if we find (as we do in fact find) that the actual origin of some of Weber's sociological concepts (such as his 'ethic of ultimate ends' and his 'ethic of responsibility') can be traced to the transposition of concepts derived ultimately from certain diverse — but diversely *erroneous* — philosophies or ideologies, then we must conclude that such defective sources will tend to vitiate in varying ways and varying degrees the validity of his sociological analysis.

Weber's ideology of the ideologies

From our brief consideration of the significance of the relationship between sociology and philosophy for any critical analysis of Weber's sociological methodology, we must return to outline an important conclusion which can now be drawn about the main subject of our study which is Weber's ideology itself. We can already see that Weber's ideology includes those so-called 'value-judgements' which he makes in the spheres of morals, politics and religion. We have seen that Weber admits *in effect* that his value-judgements are ideological in so far as he envisages them as having no objective foundation. Again, we have seen that Weber has a certain perspective from which he views the 'value-judgements' of others as well as his own. We have to consider whether Weber's doctrine about the entire 'realm' or 'arena' within which [he supposes] human value-choices are made is an ideological doctrine or not.

In order to understand the real character of Weber's doctrine about the entire realm of 'value-choice', we need to consider the status of certain postulates or presuppositions which Weber uses in distinguishing the two vocations of science and politics.[35] Unfortunately for Weber, there is no room in his overall system of thought about science and value for a truly *philosophical* theory of the relations between the two vocations. However, the very terms of Weber's distinction between the subject-matter of values *considered as facts* (scientific sociology) and the realm of values *considered as choices* ('value-judgements' within the arena of 'value-choice') prevent him from giving a *scientific* account of the relations between the two spheres. Therefore, in so far as Weber endeavours to take a bird's eye view of the relations between the vocation of scientific sociology and the vocation of moral, political and religious choice, his judgements will be non-scientific. If these judgements are non-philosophical and non-scientific (and since they are certainly not judgements in formal logic) what else can they be but ideological judgements?

We have seen that certain types which have a role in Weber's sociology are also found in Weber's characterisation of the realm of 'value-choice'. Indeed, with the aid of some process of transposition and transmutation, Weber arranges a certain two-way traffic of concepts between his sociology and his discussion of ideological value-choice. Yet, just as the ideological origin of Weber's sociological concepts can vitiate his sociology, so also the sociological origin of those concepts (however transposed or transmuted) cannot afford any rational basis for his account of the whole realm within which men are supposed to make their choices and impose their values. Weber's account of this realm is therefore neither a philosophy nor a science of the ideologies, it is simply an ideology of the ideologies. If Weber sometimes seems to give the impression that he has transcended the limitations of an irrational ideology in expounding the realm for human value-choice, this supposed transcendence is spurious.

Notes and references

1 See my discussion of Lenin's position in chapter 7.
2 Y. Simon, *The Tradition of Natural Law*, New York, 2nd printing, 1967, pp.16—27.
3 W.O. Martin, *Metaphysics and Ideology*, Milwaukee, 1959, p.72.
4 A.W. Gouldner, 'Anti-Minotaur: The Myth of a Value-free Sociology' in I.L. Horowitz (ed.), *The New Sociology*, New York, 1964, p.212.
5 Gouldner, 'Anti-Minotaur', p.216.
6 See my discussion of ideological substitution for human intelligence in chapter 8 and of ideological substitution for the 'economies' of the eternal law in my article 'On "Substitute Intelligences" in the Formation of Atheistic Ideology', *Laval théologique et philosophique*, October 1980, pp.239—53.
7 W.J. Ong, *Ramus: Method and the Decay of Dialogue*, Cambridge, Mass., 1958, p.165.
8 J. Wellmuth, *The Nature and Origins of Scientism*, Milwaukee, 1944, p.19.
9 Modern discussions of this general subject include J. Maritain, *The Degrees of Knowledge*, (second translation), London, 1959; E. Gilson, *The Unity of Philosophical Experience*, New York, 1950; and W.O. Martin, *The Order and Integration of Knowledge*, Ann Arbor, 1957.
10 N.W. Gilbert, *Renaissance Concepts of Method*, New York, 1960, pp.112—13.
11 W.J. Ong, *Ramus*, p.251.
12 See E.B.F. Midgley, *The Natural Law Tradition and the Theory of International Relations*, London/New York, 1975.
13 W.O. Martin, *Metaphysics and Ideology*, pp.57—8.
14 E. Gilson, *Unity of Philosophical Experience*, ch.IX.
15 See fuller treatment of Kant's teaching in Midgley, *Natural Law Tradition*, ch.10 and also G.G. Grisez, 'Kant and Aquinas: Ethical Theory', *The Thomist*, XXI, 1958.
16 Schopenhauer, *On the Basis of Morality*, Indianapolis, 1965.
17 L. Krieger, 'Kant and the Crisis of Natural Law' in *Journal of the*

History of Ideas, 26, 1965, pp.191—210.
18   Taparelli d'Azeglio, 'L'Aristocrazia del Diritto' in *Civilta Cattolica*, XII, ser.II (1853—5), p.260.
19   F.P. van de Pitte, 'Kant as Philosophical Anthropologist' in *Proceedings of the Third International Kant Congress*, L.W. Beck (ed.), Dordrecht, 1972. See also E.B.F. Midgley, 'Natural Law and Fundamental Rights' in *American Journal of Jurisprudence*, XXI, 1976.
20   R. Aron, 'What is a Theory of International Relations?' in *Theory and Reality in International Relations*, J.C. Farrell and A.P. Smith (eds.), New York, 1968.
21   L.W. Beck, *Studies in the Philosophy of Kant*, New York, 1965, p.227; and *La Philosophie Politique de Kant*, Paris, 1962, p.134.
22   E. Fleischmann, 'De Weber à Nietzsche' in *Archives Européenes de Sociologie*, 1964, pp.190—238.
23   J. Freund, *The Sociology of Max Weber*, London, 1968, p.6.
24   Ibid.
25   A. Dawe, 'The relevance of values' in *Max Weber and Modern Sociology*, Sahay (ed.), London, 1971, p.39.
26   Ibid., p.41 quoting Weber, *The Methodology of the Social Sciences*, New York, 1949, pp.81—2.
27   See E.J. Roesch, *The Totalitarian Threat: The Fruition of Modern Individualism, as seen in Hobbes and Rousseau*, New York, 1963.
28   *From Max Weber*, trans. and ed. H.H. Gerth and C. Wright Mills, London/Boston, 1948, p.143.
29   E. Gilson, *The Unity of Philosophical Experience*, New York, 1950, pp.292—3.
30   E.B.F. Midgley, *Natural Law Tradition*, pp.234—5.
31   St Thomas Aquinas, *Summa theologiae*, Ia IIae, q.91, art.6 and q.90, art.1, reply to obj.1.
32   A.M. Parent, 'Le Marxisme, comme tentative de soustraire l'homme à la loi de la concupiscence déréglée, *lex fomitis*' in *Sapientia Aquinatis*, vol.2, Rome, 1956, pp.149—58.
33   See discussion in chapter 3 and also in my article 'Authority, Alienation and Revolt', Aberdeen University Review, 1976, pp.372—83.
34   See M. Weber, *The Methodology of the Social Sciences*, pp.21—2.
35   *From Max Weber*, p.143 and elsewhere.

3 Weber versus moral and political philosophy

Since both Nietzsche and Marx explicitly reject preceding philosophy, they can reasonably be considered to be fundamental opponents of moral and political philosophy. The positions of Weber seem more obscure but, in an important statement, he indicates his solidarity with the modernist intellectual 'world' which he considers Nietzsche and Marx to have created. This basic solidarity is so strong that Weber will question the honesty of any contemporary philosopher who does not admit a fundamental intellectual indebtedness to the two great enemies of right reason. Weber observes:

> One can measure the honesty of a contemporary scholar, and above all, of a contemporary philosopher, in his posture toward Nietzsche and Marx. Whoever does not admit that he could not perform the most important parts of his own work without the work that those two have done swindles himself and others. Our intellectual world has to a great extent been shaped by Marx and Nietzsche.[1]

Although Weber's opposition to moral and political philosophy is fundamental and radical, its specific formulation and its nuances are partially characterised by pre-Marxian and pre-Nietzschean thinking. We have already recognised that Raymond Aron was not wrong in suggesting that the Weberian 'philosophy of values' has its origin in the Kantian philosophy.[2] With Kant, Weber abandons metaphysics, the natural law and also natural theology. The rejection of natural theology is crucial for Weber's perspective on natural law and for his entire ideology. Like Kant, Weber concurs in the rejection of natural theology by the Protestant pietist theologian, P.J. Spener. It is not that either Kant or Weber accepts Spener's theology as true. It is rather that they accept from Spener that, if there were such a thing as true Christian theology, it could only be of a kind which affords no place for natural theology. Accordingly, Weber announces somewhat complacently that, 'All pietist theology of the time, above all Spener, knew [sic!] that God was not to be found along the road by which the Middle Ages had sought Him'.[3]

Following Kant's denial of both natural theology and natural law, the Kantian secular ethics are rightly seen to be a doctrine without any real foundation. This is the testimony of Hegel, Schopenhauer and Nietzsche and — despite their numerous fundamental errors — these writers were, on this point, not wrong. Schopenhauer accuses Kant of purporting to provide, in effect, a substitute for theology in the doctrine of duty for duty's sake. Nietzsche regards Kant's ethics as merely Christianity in disguise. Schopenhauer, the great pessimist, and Nietzsche, the great optimist, of the radical successors of Kant, are both ideological thinkers whose point of departure is the supposed basic irrationality of the human will.

Weber's views on ethics have an ancestry which can be traced back both to Kant and to Machiavelli. Because Weber is eventually a post-Nietzschean ideologist and not a philosopher, he is disinclined or even unable to address himself seriously to the philosophical explanation of the complex relationship which subsists between his own ethical doctrine and the positions of both Kant and Machiavelli. His ideological appraisal sometimes presents more or less Kantian and more or less Machiavellian positions as opposed value-stances in ethics. Occasionally, these positions are represented as if they were in some way complementary to each other. Weber certainly tends to prefer Machiavellianism to Kantianism — especially in commending action in view of the 'necessities' of politics. Yet this preference is not justified philosophically: Weber tends rather to criticise ethical systems of the Kantian type as unserviceable. At the same time, Weber finds a certain place for ethics of the Kantian type as an element within his own post-Kantian system.

Weber's very limited acceptance of an element of a kind of Kantian ethical stance within his own post-Kantian system does implicitly remind us that Kant himself incorporated within his own doctrine something of the essence of the Machiavellian thought itself. H.V. Jaffa has rightly pointed out that it was one of Leo Strauss's achievements to draw attention to the fact that 'in the decisive respects, Kant too was a Machiavellian'.[4] Elsewhere, we have attempted to analyse those orientations of Kant's thought which approximate to the Machiavellian teaching and even carry it further in the direction of a more radical modernism.[5] Weber's ideological manoeuvres cannot help taking place against the background of the true philosophical relationships between the errors of Machiavelli and the errors of Kant. However, Weber himself does not have a clear insight into these relationships because he judges them in part in a distorted post-Nietzschean perspective. Accordingly, although Weber is not a faithful disciple of either Machiavelli or Kant, he will find himself sometimes opposing an element of Kantianism in the name of Machiavellianism and sometimes accepting an element of Kantianism into his own post-Kantian system. Similarly, he will occasionally seem to represent some combination of elements from Kantianism and Machiavellianism as essential for the completeness of his own thought.

Of course, if Weber had correctly understood the rapports between Kant and Machiavelli philosophically in the light of fundamental truth, he would *eo ipso* have abandoned his eclectic ideological stance in the process of really understanding what it involved. As a matter of fact, we know that Weber does not abandon his idiosyncratic stance but rather seeks to sustain it by balancing his ideology, as it were, between the optimism of Nietzsche and the pessimism of Schopenhauer.

Weber's sociological scholarship serves as a pabulum to moderate some of the excesses of more extreme positions. Weber is no doubt protected by his preoccupation with 'science' from a too frequent preoccupation with those tendencies towards a doctrine of irredeemable pessimism which Schopenhauer inconsistently sought to keep at bay through his preoccupation with a 'morality' and an 'art' which, on Schopenhauer's premises, could no longer retain their true *raison d'être*. Similarly, Weber's preoccupation with 'science' may have served to restrain him from some of the more exultant posturings of Nietzsche. Nevertheless, there is no doubt that Weber cannot offer any real solution to the problems of ethics with which the German philosophers of the time had vainly struggled. Since Weber could not solve the problems of moral philosophy, nor in consequence could he resolve the problems of political philosophy.

Weber's rejection of a hierarchy of values; and his notions of consistency

By rejecting every theory of the natural moral law, Weber implicitly rejected the Thomist doctrine of the natural law although there is no reason to suppose that he properly understood what he was rejecting. However, given this rejection, it is not surprising that Weber will presuppose that a hierarchical ordering of values — as the basis of a coherent morality — cannot be attained without appeal to ecclesiastical dogmas.[6] Here we encounter a non-scientific judgement about the supposed inability of philosophy to provide basic guidelines for the hierarchical ordering of values. It must be emphasised that Weber is not simply saying that he does not personally accept a philosophy which claims to provide a basis for a hierarchical ordering of values; he is claiming that it is logically impossible from any standpoint to uphold a philosophical morality. Yet, we may well ask: What is the status and the methodology of this 'overall' judgement about the scope and limits of all alternative 'logically tenable' (though mutually contradictory) standpoints? Weber's formulations about this are not free from a certain hesitancy. He will say that the critical judgement involved has only a dialectical character; he will say that it can be no more than a formal logical judgement; he insists that it produces no new knowledge of facts but he will be sufficiently uncertain about its rigorously logical character that he will say that its validity is similar to that of logic.[7]

Weber's teaching certainly involves the rejection of the [Thomist] notion of the common good irrespective of whether this notion is expressed (incompletely) in terms of philosophy or (more adequately) in terms of both philosophy and dogmatic theology. Raymond Aron recognises this implication of Weber's thought when he says that:

> political decisions will ... always be dictated by a commitment
> to values which cannot be demonstrated. No-one can decree
> with assurance to what extent a given individual or group must
> be sacrificed ... in Weber's mind it is as if the Catholic notion of
> the common good of the polity were not valid, or in any case
> could not be rigorously defined.[8]

Aron's interpretation here is too cautiously qualified. Certainly, Weber's objections to the notion of the common good do not rest upon merely practical difficulties about determining with precision what the common good may specifically require in particular cases. Moreover, Weber's fundamental theoretical objections to the [Thomist] concept of the common good do not merely consist in preferring not to use this concept as an ideal type for the purposes of a fruitful analysis (in scientific sociology) of conflicting ethical standpoints. Nor is Weber simply saying that the [Thomist] concept of the common good is not a value which he personally chooses to prefer. Rather does he imply that, quite apart from his own particular private value-judgement, there is something illogical about the notion of the common good. He seems to hold — on the basis of a procedure which is alleged to be either purely logical or purely 'quasi-logical' — that the internal consistency of a value-system requires it to be necessarily internally inconsistent. How then does Weber arrive at this astonishing — not to say paradoxical — conclusion?

The occasion of this absurdity is to be found in Weber's conception of the tragedy of the human predicament. Man is gifted with logic: a logic or 'quasi-logic' which enables him to apprehend ideal types of value positions and to test the internal consistency of value systems which might be presented for scientific investigation. If follows from the coexistence of logic and human life that each act of the moral life can come to be exposed to a relentless analysis of the coherence or incoherence of its value orientation in terms of logic or quasi-logic. Evidently, however, Weber does not suppose that the moral life of a man can ever withstand this kind of criticism either in practice *or even in theory*. Total logical consistency over time in adherence to totally consistent ethical norms is not to be expected. The Weberian sociologist should not expect to find such total consistency among the empirical phenomena which he studies. Nor does Weber in his private value-judgements assent to an ethical system possessed of a total consistency. Yet the norms of logic at least remain and so we cannot avoid asking: In what way and to what extent can one take account of logic in the living of the active life?

In answering this question, Weber — in company with a great part of the modern world — falls into the trap of supposing that the challenge of logic can be met — so far as it can be met at all — by postulating an autonomous virtue of honesty or sincerity which is unconnected with the other virtues. In effect, a man is advised to take account of the challenge of logic by honestly and explicitly recognising — and even affirming — the heterogeneity of his own private value-judgements. It therefore appears that the whole realm of mutually incompatible values is characterised not only by the Weberian framework of ideal types and the laws of logic or 'quasi-logic' but also by certain exclusions. A value system is, in a sense, excluded if it claims — and in so far as it claims — to challenge the Weberian postulate of the ultimate incommensurability of the goals and values of any and every value-position held — or capable of being held — in the actual world.[9] The Weberian thesis comes to this: that whichever values, whichever gods, whichever devils, might compete for our allegiance, the one thing which seems to be ruled out is an *ordered* allegiance. In other words, the only notions — namely, the notion of a hierarchy of goods and the notion of the common good — which can begin to provide a consistent basis for rational human action are, as it were, ruled out as lacking in internal consistency.

To sum up, we have seen that Weber wants to envisage a range of logically legitimate choices among various value-judgements — including some of which he privately disapproves — but that he considers that the [Thomist] concept of the common good (whether philosophically or theologically expressed) is, somehow, to be rejected, as it were, on grounds pertaining to the logic of the realm of value. This 'logic' does not belong to social science, nor is it supposed to belong to Weber's own value system in so far as this is envisaged as differentiated from other 'legitimate' value systems. Accordingly, the [Thomist] concept of the common good is, in reality, excluded by Weber on the basis of an initial prejudice of which Weber himself seems to be imperfectly aware. This prejudice is evidently an element in his ideology of ideologies.

The ideological role of Weber's ideal types

Having excluded, on ideological grounds, the only viable principles upon which a solution of the problem of values could have been achieved, Weber then declares, in effect, that the problem of moral and political norms for the purposes of action is insoluble. In order to consider what Weber will construct as a substitute for right reason, we must notice that he offers a fourfold classification of actions: two forms of rational action (one directed to a goal; the other directed to a value) and two forms of non-rational action (affective action and traditional action). Of course, the significance of this classification is not confined to the field of sociology alone. The postulation of heterogeneous forms of action — in so far as it envisages heterogeneous forms of 'rational action' — has implications for Weber's ideology of the realm of values.

More specifically, as we have seen, the formation of Weber's ideology owes much to an intellectual climate in which there had been a debate between a more or less Kantian position and a more or less Machiavellian position. It is obvious enough that Weber regards the conflict between these two kinds of positions as having importance not only in his scientific sociology but also in his non-scientific reflections on morals and politics. Accordingly, some of the ideal types which are sometimes used as instruments of analysis in scientific sociology may also be seen to have a constitutive role in establishing the scope of the Weberian realm of values. Although Weber's ideal types are intended to be used in a value-free 'science', some of them are found to have suffered a sea-change when they reappear as parameters of the non-scientific realm of values. Accordingly, as we have seen, the Weber who does not prescribe for anyone what values one should choose will nevertheless announce to his readers what value realm there is from which they must make their choices. Moreover, Weber purports to do this without resort even to philosophy. Certainly, the flaw in such a theory of the realm of values which purports to avoid philosophical principles is somewhat analogous to the flaw in those celebrated theories of 'things indifferent'[10] which purported to determine the realm of those things neither forbidden nor commanded by natural or divine law, without thereby claiming any competence to declare either the natural or the divine law.

We know that Weber does not consider that the categories of true and false are properly applicable to value systems. The closest approach to the construction of a substitute for truth or right reason in Weber's 'ideology of ideologies' is to be found in his notion — also used in his sociology — of an 'internally consistent value system'.[11] It would appear, however, that, from the standpoint of right reason, the notion of *internal* consistency of objectively erroneous 'value systems' is, at best, a somewhat relative one. Given that Weber does not envisage even the possibility of a homogeneous value system, his procedure for the 'deduction of implications'[12] of [internally heterogeneous and therefore erroneous] value positions is ambiguous, precarious and, properly speaking, not fully tenable. More importantly, all value systems — true or false — evidently claim to be actually applicable to the life of men who really exist in the world which really exists. Hence, any value system which is not consistent with whatever norms are built into human nature could only claim to be 'internally consistent' — if it could plausibly make that claim at all — by detaching itself from any application to the real world and adopting the rationale of a rationalistic fantasy about merely possible creatures who are not human beings.

It is therefore necessary to insist, over against Weber, that the only 'value system' which could claim perfect consistency in its application to the real world would be a system rooted in the truth. The truth requires the proper ordering of all subordinate goods according to an objective moral order which is determined in principle and in its specific tendencies by human nature itself — and its natural relation to the rest of nature and to the Author of nature — and which is open to the reception of its gratuitous completion in the supernatural order. Any other 'value system' will be either incomplete or to some extent erroneous. In the absence of any reference to the supernatural order, the value system proposed by valid philosophy will be incomplete and, in the actual world, some degree of error would, practically speaking, be virtually inevitable. In the absence of even a valid philosophy, any proposed value system will be *eo ipso* somewhat erroneous, since what is not in accord with valid philosophy will be somewhat inconsistent with valid philosophy. Finally, since the whole field of philosophical truths accessible to human reason belongs to that order of values with which man is, in principle, orientated, no system of value which rejects a valid element of the ordered realm of human morality can be truly consistent with human nature. If follows that any value system which is not in accord with human nature cannot be held with true consistency by a being who is constituted by that nature.

Weber's ideological misconceptions about natural law and Christian ethics

An examination of Weber's teaching indicates that his misunderstanding of natural law is inextricably connected with his misunderstanding of Christian ethics.[13] Moreover, Weber's views on both natural law and Christian ethics are connected with the opinion, which he shares with Machiavelli, that, in many cases, the ruler must ignore morality in the course of acting in the political arena. There is certainly a connection between Weber's political ideology and his sociological analysis of the State in terms of coercive force.[14] In his political ideology, Weber tends to ignore certain factors — which are excluded also from his sociological analysis which does not refer to the ends of the State — such as the moral and legal distinctions between just and unjust police action and between just and unjust war. Accordingly, outside social science, as well as within it, Weber is primarily concerned not with the concepts of just and unjust force but with the concept of force as such abstracted from its moral and legal character.

Of course, it might be objected that Weber discusses the legitimation of political force in his sociological studies. However, this discussion does not advert to the problem of objective legitimacy. Indeed, even when Weber refers to 'inner justifications' pertaining to legitimacy, his thought cannot reasonably be interpreted as specifically concerned with the objective philosophical justification of political authority either in general or in the case of a particular régime.[15] Weber is concerned with alleged 'justifications' (irrespective of whether these are valid or invalid) which, Weber suggests, claimants to political power commonly use in seeking to establish (in the minds of the people) a supposition (irrespective of whether this supposition is right or wrong) of the legitimacy of their claims to power.

Weber's acceptance of a *Realpolitik* contrary to political morality is forcibly stated in his inaugural lecture of 1895 and it remained an essential element of his teaching throughout his life. In the lecture, he even went so far as to suggest that the ultimate goal of scientific sociology itself was political education directed to the social unification of the nation for 'the difficult struggles of the future'.[16] It is sufficiently evident that these 'difficult struggles' were envisaged in relation to a German politics of world power. More commonly, against the background of his sociological analysis of force as such, Weber formulates the moral problem of politics in this sense: Is the use of force as such justified or not? He seeks to defend this oversimplified formulation by suggesting that those who employed force differed only with regard to their intentions or the ends which they pursued since the means, namely, coercive force, is identical in each case. In supposing that all coercive force has an identical character as a means, Weber is implicitly rejecting the traditional view that some kinds of violent means (for example, the killing of an unjust aggressor in necessary self-defence) may be morally lawful whereas other kinds of violent means (for example, the direct and deliberate killing of the innocent) are immoral even if they are employed in order to secure some good or other.

In proposing a false dichotomy between a quasi-Machiavellian use of physical coercion and the general repudiation of coercive force in all circumstances, Weber may have been unduly influenced by a lively sense of the moral dangers involved in the use of any kind of violence for any purpose whatsoever.[17] Weber then finds himself disinclined to uphold the valid distinction between those uses of physical force which are morally wrong and those uses which, though not immoral, can hardly be done without there being some incidental temptation to immorality.

Weber tells us that Christian ethics are inapplicable to political life because they supposedly fail to take account of the average deficiencies of the people.[18] This opinion is not really justified. Obviously, the Christian ruler is not bound to make every grave sin liable to criminal punishment. However, the Christian ruler is not forbidden to correct, by means of coercive force, certain wrongs committed by his subjects. Weber does not accept the validity of this Christian approach to politics because, like Machiavelli, he entertains a concept of the moral and religious values of Christ's teaching which is, in a certain sense, sentimental and even naive. Indeed, Weber seems to envisage the authentic Christian as, amongst other things, a pacifist pure and simple. In formulating the moral problems connected with physical coercion in terms of all or nothing, Weber ignores the distinction between the licit and illicit uses of force and simply says that 'fighting is everywhere fighting'.[19]

Weber concludes that the ethic of the Sermon on the Mount contains unconditional prohibitions of the use of physical force (even in legitimate defence of the common good) and of the ownership of property and so on. According to this rather idiosyncratic interpretation of the 'absolute ethics of the gospel', unconcern is said to be the essence of the ethical commandment.[20] Weber seems to envisage, in the doctrine of Jesus, the Apostles and St Francis, a universal prohibition of physical coercion which is contrary to St Paul's teaching (in the Epistle to the Romans) that the political authorities use the sword as ministers of God against evil-doers.

Given this preconceived assumption about the nature of authentic Christian ethics, Weber implies, without proof, that Catholic ethics (and especially the Catholic distinctions between precepts and counsels) are indefensible and that this 'gradation of ethics and its organic integration into the doctrine of salvation is less consistent than in India'.[21] In considering this judgement of Weber's, we must bear in mind that his knowledge of the various schools of natural law seems to have been almost entirely confined to the post-Reformation Protestant and Rationalist writers on the subject. He never seems to show any real grasp of the Thomist teaching. Even when he appears to be writing very generally about the adoption of natural law by 'Christianity', his approach is governed primarily, if not exclusively, by his preoccupation with an image of Christianity which he draws from Protestant sources.

In his work *On Law in Economy and Society*, Weber suggests that the *lex naturae* is 'an essentially Stoic creation which was taken over by Christianity for the purpose of constructing a bridge between its own ethics and the norms of the world'.[22] Despite the oversimplification involved, it might, with some plausibility, be attempted to characterise (say) the natural law theory of Pufendorf in some such terms as these. However, one certainly could not dismiss the Thomist teaching on natural law in this fashion. The rashness of Weber's discussion of Christian natural law in general emerges again in the sentence in which he says that the natural law was 'the law legitimated by God's will for all men of this world of sin and violence, and [which] thus stood in contrast to those of God's commands which were revealed directly to the faithful and are evident only to the elect'.[23] The phraseology of this whole sentence is redolent of Protestantism and is alien to Catholic thought. Weber attributes the legitimacy of the natural law to a particular state of mankind and not to human nature as such. He envisages the natural law as secularised in such a way that it is not coherent with revealed law. He implies that the revealed law is known only to the elect or to the faithful in so far as they are deemed to be included among the elect. All these three presuppositions are contrary to the mind of St Thomas.

Despite the degradation of the concepts of natural law and Christian ethics in the thought of Weber, we need not suppose that he is committed to the view that the ethical life is derivative from and simply dependent upon the economic life. Dorothy Emmet has suggested, not without reason, that the more fruitful approach to Weber's work on *The Protestant Ethic and the Spirit of Capitalism* is to interpret it as suggesting the *mutual* conditioning of the economic and the ethical life. Accordingly, she envisages sociology of the Weberian type as postulating a 'soft' form of relativism which 'is not committed to denying that there may be *special* ethical interests and motives' but which 'is only committed to saying that the form of their expression and the behaviour to which they give rise is conditioned by other factors in their social context'.[24]

If this is not an incorrect interpretation of Weber's position, it still does not resolve the difficulties inherent in that position. Of course, no-one will deny that social observation and experience commonly show that moral and religious practice and even the moral and religious opinions of many people are commonly defective and improperly influenced and conditioned by factors contrary to true religion and morality. Again, examination of defective manifestations of moral and religious belief and practice may indicate that the spheres of morality and religion are often treated as if they were merely special departments of life coexisting but not in harmony with incompatible norms held and put into practice in other departments of life. Certainly, a sociologist may sometimes discover that, *in a sense*, a particular moral or religious practice and a particular heterogeneous economic practice may mutually reinforce each other. However, such *mutual* conditioning is incompatible with the true architectonic supremacy of theology and moral philosophy *vis-à-vis* the special science of economics. Any economic practice or theory which is not fully in accord with true moral philosophy and theology may happen to reinforce some sort of defective religious and moral practice and theory but it will, at the same time, tend to reinforce actual disorder or error in that religious and moral practice and theory.

The fact that defective moral and religious practice and its doctrine is partially exposed to reductive sociological analysis does not suffice to justify Weber's perspective. For, certainly, there exists — somewhat obscured no doubt by the confused practice and the strange conflicts found in actual human life — a law deriving from man's nature and a vocation belonging to the supernatural order which claim a universal jurisdiction over the whole man. It is this natural law and this Christian vocation together which not only defy sociological reduction but which claim the right to determine the scope and the rule of the other departments of life including the moral principles applicable to the economic life itself. This jurisdiction is not that of one power among many but of one which is, by right, superior to all and which, in a sense, pervades all. The serious denial of this architectonic status of moral philosophy and theology in the name of ethical interests considered to be special and heterogeneous in relation to other, supposedly legitimate, human interests will inevitably lead to the ideological distortion of ethics and religion.

Nevertheless, Mommsen has sought to insist,[25] perhaps more strongly than Dorothy Emmet, that 'Weber always insisted that every genuine religious ethic should, at least in its highest postulates, derive from purely religious roots and not originate in economic or social or psychological considerations'. If we were fully to accept Mommsen's arguments, we might be led to surmise that Weber could have upheld a proper distinction between 'genuine religious ethics' and 'ideological pseudo-religious ethics'. However, it is necessary to ask what Weber really means by 'an ethic which derives from purely religious roots'. Certainly, Weber does not tell us what he means and Mommsen's sympathetic appraisal does not reveal to us what Weber has left obscure. Mommsen points to the difference between Weber's formulations and those of Marx but he hesitates to be definitive about the relation of Weber to Nietzsche on the point at issue.

When we cut through Weber's obscurities, we shall recognise that he is in an impossible position.[26] He seeks on the one hand to affirm that there is such a thing as a 'genuine religious ethic'. On the other hand, if all religions were false, there could be no such thing as a genuine religious ethic. Since Weber's teaching generally implies that there is no true religion, his positions can lead only to the conclusion that even a supposedly genuine religious ethic must be, in reality, an ideological ethic whose ideological origins are merely more obscure and subtle than the gross ideological origins of manifestly pseudo-religious ethics crudely motivated, conditioned or distorted by economic interest.

Weber's 'heterogeneity of ethics' *vis-à-vis* the philosophy of man

Weber seems to suggest that what he would call a 'genuine religious ethic' is an instance of a class of ethical standpoints which he designates as 'ethics of ultimate ends'. We have already seen that Weber's concept of a 'genuine religious ethic' is philosophically and theologically arbitrary. We find further evidence of the philosophically arbitrary character of Weber's notion of the 'ethics of ultimate ends' when he tells us that it is not simply the devotees of the [Weberian version of the] Sermon on the Mount but also the revolutionary syndicalists who fall into the category of 'absolute moralists'. Again, there is the implication in Weber that the 'ethics of ultimate ends' is to be found in the 'Kantian ethical judgement'. Elsewhere, Weber suggests that a man is following 'a pure ethic of absolute ends' when he is not a pacifist, nor a disciple of Kant, nor a revolutionary syndicalist but when he 'chases after the absolute good in a war of beliefs'.[27]

When we reflect upon this pastiche of mutually incompatible points of view which Weber has presented to us, we are bound to recognise that his expression 'the ethics of ultimate ends' is not a philosophical concept but a term which is the reflection in Weber's 'ideology of the ideologies' of a rather simple sociological type: the type of unconcern. More generally, it can be said that, in Weber's essay on 'Politics as a Vocation', the two types of ethics — the 'ethics of ultimate ends' and the 'ethics of responsibility' — are elements of an erroneous ideology which takes its origin from the illicit transposition of a sociological typology which, even in the field of sociology itself, is oversimplified and misleading.

Certainly, the typology of the two types of ethics which Weber advances is somewhat unoriginal. Something of this sort is to be found in Machiavelli. Moreover, like Machiavelli, Weber seems to have an ambiguous attitude involving some respect mixed with his contempt for the type of absolute morality which he has characterised. Nevertheless, when Weber announces that absolute ethics is a serious business, he will go on to prefer an 'ethics of responsibility'. For example, he will tell us that he finds beauty in Machiavelli's praise for those who 'deemed the greatness of their native city higher than the salvation of their souls'.[28] It is then no surprise to recall that Weber holds that 'one cannot prescribe to anyone whether he should follow an ethic of absolute ends or an ethic of responsibility, or when the one and when the other'.[29] Again, this is in accord with Weber's statement that all ethically orientated conduct may be guided by one of two fundamentally differing and irreconcilably opposed maxims'[30] corresponding with the two types of ethics. Hence, Weber goes on to say that 'the ultimately possible attitudes towards life are irreconcilable and hence their struggle can never be brought to a final conclusion'.[31]

Of course, the fundamental objection to all this is concerned not merely with the spurious simplicity of Weber's distinction between the two types of ethics. Since Weber envisages many differing ethical doctrines under each type — and since he envisages that a man may sometimes act from an ethic falling under one type and sometimes according to an ethic of the other type — our fundamental objection is concerned with Weber's ideological approach to the so-called *heterogeneity* of each and every value system. This radical heterogeneity will manifest itself in various forms and under diverse aspects which we shall examine in later chapters of this study. We shall examine the fallacies underlying Weber's preoccupation with a supposed synthesis of blind bureaucratic discipline and individual 'charisma' in chapters 4, 5 and 6. We shall also see — in chapter 7 — that there is no tenable foundation for Weber's attempt to formulate a political theory by conjoining an erroneous individualism with an erroneous collectivism. Although Raymond Aron does not discern the true nature of these errors in Weber, he aptly sums up the ideology which contains them when he says that 'The heterogeneity of ethics ... makes our whole existence "a series of ultimate choices by which the soul chooses its destiny". The multiplicity of gods expresses an ineluctible struggle ... Existence consists in choosing between different gods'.[32]

Despite this basic heterogeneity — which requires that 'Each of us must impose our own meaning upon an otherwise meaningless world',[33] Weber cannot avoid seeking some resolution of his antinomies. Even in considering the uses of scientific sociology, he will write, with obvious approval, of its value in helping a man 'to give himself an account of the ultimate meaning of his own conduct'.[34] Although he has opted, in general, for an ethic of responsibility, he will still hold that 'man would not have attained the possible unless time and again he had reached out for the impossible'.[35] Eventually, Weber purports to synthesise his two types of radically divergent and incompatible ethical ordinations. He imputes to them a supposed 'unity' by merely asserting that, after all, the two types of ethics are not absolute contrasts but rather supplementary to each other! Weber does not explain how this could be shown. Indeed, since he has previously emphasised that no-one can prescribe in this matter, it would seem impossible for him to devise any plausible argument in favour of his unexpectedly triumphant conclusion that absolute ethics and responsible ethics 'in unison constitute a genuine man — a man who *can* have the "calling for politics" '.[36]

It is interesting that, in this last passage, Weber seems to presuppose that there is a link between the validity of his ethical 'synthesis' (of the two types of ethics 'in unison') and the validity of his doctrine of man as an authentic being. This (unwittingly profound) presupposition of Weber naturally leads us to surmise that, if his ethical 'synthesis' is spurious, his doctrine about 'genuine man' will also be spurious. Certainly, it is not merely that Weber cannot advance an authentic or adequate moral synthesis, it is rather that what he advances is not really a moral theory at all. Consequently, we find — as we should expect to find — that Weber not only fails to advance a doctrine which adequately expounds what it is to be authentically human, it is rather that what he does advance is not even a doctrine of man as a being which could really exist!

In other words, we must conclude that the ontological consequences of Weber's teaching are grave and irremediable within his presuppositions. For, if 'human nature' were *per impossibilia* subject naturally and properly to the incompatible ordinations which Weber has arbitrarily postulated, then it would follow that there could be no such thing as a real human being. St Thomas Aquinas would explain the difficulty here by recalling that man cannot have fundamental inherent natural inclinations towards logically incompatible ends, that he cannot naturally desire evil as such and that he cannot naturally desire to be another kind of being.[37] Indeed, St Thomas goes so far as to say that a being embodying such contradictions could not be brought into being even by Omnipotence.[38] We shall see, in later chapters, that, lurking behind Weber's abandonment of the exigencies of a true philosophy of man, there is to be found the spirit of the Nietzschean superman who purports not only to usurp the prerogatives of God but even to accomplish those things which God cannot do because they cannot be done!

Notes and references

1   Quoted by E. Baumgarten and discussed in A. Mitzman, *The Iron Cage: An Historical Interpretation of Max Weber*, New York, 1970, p.182ff.
2   R. Aron, *Main Currents in Sociological Thought*, vol.2, p.206.
3   *From Max Weber*, p.142.
4   M.V. Jagga, *The Conditions of Freedom*, Baltimore, 1975, p.4.
5   E.B.F. Midgley, *The Natural Law Tradition and the Theory of International Relations*, London, 1975, pp.276–99.
6   Having maintained that there is no (rational or empirical) scientific procedure which can yield a practical moral decision, Weber says: 'there is, in general, no logically tenable standpoint from which it could be denied except a hierarchical ordering of values unequivocally prescribed by ecclesiastical dogmas', *The Methodology of the Social Sciences*, p.19.
7   Weber suggests that scientific criticism of historically given value-judgements consists in a 'formal logical judgement' (Ibid., p.54). He also says of this scientific procedure that: 'Its "validity" is similar to that of logic'. (Ibid., p.20).
8   Aron, *Main currents in Sociological Thought*, vol.2, p.209.
9   Weber does suggest that the actions prescribed by an ethic of absolute ends and an ethic of responsibility might, accidentally and occasionally, coincide. This suggestion does not achieve any resolution of the Weberian antinomies.
10   See, for example, the erroneous theory advanced in John Locke, *Two Tracts on Government*, P. Abrams (ed.), Cambridge, 1967.
11   Weber will envisage *divergent* attitudes — involving mutually contradictory 'values' — as each being based upon 'ultimate, internally "consistent" value axioms', *The Methodology of the Social Sciences*, p.20.
12   Ibid., p.20.
13   See also later discussions in chapters 4, 5 and 6.
14   *From Max Weber*, pp.77–8.
15   Ibid., pp.78–9.
16   M. Weber, 'Der Nationalstaat und die Volkswirtschaftspolitik' in

Gesammelte Politische Schriften, Tübingen, 1971, pp.23—4.
17   *From Max Weber*, pp.121—2, 125—6.
18   Ibid., p.121.
19   Ibid., p.119.
20   Ibid., p.119.
21   Ibid., p.124.
22   M. Weber, *On Law in Economy and Society*, M. Rheinstein (ed.), Cambridge, Mass., p.287.
23   Ibid.
24   D. Emmet, *Rules, Roles and Relations*, London, 1966, pp.91—2.
25   W.J. Mommsen, 'Max Weber's Political Sociology and his Philosophy of World History', *International Social Science Journal*, vol.17, 1965, p.30.
26   See further discussion of the relation of Weber's position to Nietzsche's evaluation of religious ethics, in chapter 6.
27   *From Max Weber*, p.126.
28   Ibid., p.126.
29   Ibid., p.127.
30   Ibid., p.120.
31   Ibid., p.152. See also Weber, *The Methodology of the Social Sciences*, pp.17—18.
32   R. Aron, *German Sociology*, p.84.
33   See discussion in A. Dawe's article in *Max Weber and Modern Sociology*, Sahay (ed.), London, 1971, p.42.
34   *From Max Weber*, p.152.
35   Ibid., p.128.
36   Ibid., p.127.
37   See St Thomas Aquinas, *Summa theologiae*, I, q.76, art.1 and I, q.63, art.3; *Quaest. Disp. De Anima*, Art.XI; *Summa contra Gentiles*, II, c.58(5); and so on.
38   See St Thomas Aquinas, *Summa theologiae*, I, q.25, art.3 and further discussion in chapter 6.

4 Protestantism and the spirit of Weberian secularism

Max Weber is not a theologian. Yet, despite this deficiency, there is a certain sense in which we can say that Weber, no less than Bossuet himself, is aware of the variations of Protestantism. Weber has not an adequate understanding but he does have a peculiar sensitivity to the spectrum of mutually incompatible positions which constitutes Protestantism. At the same time, it is to this spectrum to which Weber habitually returns when he thinks of Christianity. An acute awareness of the contradictions within the ambit of Protestantism has led many people to the Catholic faith but, for Weber, it is as if the rejection of Protestantism were identical with the rejection of Christianity as such. Accordingly, the incompatibilities within Protestantism provide part of the occasion of — and the reinforcement of — his unbelief.

It would not be correct to suggest, however, that Weber's attitude to the Protestant variations has absolutely nothing in common with the Catholic attitude. R.S. Devane, in a spirited criticism of modern individualism, has quoted with approval the passage in *The Protestant Ethic and the Spirit of Capitalism* in which Weber recognises the extreme inhumanity of religious individualism which imposes a feeling of unprecedented inner loneliness within the isolated individual.[1] Weber recognises varying degrees of religious individualism within Protestantism. He observes, for example, that the complete elimination of salvation through the Church and the sacraments was not developed to its final conclusions in Lutheranism. Yet, Weber's evaluation of Protestantism has this also in common with the Catholic evaluation:

Weber does not disapprove of Protestant positions simply and solely in proportion to the apparent degree of individualism involved.

From the standpoint of Catholicism, the varieties of Protestantism are seen to have very complex relations with the faith from which they variously deviate. It cannot be affirmed, without qualifications, whether Luther or Kierkegaard is further away from Catholicism. Weber's standpoint is analogous to the Catholic standpoint in this one respect: that it cannot be said, without qualifications, whether Lutheran Protestantism or Kierkegaardian Protestantism is the further away from Weberianism. With this in mind, let us consider how the nuanced position of Weber *vis-à-vis* these types of Protestantism leads him not to Catholicism but to atheism.

It must be recognised that Kierkegaard sometimes seems to press religious individualism — the quest for God of the isolated soul — to the utmost limits. Moreover, before his 'conversion', there is a background of revolt against the divine order which is of such intensity and persistence that more than one learned writer has gone so far as to deny the genuineness of Kierkegaard's 'conversion' to any species of Christianity.[2] Although this would seem, perhaps, to be an extreme interpretation, it cannot be denied that there is, in Kierkegaard's writings, a certain relentless spirit of paradox which is not, in fact, in accord with the Christian revelation. However, there are certain moments in the thought of Kierkegaard which seem to represent something of a return to the spirit of Catholic thought. Kierkegaard was not unwilling to reproach the teaching of Luther with having falsified Christianity on the pretext that mankind would otherwise have to despair. Kierkegaard is, accordingly, inclined to resist that dilution of the evangelical counsels which was endemic in Lutheranism. However, Kierkegaard's emphasis on the counsels occurs in a setting in which there is no account of human nature or society.

Against this background, let us try to expound Weber's predicament *vis-à-vis* the Lutheran and Kierkegaardian types of Protestantism. First of all, Weber admits his frank admiration for Luther who (Weber asserts) 'towers above all others'. Certainly, even Lutheranism brings the tragedy of religious individualism in its train and, certainly, Protestantism of the Kierkegaardian type is an aggravation of Lutheranism by way of an extremity of inner loneliness. In this respect, Weber is bound to prefer Luther to Kierkegaard. However, Weber observes that there is in Lutheranism a rejection of part at least of the Christian teaching on morality. Weber observes in a letter to Harnack in 1906 that 'Much as Luther towers above all others ... Lutheranism, in its historical manifestations, is for me, I can't deny it, the horror of horrors'.[3] In the same letter, Weber goes so far as to say 'That our nation was never schooled by rigorous asceticism is the root cause of all that I find despicable in it (as well as in myself)'. It follows that Weber would be obliged to regard Kierkegaard as a teacher of the purification (by way of asceticism) not only of Lutherism but even of the morally lax teaching of Luther himself. In this respect, at a certain stage, Weber is bound to prefer Kierkegaard to Luther. Later in his professional life, Weber (like Luther himself) relaxed the disordered 'ascetical' rigour of his views on the control of the passions in favour of a disordered kind of indulgent view idiosyncratically associated with a bogus 'mysticism'.

Certainly, Luther's teaching provides a preparation not only for the Calvinism of Calvin but also, to some extent, for that 'carnal Calvinism' (to use Leo Strauss's apt phrase) which is, for Weber, sociologically interesting and economically serviceable. Despite the fact that Weber seems to be interested in ideologically distorted manifestations of Christianity, which are closely correlated with social and economic change, Weber seems — implicitly at least — to recognise that these ideological forms of Protestantism have become far removed from the teaching of Jesus Christ. Consequently, Weber seems to be not un-aware of the fact that even 'Lutherism' itself is considerably removed from the ethical teaching of Christ.

When we consider the dilution of ethics in Luther[4] and the secular-ising effect of his resort to an Erastian solution of the problem of Church order, it is evident enough that Luther, despite his dramatic stand, is not the one who is going to provide Weber with the type of Christian who upholds the Christian revelation as a truth which remains inviolate despite the attempts made by human mediocrity to emasculate it. Indeed, despite the extremely idiosyncratic elements in Kierkegaard's thought, it is Kierkegaard (rather than Luther) who seeks — in his own way — to uphold the Christian revelation as a God-given datum over against those religious entrepreneurs who merely offered what the fashionable mediocrity of the time might happen to demand. He sought to uphold Christianity as the norm which was absolutely valid and which rightly claimed to judge those theories which sought to explain it away. Against those who had lost the sense of Christianity as a true divine revelation and who had replaced it with an indulgent pleasure in picking this or that from a doctrinal commodity market, he uttered this grave admonition:

> All that has been thought up by human ingenuity to make of Christianity merely a merchandise is false and mistaken. Do we need to have our pastors adapt Christianity to the changes in the times? Is Christianity exaggerated in its demands upon us? Does God not know man?

Of course, despite the nobility of these words and the zeal which they express, Kierkegaard was unable to provide that intellectual synthesis which is required in order to defend the Christian revelation against secularist reductions. In the course of rejecting any attempt to convert Christianity into a socio-political ideology, he seems to go to the point of making any Christian social teaching (however uncontaminated with ideology it might be) appear impossible or unacceptable. Certainly, if Kierkegaard had adequately considered the social teaching of Christianity, he would have had to recognise that the immutable doctrine does admit of a certain *homogeneous* development and application to varying conditions of human life. Again, in theology, Kierkegaard fails to develop an adequate doctrine of the Church. So far as philosophy is concerned, the inadequacies of Kierkegaard's thought have led some writers to regard him as a kind of father to existentialism. This is the misfortune of one who discerned so clearly the errors of rationalistic essentialism but who failed to grasp that moderate realism which is the foundation of an adequate metaphysics of being.[5] Accordingly, Kierkegaard maintained not a harmonious synthesis between reason and faith but rather a conflict and a paradox. It is true that every Christian writer must recognise in the Gospels a doctrine which is felt as a 'paradox' and a 'scandal' to average human mediocrity. In taking this point, Kierkegaard seems to have gone astray by failing to recognise that right reason, which is itself superior to human mediocrity, is in accord with, and is properly preferred by, faith.

Accordingly, in the very act of resisting the conversion of Christianity into an ideology, Kierkegaard promulgates Christianity in a way in which it could hardly be envisaged as anything else but an ideology. In the very act of insisting upon the absoluteness of Christianity — and in uttering his justified condemnation of those who treat Christianity as a merchandise — he manifests a general individualism and scepticism which would constitute a fatal threat to his entire enterprise. If we were to take seriously the logical consequences of Kierkegaard's epistemology, we should only be able to hold Christianity as the 'heroic' ideological choice of the individual soul: a choice which, however 'valid', 'authentic' and 'sublime', could not exactly characterise itself as true! In other words, whatever Kierkegaard may or may not have intended, his epistemology points not towards the upholding of Christian truth but towards the nihilism of Nietzsche.

Accordingly, Weber is confronted with many various and mutually contradictory tendencies within Protestantism which each lead separately and which all lead collectively to the conclusion that Protestantism does not make sense. Moreover, in aggregate, the Protestant positions lead Weber to suppose that it is impossible that there should be a Christianity which is not ideological in one or other of the two senses which we have discussed in chapter 3. A Protestantism which embodies a socio-political role can be unmasked as incorporating a socio-political ideology. On the other hand, a Protestantism which is radically individualistic, which rejects a social dimension, may well entertain a 'profound' velleity towards an absolute commitment but this absoluteness can only be an ultimately arbitrary subjective value-choice.

To put the matter simply, in terms of the positions of Luther and Kierkegaard, we can see that, from Weber's perspective, Luther is vulnerable to Kierkegaard but the triumph of Kierkegaard leads to Nietzsche. At the same time, from Weber's perspective, Kierkegaard is vulnerable to Luther but the triumph of Luther leads not only to Calvin but to a carnal 'Calvinism' which has nothing much to do with the teaching of Jesus Christ. Accordingly, on Weber's premise that Christianity is Protestantism, all roads lead not to Rome but to atheism. However, despite Weber's commitment to disbelief in every kind of Christianity, there is a series of rapports between the themes of Weber's secular ideology and certain elements in the Protestant cultural background. As in so many other cases, there survive, in the mind of Weber, certain reactions both favourable and unfavourable to elements of a religious culture which received its significance from a belief which he no longer accepts. Indeed, without reference to this general background, it would be impossible to account for the specific formulations of the paradoxes in Weber's ideological secularism.

Accordingly, although it is possible to consider Weber as a 'poly-theistic' atheist and as a 'Manichean' atheist, there is also certainly an important sense in which Weber can be envisaged as a Protestant atheist. Despite his rejection of Protestantism in every shape or form, Weber transposes and transvalues elements drawn from various parts of the Protestant spectrum and incorporates them in his own atheistic ideology.

Sometimes, the Protestant influence, even when it is undoubtedly present, is not an essential or crucial factor in Weber's ideology; in such cases, Weber could have arrived at the same position in response to non-Protestant influences if he had lived in a secular but non-Protestant culture. For example, let us recall the Erastian element in Protestantism which was undoubtedly an important factor in the historical formation of German nationalism. This factor is certainly an influence which plays its part in the German culture which occasions Weber's own excessive nationalism. However, excessive nationalism is a common fault in cultures of many types including cultures which have no knowledge of Protestant Erastianism. Certainly, it is a social fact that many Prot-estants, in Germany and elsewhere, had 'learned to live with' the tensions created by the dominance of the secular power of the State over Protestant theological doctrine. This may well have accustomed a nationalist like Weber to accepting that so-called 'heterogeneity of values' whereby Weber came to acquiesce in the suppression of a (supposedly legitimate) value in one order in the name of another (supposedly legitimate) value in another order.

Again, one accepts that anyone who embraces an atheistic ideology will *eo ipso* reject true philosophy and natural theology. Nevertheless, Weber's atheistic ideology is specifically conditioned by the teachings of those sectors of Protestantism which rejected philosophy and natural theology in the name of an exclusively dogmatic theology. But from these general rapports between Protestantism and the ambiguous ideology of Weber, we must now turn to consider some more specific relationships.

The concept of 'vocation without mission'

It is characteristic of Protestantism in all its forms that it does not fail to encounter difficulties concerning the nature of the Christian mission. Indeed, it was the first and generic argument of St Francis of Sales[6] in his controversy with the Calvinists of the Chablais that the Protestant revolt could not be legitimately sustained because the Protestant churches lacked the divine mission conferred upon the Holy Church which is Catholic and Roman. St Francis held that the Protestants could not lay claim to the *ordinary* mission of the Church which derived from the apostolic succession of bishops in communion with the See of Peter. He went on to deny that the Protestants could lay claim to an *extraordinary* mission, since, unlike the extraordinary mission of Christ's Apostles, the acts of the Protestant reformers had not been vindicated by evidence of miracles and extraordinary sanctity.

The Protestant theologians were in difficulties in dealing with the Catholic claim that 'the Church of history is not Protestantism'. If they tried to argue that the reformed churches — or some selection of them — constituted the one true visible Church, they found this hard to prove. Again, it was difficult to show that Jesus Christ really wanted a miscellaneous collection of politically organised State churches holding whatever doctrine might please the prince or the local people. If recourse was had to a doctrine of an invisible church, it was not easy to show how the particular visible ecclesiastical organisations of Protestantism were connected with it. However they might twist and turn, the Protestant theologians found it difficult to connect the vocation of the individual Protestant believer with the divine mission of the one Church instituted by Jesus Christ.

In Weber's intellectual formation, the historic background of the dilemmas of Protestant ecclesiology was complemented by the Protestant sociology of Ernst Troeltsch. To understand this, it suffices to recall Troeltsch's classification of ecclesiastical bodies into 'Church-type' and 'sect-type'. Certainly, this questionable distinction in Protestant sociology fails to give due recognition to the unique character of the Catholic Church which cannot be properly classed (even sociologically) with the Protestant national churches any more than it can be identified with the Protestant sects which are not politically organised on a national basis. Yet, it is in the shadow of Protestant theology and Protestant sociology that Weber undertakes his task of developing a completely secularised notion of 'vocation'. For Weber, Christianity is, in effect, Protestantism and Protestantism comprises men whose 'vocations' are not obviously related to any definitive doctrine of the divine mission of the Church. Already within Protestantism there are men who regard themselves as 'called' but of whom it may fairly be asked: Who has called them? Is this call really a call from God or is it in whole or in part an illusion? Weber is not the man to concern himself closely with questions of theological discernment since his own peculiar idea of authenticity does not really enter into such questions.

In much of his work, Weber is not primarily interested in traditional forms of Protestantism. As Strauss has rightly pointed out,[7] Weber sought out among the Calvinisms not the Calvinism of John Calvin but a 'carnal Calvinism' which he sought to relate to the development of capitalism. The final stage of ideological secularisation is reached when Weber adopts the notion of 'vocation' in a sense which is completely separated from its original Christian origin and basis. Indeed, accustomed as he was to the recognition of secularised versions of religious commitments, Weber formed the habit — to the point of its becoming second nature — of transposing religious doctrines into secular positions. In particular, when dealing with religious positions which were sometimes little more than ideological attitudes ill-supported by questionable doctrines, the process of transposition could become for Weber a matter of almost effortless routine.

The concept of 'faith without credibility'

If Weber is exposed, in his sociological research, to the occupational hazard of engendering in himself an ideological notion of 'vocation without mission', he was similarly vulnerable in relation to the concept of 'faith without credibility'. Again, the occasion of the acceptance of this concept was the background of Protestant culture. If Protestantism had found itself in difficulties in attempting to give an account of the universal mission of the Church, it found itself in similar difficulties

64

concerning the rule of faith.

St Francis of Sales maintained, in response to the Protestant reformers, that the true rule of right-believing is the Word of God preached by the Church of God. In breaking with the Catholic Church, Protestantism rejects the authority of the Church as a whole and hence the authority of the Pope, the authority of General Councils of the Church as well as the consent of the Fathers. At the same time, Protestantism is led to undertake the partial dismemberment and distortion of the Word of God by rejecting Apostolic Traditions and by violating in various ways the integrity of the Sacred Scriptures themselves. St Francis also observes that the reformers rejected the extraordinary testimony given by miracles to the truths of Catholic teaching which Protestantism had denied. Finally, St Francis observes that natural reason is also a rule of right-believing but that it is so negatively: that is, if something is an article of faith, it cannot be against natural reason. Again, the reformers failed to uphold the harmony between faith and reason.

In rejecting the rule of Catholic faith which St Francis thus expounds, Protestantism found itself in a state of disintegration in which the continual proliferation of mutually incompatible teachings on what constitutes right belief was inevitable. Since, outside of Catholicism, no certain means was available for resolving the doctrinal controversies of Protestantism, Christianity outside of Catholicism found itself becoming increasingly incredible. At no point could Protestantism call a halt and develop a plausible set of evidences or find motives of credibility for any one of the various doctrinal positions into which it had divided itself. Hence, there arose diverse trends: either towards a pseudo-ultra-supernaturalism which was unable to give any reasons why anyone should believe its 'ineffable' faith, or towards a rationalistic simplification or secularisation of Christianity in a sense which involved the eventual abandonment of the very idea of divine revelation. The ultimate and extreme consequences of the rejection of that supernatural faith which was above reason but in harmony with it were the acceptance either of a pseudo-'ultra-supernatural'-faith contrary to reason or of a pseudo-faith rationalistically transposed by a debased misuse of reason into a kind of more or less secular 'Christian' ideology. Both these diverse trends were accelerated as responses to the rise of rationalistic Protestant biblical criticism in the nineteenth century.

Accordingly, the Protestant religious culture of the nineteenth century presented for Weber's consideration was one of somewhat extraordinary intellectual disorder. If some forms of 'Christianity' had been diminished to the point of being little more than secular ideologies with a 'religious or mystical allure', it is not surprising that Weber's sociological analysis should treat them as such. If other kinds of Protestants regarded faith as a kind of irrational leap in the dark — without motives of credibility, without coherence with conclusions of reason, without evidence and without a divinely ordained rule of faith — it is not astonishing to find that Weber will totally secularise this emasculated notion of faith and present it as an arbitrary choice resting upon the will and not the intellect.

We have already seen, in chapter 3, that Mommsen endeavoured to defend Weber against the anticipated criticism that Weber's teaching is opposed to authentic religious ethics. This defence showed itself to be spurious in so far as Mommsen — like Weber himself — can only characterise religious ethics as 'authentic' according to the false quasi-Nietzschean concept of 'authenticity'. Just as Mommsen sought to argue that Weber's teaching could respect 'authentic' religious ethics, so Karl Jaspers sought to argue that Weber's teaching is not inimical to 'authentic' religious faith. Again, Jaspers's defence is spurious because he uses 'authentic' in a quasi-Nietzschean or existentialist sense.

Karl Jaspers seeks to claim that 'it is characteristic that true believers take no umbrage at Max Weber's analytical sociology of religion'. This claim is strange because, although a true believer may take no umbrage at certain sociological reductions of religious errors and deviations, he can hardly (without apostasy) accept a sociology which claims to provide a sociological reduction of even the true faith. Jaspers indicates why this consideration does not concern him when he suggests that 'Recognition of the fact that knowledge is relative only enhances the purity of faith'.[8] Certainly, Jaspers's radical division between knowledge and faith would deprive faith of its content so that it would no longer be possible to speak of the truth of faith. Moreover, if Jaspers's 'faith' is neither true nor false, there can be no obligation to believe it on the grounds that it is true! In this perspective, it is no longer possible to sustain the distinction between a true prophet and a false prophet and, consequently, Jaspers can have no reason — in terms of his own presuppositions — to object to Weber's view (formulated accurately by Jaspers himself) that 'We are free to believe a prophet or not to believe him'.[9] Evidently, the religious existentialism of Jaspers finds itself at the point of contact between a belief diminished asymptotically to unbelief and an atheism (like Weber's) which is contaminated with an ideological nostalgia for a belief that has been lost.

If we listen not to Weber nor even to Jaspers but to Jesus Christ, we learn that the Christian revelation carries with it the obligation to believe. This obligation is an obligation not in the political order but in the moral and spiritual order. If there is a sense in which God leaves us free to believe or not to believe His revelation, it is only in the sense that the act of faith must be made willingly by the believer. Given sufficient promulgation, God does not leave man free to reject revealed truth without fault. Accordingly, when Weber holds that any man may properly determine at will whether or not a prophet shall be believed by him or not, he is secularising a radical religious heresy. If certain Protestants began the process of disintegration by promoting a notion of 'faith' without credibility, Weber's teaching emerges as a later stage in the reductive process in the form of an ideological commitment without faith.

The concept of 'charisma' without the testing of spirits

For Christianity, from the very beginning, the manifestations of the Holy Spirit were subject to the testing of spirits to distinguish the authentic manifestations from the spurious.[10] For Christianity, the separation of the exercise of charisma from the discernment of spirits is contrary to faith. If it were not so, then, any bizarre psychological manifestation would be liable to be accepted as being from God. Within Catholicism, the discernment of spirits had been achieved through the spiritual direction of the individual and through the intervention of the teaching authority of the Church. Moreover, the teaching authority was itself possessed of a divine charisma to teach, rule and sanctify. There was no question of regarding the saints and the recipients of gratuitous graces as alone possessing the charisma or of conceiving the ecclesiastical structure as having a purely human character.

The problem for the Protestant Reformers was to know how the discernment of spirits could be accomplished once they had abandoned the Church which had claimed the divine commission to perform this task. It is not our purpose to review the struggles of those who sought to retain some established kinds of Protestant beliefs and practices in the face of divergent leads given by others who claimed to be luminaries, prophets or enthusiasts. It suffices to observe that it is against the background of such historic struggles that Weber succumbs to the temptation to abstract from the distinction between authentic and spurious charisma and thus to advance a fundamentally secularised concept of 'charisma'. Employed in Weber's supposedly value-free sociology, one 'charisma' (given that it has some social effects worth studying) is (sociologically) as good as another. Every 'charisma' is thus supposed to be an ideological manifestation which happens to have been chosen.

Nevertheless, despite this supposedly value-neutral approach, Weber will implicitly presuppose a certain false assumption about what charisma might appropriately be disdained or not preferred. Given that Weber abstracts from the real criteria required for the discernment of spirits, he will also proceed as if the charisma of *magisterium* of the Church could be considered minimal or in some way inferior. He seems to regard ecclesiastical institutions (treating them all indifferently) as if none of them could be regarded as an appropriate receptacle of charisma. This seems to be implicit, for example, in Weber's distinction between the discipline of an organisation and a charisma considered to be the gift of an individual. Mommsen rightly draws our attention to Weber's view that there is a 'shifting battle between discipline and individual charisma'.[11] If an institution claims to manifest charisma, Weber does not seem disposed to consider whether such a claim is justifiable. He seems to regard any supposed institutional charisma as necessarily a more or less spurious attempt to organise something which is not specifically or properly susceptible of being organised, namely, the 'charisma' considered by Weber to be appropriate not to any bureaucracy but rather to the individual. Leo Strauss bluntly draws our attention to the sources of this kind of ideology of 'charisma' in the following passage:

> [The] very expression 'routinization of charisma' betrays a Protestant or liberal preference which no conservative Jew and no Catholic would accept; in the light of the notion of 'routinization of charisma' the genesis of the Halakah out of Biblical prophecy on the one hand and the genesis of the Catholic Church out of the New Testament teaching necessarily appear as cases of 'routinization of charisma ....'.[12]

The concept of 'private judgement'

St Gregory the Great once likened Sacred Scripture to a river that is both deep and shallow in which an elephant may float and a little lamb may find its feet. In spite of a certain Protestant appeal simply to the alleged 'clarity' of Scripture, Gregory's judgement can hardly be seriously questioned. Whilst the Scriptures contain passages of child-like simplicity, they also contain passages whose meaning lies hidden behind strange and mysterious imagery. It would not be very plausible to speak of the 'clarity' of the entire text of the last book in the canon of the New Testament. Accordingly, since the Protestant appeal to Scripture as the interpreter of Scripture does not provide the individual Christian with a serviceable criterion of the true meaning of Scripture, Protestantism was inevitably forced back upon the admission of 'private judgement' in the interpretation of divine revelation. The Catholic Church was not slow to point out the contradiction which is seen to exist between the idea of a public divine revelation and the idea of a private judgement of its meaning. The multiplication of mutually incompatible private judgements tended to produce a state of affairs in which the individual would pick and choose what he would believe according to his own fancy rather than submit to the objective revelation truly promulgated by God.

Taparelli d'Azeglio was so conscious of the subversive effects of the principle of private judgement that he went so far as to suggest that the principle of the Protestant Reform was the principle of pure rationalism.[13] Some of the Reformers themselves were not wholly insensible of the dilemma in which they found themselves. Luther's notorious attack upon reason as 'the greatest prostitute of the devil' might seem to represent an unavailing and misguided attempt to uphold a Protestant interpretation which would not involve a subjective human *rationalistic* judgement upon what God had revealed. Certainly, it was impossible for Luther to save the truth of faith by means of an attack upon reason and the validity of philosophy. Moreover, Luther diminished the truth of faith in so far as he regarded teaching as accidental to Christ's mission. It is characteristic of Luther's negative attitude to Christ's own teaching office that he not only rejects the divinely instituted teaching office of the Vicar of Christ but even condemns the Vicar of Christ as the antichrist. In undertaking his comprehensive revolt against the *magisterium*, Luther refused to admit that his own doctrine (supposedly necessary for salvation) could be judged by anyone. J. Maritain and J.A. Moehler are agreed that, in locating the criterion of doctrine in himself, Luther was putting himself in the place of Christ.[14] Following this subjectivism of Luther, subjectivism of one sort or another is found to be endemic in Protestantism: manifestations of 'pseudo-ultra-supernaturalism'[15] were not less subjective than a crude Erastianism and no less subjective than those private interpretations which were evidently rationalistic in character.

Very generally, the Protestant principle of private judgement has played its part in preparing an intellectual climate in which men would come to regard religion as a matter of private choice which depends for its authenticity simply upon the particular person concerned. If one's private judgement were the real criterion of revelation, eventually it would be considered to stand *above* the revelation in order to judge it. From this height, the purely human private judgement would eventually find itself implicitly rejecting — either rationalistically or irrationalistically — the very idea of revelation and the very idea of God as the Author of revelation.

Within the ambit of Protestantism, it can be said that fideism has had a role in the development of the idea that the individual may and should make ideological choices for which no reasonable justification can be given. A certain Protestant notion of conscience is similarly susceptible of the secularising subversion to which fideism is vulnerable and which the principle of private judgement cannot help facilitating. Sometimes, the Protestant notion of conscience will take the form of a supposedly autonomous 'inner light' or moral sense or moral feeling which claims to furnish its own inner justification. Even in less extreme forms, however, Protestant notions of conscience, whilst rightly insisting upon the need to follow conscience, will tend to diminish or minimise the importance of ensuring that one's conscience is soundly formed on the basis of objective principles.

Traditional Protestantism does not provide Weber with his specifically atheistic 'vocation' to undertake the free attribution of subjective ideological 'values' upon a universe which [supposedly] has no real meaning either in itself or in relation to God. However, a Protestantism which rejects Catholic teaching has tended to choose between a liberal Christianity (which, in effect, subverts the very concept of divine revelation) and a somewhat arbitrary fideistic Christianity whereby the believer resists the solvent of liberalism mainly by the exercise of will-power. This misconceived primacy of the will results from the unresolved problem — ubiquitous in Protestantism — of the source and validity of the proximate rule of faith.

Weber inherits elements from both 'dogmatic' Protestantism and from liberal Protestantism. He secularises both and implies, first, that quasi-dogmatic ideological choices have to be made if we are to act at all and, secondly, that there is no real justification for those choices since they are ultimately arbitrary.

The concept of 'necessary sin'

In denying any objective moral order in the universe, Weber is adopting a position which, *in its complete formulation on the basis of atheism*, is opposed in some way or other to every species of Christianity. Nevertheless, Weber's notion of the heterogeneity of ethics — which involves a deeply secularised concept of 'necessary sin' — does not fail to lay under contribution a certain Protestant doctrine concerning the justification of the ungodly.

We should first recall that, although the Council of Trent taught that faith is the *root* of all justification, Catholicism holds that the justification of man is a real justification which is effected not by supernatural faith alone but by sanctifying grace. The Protestant doctrine of justification by faith alone involved the notion of an imputed justification whereby a man was not made just but merely accounted just so far as his eternal destiny is concerned. Implicit in this Protestant doctrine is a certain pessimism concerning the effects of original sin and about the efficacious operation of divine grace. These theological differences between Catholicism and Protestantism have commonly been reinforced by a Protestant unwillingness or inability to hold to either a really substantive metaphysics of being or a really substantive doctrine of natural law.

In conjunction with the differences already mentioned, we find that Protestantism — unlike Catholicism — will often regard the very first motions of concupiscence as morally culpable. This doctrine, which renders sin unavoidable, leads inevitably to scrupulosity unless scrupulosity can be averted by some doctrine or other which makes sin somehow permissible. It is well-known that Luther's way of breaking out of this scrupulosity was to adopt the doctrine of justification by faith alone and even to offer, in one fatal passage, that ominous prescription: *pecca fortiter*. If sin is necessary, so the argument runs, what is to be done except to sin boldly? There seem to be secularised elements of a similarly false scrupulosity and false laxity in the various phases of the thought of Weber himself. Although Leo Strauss does not deal extensively with the Protestant background to Weber's thought, the very terms of the following passage from Strauss reveal the rapports between Weber's positions and the Protestant doctrines which we have been considering here 'failure, that bastard of forceful sinning accompanied by still more forceful faith instead of felicity and serenity, was to be the mark of human nobility ...'.[16]

The concept of 'necessary commitments'

We cannot complete our review of the rapports between Weber's secularism and the Protestant background without turning our attention to the drama of Luther's fundamental revolt against the Catholic conception of the Church. In admitting the possibility that there are times in which even the adherent of an 'ethics of responsibility' may choose the way of an 'ethics of ultimate ends', Weber actually quotes the very words of Luther: 'Here I stand, I can do no other'.[17]

The mediaeval canonists had described the act of faith as the one necessary vow. The necessity of the act of faith was seen to have an inseparable connection with the truth of the faith. When Luther revolted against the Catholic faith, he claimed, over against the Church, that it was his own stand that was really necessary. Since Weber is neither a Catholic nor a Protestant, he cannot identify himself with the religious positions adopted by either of the parties to the controversy. Weber secularises the notion of the 'necessary stand' or the 'necessary commitment' by abstracting it from the merits or otherwise of the positions actually held.

Since Christ's teaching and His Church pertain to the order of divine revelation, it is evidently not consistent with the acceptance of that revelation to revolt against what has been divinely instituted in respect of the Church. Luther himself admitted, in the Leipzig dispute of 1519, that he was in revolt against the Catholic conception of the divine institution of the Church. Indeed, Luther's break with the Church has been the occasion of recurring meditation and inquietude even within the Protestant churches themselves.[18] Since no-one could seriously suppose that all Christians agreed that Luther had not rebelled against what God had instituted, Luther's stand presents itself to Weber as, at best, a problematical stand even within the ambit of the Christianities. If Weber's background of Protestant culture inclined him to admire Luther's stand, his admiration could only be accommodated within the atheistic ideology of Weber by confining it to admiration of the dramatic (and purportedly 'necessary') decision as such, in abstraction from its objective validity or invalidity.

Although it is clear that Weber has reduced Luther's stand to a sociological type which will then be transposed to serve as a category in the Weberian ideology, it seems not unfair to say that Luther's stand is apt, in a certain way, to be secularised. Luther did not accept the Catholic teaching that the act of faith is primarily an act of the intellect which is supernatural, free and certain. Given Luther's view of the primacy of the will, the suspicion must arise that the drama of his revolting will, claiming necessity for its rebellion, is a revolt which proceeds in spite of, and not in accord with, the proper act of the intellect. The drama of such a revolting will, as secularised in the ideology of Weber, is a drama in which neither the intellect nor reason nor faith are supposed to be able to form the act of the will. The religious revolt (purporting to be necessary but suspected of being arbitrary) is secularised and transposed, by Weber, into the ideological choice purporting to be necessary whilst actually conceding that it is arbitrary.

The concept of 'necessary intellectual sacrifice'

The idea that the acceptance of Christianity involves the rejection of reason is a theme which recurs regularly in the writings of Luther. Luther himself does not represent this as a dilemma because he wills his faith and wills his contempt of reason. Nevertheless, Luther (no less than the mediaeval exponents of the double truth theory) is bequeathing a paradox to his successors and to those who were influenced by him, including such an unbeliever as Max Weber.

Strauss[19] has rightly argued that Weber's scepticism is connected with the fact that, in the search for the guiding principles of our lives,

Weber felt that it is necessary to choose between human reason and divine revelation but that there are no real grounds which would justify the one choice or the other. Corollaries of Weber's position would be:

i. that the choice of revelation involves an 'intellectual sacrifice';
ii. that the choice of reason alone cannot enable us to establish objectively valid rational principles for the guidance of our lives;

and, therefore,

iii. that every human choice of values whatsoever necessarily involves an 'intellectual sacrifice'.

It is not difficult to follow this sequence of thought starting from its first premises. The interesting questions begin to arise when we ask why Weber supposed that he could not choose both reason and revelation, both philosophy and theology, both human guidance and divine guidance. It would appear that Weber's starting point derives from a certain implicit assessment of the conflict between the Christian confessions. Weber is aware of the failure of Protestantism, in the midst of its variations, to eliminate fundamental inconsistencies in its own teachings. On the other hand, Weber felt that Protestantism had succeeded in revealing to the post-Reformation world certain fundamental inconsistencies in the teachings of Catholicism. Weber seems to have regarded Protestantism as if it were a kind of insect which dies in the very act of inflicting a fatal sting upon its enemy. Or, it is, for Weber, as if the two confessions had unwittingly found themselves linked by a kind of suicide pact whereby each is in some way responsible for the death of the other.

Such a diagnosis of the post-Reformation theological predicament would have received a measure of support from the analyses of Weber's friend, the Protestant theologian, Ernst Troeltsch. Troeltsch's writings, which were somewhat unsympathetic towards Catholicism, certainly contained some serious misunderstandings of Catholic teaching. Of Thomism, Troeltsch argued that 'The inconsistencies which it contains belong to life itself, and they are bound to emerge again and again ....'. Even in this misconception of Thomism, Troeltsch seems to be saying that there are not inconsistencies in it which he [Troeltsch] would deem to be really avoidable. Accordingly, Troeltsch seems to pay reluctant ideological tributes to that very Thomist doctrine which he regards — as he regards any possible teaching whatsoever — as necessarily inconsistent. He suggests that Thomism possesses a greater measure of coherence than Catholic Modernism[20] and he concludes with the obscure paradox that 'So far as one can see, Thomism will invariably conquer until it dies in the act of victory'.[21]

The objection might be raised that, whilst Weber certainly concluded that Protestantism involved an 'intellectual sacrifice', this fatality could not have been caused in any way by Catholicism. It might be argued that Protestantism — like Catholicism — was seen, in Weber's eyes, merely as a victim of the corrosive power of 'rational thought' in the sense in which Weber understands human rationality. Although it is at first sight plausible, this objection is found to be inconclusive. The reason is that 'human rationality' is not, for Weber, an unassailable criterion for the definitive rejection and replacement of any doctrine. It would appear to be Catholicism considered as an *ideal* — which Weber, like Troeltsch, believes to be unattainable — which constitutes, even in the mind of Weber, a standing criticism of any doctrine of revelation which rejects human reason and of any human reasoning which rejects 'extra-rational' evaluations such as divine revelation. Although the supposed 'reality' of Catholicism is, in Weber's opinion, intellectually powerless to prove its validity definitively over against Protestantism, the Catholic *ideal* of the harmony of reason and revelation seems to function, in Weber's perspective, as a catalyst which facilitates the reduction of the Christianities (Protestant and Catholic alike) and the post-Christian evaluations of those who rejected revelation in the name of 'rational thought', to the status of mere particular or private ideologies.

Maritain has pointed out that, whilst the spiritual principle introduced by Luther was directed, in its fundamental orientation, towards individualism, the concrete social consequences were often found to operate, accidentally, in the direction of delaying the emergence of radical individualism.[22] Luther gave rise then to a spirit of romantic religious choice and, accidentally, to the imposition of an Erastian type of national politico-religious uniformity. We shall see that Weber's evaluation of Christian ideologies envisages these two types which both involve (each in its own way) an 'intellectual sacrifice' which is supposed to be inherent in the acceptance of any kind of revelation whether Christian or not.

The supposedly necessary 'intellectual sacrifice' involved in Protestant Erastianism is associated historically with a certain religious indifference which became endemic in European culture in consequence of the Reformation. To illustrate this point, it must suffice to select from many examples the case of Emmerich de Vattel. Vattel will inform us that since God desires the [temporal] welfare of states, he may be presumed to desire that religious matters be determined in accord with what that [temporal] welfare might [superficially] appear to require.[23] In making this inherently political approach to religion, Vattel was not unaware that he would be accused of tepidity.[24] He cannot give any plausible account of the universal mission of the

Church. In difficulties, he presents his [presumably Protestant and secular] readers with this choice: either each State is master of its own faith or Pope Boniface VIII is right after all.[25] The reader will not fail to receive the message that Vattel does not have it in mind to embrace the faith of Boniface. The choice is presumably presented with the intention of converting non-Erastian Protestants into Erastian Protestants.

In resisting secular domination of religion in the name of an idiosyncratic faith, the non-Erastian Protestant Reformer had sought to uphold the primacy of the spiritual over the temporal. Unfortunately, in doing so, he had romanticised faith and thus made an 'intellectual sacrifice' involving a corruption in the spiritual order. In seeking to overcome private idiosyncracies in the name of national uniformity, the Erastian Protestant merely substitutes a national idiosyncracy for a private one and he acquiesces in the 'intellectual sacrifice' of admitting the primacy of the temporal over the spiritual. Both these types of 'intellectual sacrifice' anticipate, in a certain way, the more radical 'intellectual sacrifice' envisaged in Weber's atheistic ideology.

The distinction between 'traditional action' and 'rational action'

Whilst no-one supposes that every tradition is reasonable, Weber's decision, in his sociological analysis, to subsume 'traditional action' under the heading of non-rational action leads us to suspect that he harbours some sort of prejudice against the possibility of action in accord with traditional teachings being rational in character. This impression is reinforced by the fact that Weber again distinguishes 'traditional' from 'rational' when he speaks of the three principles of legitimacy, namely, 'rational', 'traditional' and 'charismatic'. The inappositeness of Weber's threefold classification is very marked in the crucial case of the Catholic Church whose legitimate authority is (in the true senses of the words) charismatic, traditional and in accord with right reason.

In order to understand what Weber is really doing when he makes such a sharp disjunction between the 'traditional' and the 'rational', we must first recall that, in Weber's opinion, there can be no type of traditional doctrine or practice or of 'rational thought' or 'rational action' which is founded upon values having perennial validity in so far as they are objectively true. Accordingly, Weber's discussion is generally directed not towards true tradition and right reason but towards deformed traditions and deformed modernist forms of rationality. In the theological field, it is as if Weber were to concern himself exclusively with the twin heresies of traditionalism and modernism[26] which, though apparently opposed, belong to a spectrum of error which has been condemned by the teaching authority of the Catholic Church since the time of Pius IX. In so far as theological modernism and traditionalism within the Catholic fold advanced either under the influence of, or as a response to, the development of Protestantism, Weber's perspective similarly owes much to the Protestant background.

The rejection of right reason gives rise to false assumptions in Weber's classification of types of rational political action. Since action in accord with right reason cannot be adequately categorised as *wertrational* or as *zweckrational*[27] (in Weber's senses of these words), it seems to be the implication of Weber's teaching that to act in accord with right reason in politics is to undertake non-rational affective or traditional action! Certainly, right reason prescribes action *ordered to an end* (in the traditional non-Weberian sense) and not action ordered either to the 'goal' or to the 'value' of Weber's classification. It must be recognised that Weber's thought proceeds in the context of a post-Reformation tradition in which the true idea of law as ordered to the common good as an end had been lost sight of for several centuries. Indeed, Weber not only proceeds as if right reason did not exist but seems to suppose that mankind — if it desires to be in some way rational in politics — is condemned to choose either 'goals' or 'outcomes' of a more or less Machiavellian type or 'values' of a more or less Kantian or Nietzschean type, or some pastiche of both.

Certainly Luther is one of the most important remote precursors of Weber's rejection of right reason and of true tradition. This conclusion is to be inferred for many reasons. For example, the romantic individualism of Luther is a foreshadowing of the increasingly radical doctrine of the autonomy of the individual in secular liberalism. Moreover, Luther can be seen to be a precursor of both Marx and Nietzsche, who, on Weber's own admission, were the two most formative influences upon the intellectual milieu in which he worked. Marx explicitly asserts that the Lutheran revolt is to be regarded as the first step which is to be followed up by the revolution of the proletariat.[28] Similarly, the Lutheran revolt against that right reason and true tradition which derive from God is in effect an anticipation of the more radical Nietzschean revolt[29] against all preceding truth and reason and, indeed, against God Himself.

Notes and references

1   R.S. Devane, *The Failure of Individualism*, Dublin, 1948, pp.32–3.
2   See J. Malaquais, *Soren Kierkegaard: Foi et Paradoxe*, Paris, 1972.
3   See quotation in K. Jaspers, *Leonardo, Descartes, Max Weber:*

Three Essays, London, 1965, pp.206—7.

4 Luther denies the eternal import of morality. See J.A. Moehler, *Symbolism; or Exposition of the Doctrinal Differences between Catholics and Protestants*, London, 1894, pp.185—91.

5 See discussion of contrasting metaphysical errors of Kierkegaard and Hegel in E. Gilson, *Being and Some Philosophers*, 2nd edn, Toronto, 1952.

6 St Francis of Sales, *The Catholic Controversy*, 2nd edn, London, 1899.

7 L. Strauss, *Natural Right and History*, Chicago, 1953, p.62.

8 Jaspers, *Leonardo, Descartes, Max Weber: Three Essays*, p.249.

9 Ibid., p.253.

10 I *Thess.* 5:12; 19:21.

11 W.J. Mommsen, 'Max Weber's Political Sociology and his Philosophy of World History', *International Social Science Journal*, vol.17, 1965, p.37.

12 Strauss, *What is Political Philosophy?*, New York, 1959, p.21.

13 Taparelli d'Azeglio, *Essai Théorique de Droit Naturel basé sur les faits*, (French trans.), Paris/Tournai, 1857.

14 J. Maritain, *Three Reformers: Luther — Descartes — Rousseau*, London, 1928, p.15.

15 See R.A. Knox, *Enthusiasm*, Oxford, 1950, p.2.

16 Strauss, *What is Political Philosophy?*, p.23.

17 *From Max Weber*, p.127.

18 Protestants concerned about the Reformers' 'open, avowed separation from the Church' included John Wesley. See J.M. Todd, *John Wesley and the Catholic Church*, London, 1958, pp.180—1.

19 Strauss, *Natural Right and History*, pp.74—6.

20 See chapter 5.

21 E. Troeltsch, *The Social Teaching of the Christian Churches*, vol.1, London, 1931, pp.277, 280.

22 Maritain, *Three Reformers*, p.18, footnote 11.

23 E. de Vattel, *Le Droit des Gens*, 1758, book I, chapter XII, s.151.

24 Ibid., book II, chapter IV, s.61.

25 Ibid., book I, chapter XII, s.146.

26 See discussion of traditionalism and modernism in modern atheistic ideology in my Plater Memorial Lecture, 'Traditionalism and Modernism in Ecological and Liberationist Ideology', *Catholic Social Review*, vol.VI, no.3, 1977, pp.13—30.

27 Weber envisages two forms of rational action; one directed to a goal (*zweckrational*) and another directed to a value (*wertrational*) and two forms of non-rational action: affective action and traditional action.

28 See E. Voegelin, 'The Formation of the Marxian Revolutionary Idea', *Review of Politics*, 1950, pp.285—6.

29   The persistence of quasi-Lutheran elements in Weber's quasi-Nietzschean ideology has led Gouldner to suggest that Weber might be envisaged as 'half-Lutheran, half-Nietzschean'. (See A. Gouldner, 'Anti-Minotaur: The Myth of a Value-free Sociology' in I.L. Horowitz (ed.), *The New Sociology*, New York, 1964, p.214.)

Weber and Modernism

To evaluate Weber's relationships with the various forms of Christianity, we need to recognise that he did not have a thorough understanding of Catholic thought and in particular of Thomism. We have seen that, for general assumptions about the import of Catholic ideas, Weber rested heavily upon Protestant interpretations, such as those of Troeltsch, which did not represent the true character of Thomism. Another factor, not unconnected with the influence of Troeltsch, which may have encouraged Weber to think that it was unnecessary to re-examine his ideology in relation to the Catholic faith, was the rise of the Modernist movement within the Catholic Church itself.

Troeltsch's book *Die Soziallehren der christlichen Kirchen und Gruppen* was published only four years after Pius X's condemnation of Modernism in his encyclical letter *Pascendi* in 1907. At that time, Troeltsch (looking at the Church from outside) would have found it difficult to form a sound judgement as to whether or not the Papacy would eventually maintain its resistance to the Modernist challenge. In one passage, referring to the so-called 'Americanism' and Modernism, Troeltsch suggested that 'it will scarcely succeed by the adoption of the very varied modern ideas on natural philosophy, the philosophy of history, social philosophy, and metaphysics, where Thomism succeeded by the method of a simple and exclusive Aristotelianism'.[1] However, because he misconceived the genius of Thomism, Troeltsch could not radically exclude the use of the comparison (as if it were meaningful) between the Modernist challenge in the nineteenth and early twentieth century and the arrival of certain Aristotelian ideas in the West in the thirteenth century. Troeltsch made this comparison in the following terms 'Aristotelianism, with the help of which this further development took place, was explicitly rejected by the University of Paris, and then by the Popes, in exactly the same way as Modernism is rejected today'.[2] In truth, however, the two cases are not analogous. The initial hostility of Catholic authorities towards Aristotelian ideas is intelligible if we remember that some of these ideas are incompatible with the Christian revelation. The eventual approval of the Thomist synthesis is intelligible if we remember that some of Aristotle's ideas are true and therefore compatible with the Christian revelation. The comparison between the Aristotelian challenge and the Modernist challenge fails in so far as Modernism, as a whole system of ideas, is fundamentally incompatible with the Christian revelation.

Although Troeltsch conceded that Thomism was a more formidable and less incoherent synthesis than Modernism, he imagined that each of these systems of doctrine was, in the end, a pastiche which did not (and could not) finally eliminate internal inconsistencies. As we have seen, Troeltsch held that there are inconsistencies 'which belong to life itself'.[3] In sharing this view, Weber would be likely to conclude that, if Modernism is really an ideology of heterogeneous values, then, other Catholic syntheses, including Thomism, may be similarly presumed to be nothing more than rather sophisticated ideologies. In establishing correlations between the ideological principles of Weber and the doctrines of the Modernists, it will not be suggested that Weber actually worked out his ideology in relation to Modernism. He was probably unaware of the detailed correlations which are there to be found. It is rather that Weber's ideology and Catholic Modernism were both developed in an intellectual climate strongly influenced by liberal and fideistic Protestantism and by rationalism. The Catholic Modernists took a major step from Protestantism towards the ideologies of unbelief. Weber himself would not have mistaken the direction in which Modernist ideas were pointing.

Pius X observed in his encyclical *Pascendi* that the Modernists were generally disinclined to treat their doctrines in a systematic way. For this reason, he took particular care to expound the systematic structure of the Modernist doctrines in the course of declaring them to be incompatible with Christianity. It is convenient, therefore, to use in this analysis the formulations of Modernist ideas presented in *Pascendi*. Of course, it might be asked whether it is really fair to the Modernists to use (for whatever reasons of convenience) the formulations of their doctrines contained in a document promulgated by their most formidable opponent. This objection, however, can not be reasonably pressed. Certainly, one of the leading Modernists, Father George Tyrrell, did not question the undoubted accuracy of the formulations in the encyclical. In the first of two articles published in the London newspaper, *The Times* (on 30 September and 1 October 1907 respectively), Tyrrell acknowledges that the avowed purpose of *Pascendi* 'is to silence the recent allegation that the Holy Father condemns because he does not understand'. Certainly, Tyrrell considers that the encyclical contains a controversial discussion of Modernism by someone who is completely opposed to it. Nevertheless, he suggests that it comes from the pen of 'some subtle scholastic theologian unusually well versed in the literature of the subject' and that 'the picture he draws of Modernism is ... seductive to an educated mind'. It would appear then that, despite the opposed judgements made by Catholics and Modernists about the validity or invalidity of Modernism, there was not, in the end, any fundamental disagreement between Pius X and Tyrrell about the terms in which the Modernist doctrines should be systematically formulated.

One of the main points of disagreement between Pius X and the Modernists arose from the innovation whereby the Modernists adopted a peculiar opinion concerning the significance of the dogmatic definitions of faith. Instead of simply saying that definitions of dogma are always incomplete in the sense that the formulae do not comprehend and exhaust the entire riches of the divine revelation, the Modernists argued that the dogmatic formulae were radically inadequate.[4] They were then led to accept the supposition — shared by Weber and Troeltsch — that dogmas contained contradictions, compromises and heterogeneity.[5] The Modernists thus came to hold a peculiar view of the nature of doctrinal development. First, they maintained that there was a progress in doctrine which corresponded with the progress in the sciences.[6] Secondly, they envisaged a transformist development rather than a homogeneous development of dogma.[7] These positions which are incompatible with the idea of an objective divine revelation are rather vulnerable to being reduced and characterised, within Weber's realm of mutually incompatible 'values', as a value-choice of one among many purely ideological forms of 'christianity'. Furthermore, the Modernists were in a difficulty in appealing rather indiscriminately to 'religious experience' as a criterion and, at the same time, insisting that their ideas ought to be recognised as manifesting 'progress' by comparison with preceding Catholic thought. Pius X, who rejected their appeal to 'religious experience', did not fail to reveal another difficulty which Modernism faced when he asked: 'why do they not attach equal weight to the experience that so many thousands of Catholics have that the Modernists are on the wrong path?'[8] Indeed, Max Weber himself, who believed that modern man was fated to lose the faith, would have recognised that the Modernists (like the modern atheists) could not give a true objective reason for their conclusion that the doctrinal transformations which they envisaged ought to be evaluated as a progress.

Like Weber, the Modernists denied natural theology;[9] some of them seemed anxious not to be taken as philosophers;[10] they insisted upon a radical distinction between science and faith and yet, at the same time, they held for the primacy of science over faith.[11] In Modernism, as in Weber, there is the transition from agnosticism to what is in effect scientific and historical atheism.[12] Again, the Modernists were of the same mind as Weber concerning miracles and concerning arguments for the credibility of the Christian revelation. Miracles were denied to have really happened in history;[13] indeed, all arguments for the credibility of faith were denied.[14] Accordingly, the Modernists, like Weber, could not really apply the terms true and false to religious claims.[15]

Since the Modernists denied the Christian doctrine of divine revelation,[16] the Christian revelation became transvalued in their writings so that it came to be reduced — equally with every other religious belief — to the religious consciousness.[17] Consequently, the distinction between natural and supernatural religion was abandoned by the Modernists[18] and they were led to appeal simply to 'religious experience'.[19] This Modernist doctrine of 'religious experience' has something in common with the presuppositions of what is sometimes called the 'Philosophy of Religion' in secularised academic circles. Both have a common origin in certain Kantian and post-Kantian modes of thought. With regard to the 'Philosophy of Religion', there may be noted some trenchant observations of Austin Farrer who wrote:

> 'Philosophy of Religion' is the banner of a sect; for it describes its subject of study according to a Kantian or post-Kantian conception of philosophical enquiry. According to this conception, certain types of human experience and human activity are accepted as occurring, and the philosopher's business is to extract from these the *a priori* principles or universal forms presumed to be embedded in them.[20]

Farrer rightly argues against this philosophical method that 'God is not usefully defined as whatever man concerns himself with in an activity of a certain type, called religion; for the definition is circular'.

It is true that Weber did not claim to have the Modernist 'religious experience'. However, this 'religious experience' which is said, by the Modernists, to be essentially a feeling and an affirmation[21] does fit rather conveniently, in a certain sense, into Weber's realm of contradictory ideological values. After all, the Modernist holds that his 'faith' permeates the phenomena with its own life.[22] Clearly, this involves the *imposition* by the Modernist of the (ideological) values of his 'faith' upon the phenomena. Accordingly, we find that the Modernists make a sharp distinction between *real* history (which contained the Christ of history) and *internal* history (which contains the Christ of faith).[23] Obviously, this Modernist distinction harmonises, in a certain way, with Weber's own sharp distinction between facts and values.

In the light of all this, we can see that the Modernist religious life, like the Weberian ideological life, does not claim to rest upon truth nor to be in accord with logic.[24] For the Modernists, there can be an indefinite transformation of doctrine in response to man's 'inner necessities'.[25] Indeed, according to the Modernists, dogma itself (like 'value-choice' for Weber) is born of necessity.[26] Accordingly, the Modernists will transvalue the terms 'truth' and 'logic' and will refer to the 'truth and logic of life'[27] just as Weber will write of the life of a 'genuine man'[28] who knowingly acts upon contradictory principles incompatible with truth and logic.

The heterogeneity of values in Modernism is manifested again when we turn to consider the Modernist doctrine that the necessities underlying the transformation of dogma have both a collective and an individual dimension. For the Modernist, the Church is primarily a collective consciousness and the teaching authority of the Church is supposed to be subject to this.[29] Accordingly, the Modernist envisages diverse built-in necessities and, consequently, built-in conflicts within the Church.[30] Evidently this Modernist interpretation of Catholicism — if it were valid — would facilitate some sort of assimilation of its doctrine (with a minimum of qualifications) into Weber's world of mutually contradictory ideological values. Indeed, the Modernist conception of the relationship between the *magisterium* and the individual Modernist theologian is not entirely dissimilar to Weber's conception of 'the shifting battle between discipline and individual charisma'.[31]

Nevertheless, the Modernists did suppose that the indefinite transformation of dogma (supposedly driven by vital immanence) was an evolution or progress. Pius X argued that they held what his predecessor had rightly condemned, namely, that 'Divine revelation is imperfect, and therefore subject to continual and indefinite progress, corresponding with the progress of human reason'.[32] In other words, although the Modernists' view of dogma was purely symbolic and their view of dogmatic transformation was one of pure adaptation,[33] they still desired to distinguish their position from that of the unbeliever. However, the ideological character of the Modernist 'faith' emerged most clearly when, 'losing all sense of control', they went 'so far as to proclaim as true and legitimate whatever is explained by life'.[34] Indeed, in this phase of their thought, the Modernists came close to being forced to admit that the movement of vital emanation could hardly be held to be a progress since Modernism advances no satisfactory criteria for distinguishing progression from regression. Certainly, Weber would have been justified if he had said that the Modernists had no reason for their optimism.

Now it is evident that Modernism — called, by Pius X, a compendium of all the heresies[35] — is an unstable system. The Modernist conception of divine immanence is non-theistic and it leads either to pantheism or some form of atheism.[36] In seeking, despite the radical nature of their departures from the Catholic faith, to retain their connection with the Church, the ultimate recourse of the Modernist was to what Pius X properly designated as pseudo-mysticism.[37] It is instructive to note that the neo-Modernist teachings being advanced today by certain publicists who describe themselves as Catholics have been designated by Paul VI as pseudo-charismatic fideism.[38] Hence both Modernism and neo-Modernism play a part which provides an excuse (but not a justification) for the Weberian ideologist who fabricates a secularised concept of 'charisma' which can only be pseudo-charismatic in character.

Notes and references

1   E. Troeltsch, *The Social Teaching of the Christian Churches*, (English trans) London, 1931, vol.1, p.279.
2   Ibid., p.267.
3   Ibid., p.277.
4   *Pascendi*, English trans., pp.13, 22—3. (These and other page numbers refer to the facsimile reprint of the English trans. published by Carraig Books, 25 Newtown Avenue, Blackrock, Co. Dublin, 1971.)
5   Ibid., pp.14, 21, 44, 45.
6   Ibid., pp.20, 35.
7   Ibid., pp.31, 35. (See also the standard work of F. Marin-Sola, *L'Evolution homogène du Dogme catholique*, 2nd edn, 2 vols, Fribourg, 1924).
8   *Pascendi*, p.50.
9   Ibid., pp.6—8.
10   Ibid., p.36.
11   Ibid., p.20.
12   Ibid., p.7.
13   Ibid., p.19.
14   Ibid., p.8.
15   Ibid., p.16.
16   Ibid., p.8.
17   Ibid., pp.9, 10, 11.
18   Ibid., pp.9, 46.
19   Ibid., pp.15, 16, 17, 18, 43, 49, 50.
20   A. Farrer, *Finite and Infinite: A Philosophical Essay*, London,

1943.

21   *Pascendi*, p.15.

22   Ibid., p.10.

23   Ibid., pp.36, 38.

24   Ibid., pp.44, 45.

25   Ibid., p.25.

26   Ibid., p.24.

27   Ibid., p.44.

28   *From Max Weber*, p.127.

29   *Pascendi*, p.27.

30   Ibid., p.33.

31   W.J. Mommsen, 'Max Weber's Political Sociology and his Philosophy of World History', *International Social Science Journal*, vol.17, 1965, p.37.

32   *Pascendi*, p.35, quoting the Syllabus of Pius IX, prop.5.

33   Ibid., p.14.

34   Ibid., p.44.

35   Ibid., p.48.

36   Ibid., pp.50, 51.

37   Ibid., p.16.

38   Address of Paul VI to Christian philosophers, 11 March 1972, *L'Osservatore Romano*, weekly edn in English, 23 March 1972.

6 Weber *vis-à-vis* Christ and Catholicism

Marianne Weber has assured us that her husband 'always preserved a profound reverence for the Gospels and genuine Christian religiosity'. She has gone on to say that 'The parables of Jesus, the Sermon on the Mount, Paul's Epistles, and, from the Old Testament, particularly the Prophets and the Book of Job were to him [Max Weber] incomparable documents of religious inspiration and depth'. Since Marianne Weber did not go so far as to deny that her husband had been a non-Christian, it is not obvious, at first sight, what she meant by these statements. Certainly, Max Weber did not hold that 'Christian religiosity' was genuine in the sense of being the exercise of the true religion; nor did he hold that the biblical texts were documents of religious inspiration in the sense of having been inspired by the Third Person of the Holy Trinity. Although Weber says that the Sermon on the Mount is no joking matter,[1] he does not take it with due seriousness as objectively true Christian morality. With all this in mind, we shall need to consider carefully the view of Fleischmann that Marianne Weber's biography contains the 'pious reminiscences' of one who wished to transmit to posterity an image of her husband as a man who was 'pure, pious and noble'.[2]

Nevertheless, in the passages we are considering, Marianne Weber herself provides us with two clues which, properly followed, will lead us to discover something of the truth of the matter. She tells us that Weber was 'moved above all, by the [supposed] fact that on its earthly course an idea always and everywhere operates in opposition to its

86

original meaning and thereby destroys itself'. This formulation is perhaps ambiguous: it might be taken variously to suggest either an element of dialectical thinking (possibly influenced by Hegel and/or Marx) or a Nietzschean perspective on the incidence of nihilism in the intellectual life of humanity. In fact, Weber holds a position which is closely akin to Nietzsche's teaching that Christianity, as part of the history of philosophy and religion, tends inexorably towards the crucial advent of nihilism in the modern world.

The second clue which Marianne Weber's text provides is in the passage in which she records that 'the course of human destinies ... "tugged at his heartstrings" '. The 'destiny' which is especially in point here is that whereby Weber supposes that modern man is fated to lose the Christian faith. Certainly, when Weber rejects Christianity, he nevertheless retains a lasting *nostalgia* (but *only* a nostalgia) flavoured with a strange amalgam of respect and contempt for those beliefs which he has decisively rejected. We know that Nietzsche himself — the self-proclaimed assassin of God and enemy of the Crucified — had written favourably of Jesus in statements which co-exist with a fundamental rejection of the teaching of Jesus Christ. Weber's attitude to the Christianities is no less strange although, in consequence of his own peculiar kind of nostalgia for the Christian beliefs of the past, the quasi-demonic revolt against Christianity is in Weber attenuated and muted.

If then we seek to know how it came about that Max Weber could sometimes refer favourably to a Christianity which, he supposes, can-not be true and which he personally rejects, we shall find the origin of the paradox in the teaching of Nietzsche. For certainly Nietzsche was the one who rejected all preceding fundamental truth and, in doing so, purported to break decisively the necessary link between *authenticity* and fundamental *truth*. Although Nietzsche is a declared enemy of Christianity, it is nevertheless due to a certain Nietzschean influence that Weber is capable of setting aside the question of philosophical and theological truth and of concluding that Christianity can be genuine, inspired and profound even if it is not true. Let us then begin this part of our study of Weber by examining Nietzsche's own evaluation of Jesus and of the Christianities.

Nietzsche had regarded Jesus as original, not dependent upon human institutions, and as one who surpasses Socrates. He had even known that Jesus surpasses the attitude which Socrates adopted in the face of death. Nietzsche had admitted the innocence of Jesus; he had admitted that, unlike Socrates who came before and Nietzsche who came after, Jesus was free from contradictions. Yet, despite these admissions, Nietzsche's perspective is always gravely flawed and perverted. Although he had known that Jesus surpasses Socrates's attitude to death, Nietzsche was more profoundly in revolt against the Cross and the Crucified than he was in revolt against the Socrates who took hemlock. Although Nietzsche had admitted the innocence and independence of Jesus, he advanced a deeply distorted idea of their real significance. He had gratuitously supposed that the innocence of Jesus was nothing more than the innocence of immaturity. Since Nietzsche rejected the divinity of Christ, he was led to misrepresent grossly the independence of Jesus as a type of self-legislation — superseding all laws — which served as a remote preparation for the emergence of the superman. More immediately, Nietzsche envisaged both Jesus and Christianity as leading, in different ways, towards the advent of nihilism.

It belongs to the perversity of Nietzsche's thought that he purported to find a profound gulf between the life of Jesus and the teaching of St Paul, between the teaching of Jesus and Christian faith, between Jesus and His Church. Nietzsche supposed that the proper outcome of Jesus's life ought to have been some sort of Eastern religion like Buddhism. However, if we are to understand what Nietzsche was really doing, we must recognise that, despite these distinctions, Nietzsche was in revolt against Jesus just as he was in revolt against Christian faith and against the Church. Nietzsche was in revolt both against Jesus as He really was and also against the erroneous image of Jesus which Nietzsche himself had misperceived and fabricated.

Nietzsche had inherited from a false tradition which goes back to Machiavelli a sentimental image of Jesus. He supposed that a life lived according to the mind of Jesus was necessarily incompatible with political life as such. He considered that Jesus achieved a life free from contradictions by means of a preoccupation with 'the one thing necessary' at the expense of human values. Nietzsche castigated the Church for a similar preoccupation and for pursuing that preoccupation with a vindictiveness not present in Jesus. Nietzsche condemned this as the domination of faith or revealed religion which was supposed to destroy the philosophy of man by the reversal of that movement whereby Nietzsche regarded human philosophy as involving the rejection of revelation. Accordingly, Nietzsche will criticise the Church for rejecting the will to power in respect of human values and will also criticise it for [allegedly] manifesting the will to power contrary to the spirit of Jesus.

Against the historical background of the 'simplified' rationalistic and fideistic perversions of Christianity, Nietzsche considered that, if Jesus had lived in the nineteenth century, he would have been a nihilist. Nietzsche seems to have meant that Jesus would have surpassed the 'immaturity' of his actual earthly life more than nineteen hundred years before and would have recognised the culmination in the modern world of those contradictions which lead to nihilism. On this hypothesis, a nineteenth century Jesus would have prepared the way for the advent of what Nietzsche called the philosophy of the future and the emergence of the superman. Hence the Nietzschean drive to overcome the limitations of time not by reference to man's immortal soul created by God nor by reference to the eternity of God Himself but by the revolt of the irrational will of the atheistic superman.

Max Weber undoubtedly inherits this strange patrimony of Nietzshce's atheistic 'theology'. However, it must be admitted that there are important differences between Weber's and Nietzsche's responses to Jesus and to the Christianities. Not even Marianne Weber — however tendentious she might have been — could have presented Nietzsche, even with a merely superficial plausibility, as a man 'pure, pious and noble' with an 'equal love' of the Christianities. If we are to specify the ideological differences between the Weberian and Nietzschean responses to Jesus and the Christianities, we ought first to recall that the Kantian transvaluation of theology is both a precursor of — and, at the same time, a doctrine specifically different from — the Nietzschean transvaluation of theology. Weber owes most to Nietzsche but his response to Jesus and the Christianities has evidently been influenced by Kantian and other post-Kantian tendencies including the philosophy of Schopenhauer. Weber certainly partakes of the positive atheistic dynamism of Nietzshce but he also manifests something of Schopenhauer's pessimism about the futility of the operation of the human will once it is supposed to be basically irrational. Accordingly, when Weber rejects revelation, he chooses ideological values but he implicitly admits that there is no basis for an ideological substitute for revelation. When Weber contemplates the advent of nihilism, he contemplates a tragedy. Like Nietzsche, he seeks to go beyond revelation but, unlike Nietzsche, he has no *confident* commitment to a philosophy of the future. For Weber, the tragedy remains and with it an inescapable nostalgia for that former world which he believes (as Nietzsche does) to have been fated to come to an end. Similarly, with regard to the ideological suppression of the sense of sin, Weber is not so thoroughgoing as Nietzsche. Accordingly, Weber does not commit himself in such a comprehensive and consistent manner to the task of going beyond good and evil. In principle, both Nietzsche and Weber have a sense of tragedy, a sense of nostalgia, and a sense of sin and, in principle, both are committed to 'overcoming' these 'disabilities' of the past by recourse to ideological 'values'. The difference is that Nietzsche seems to have virtually no compunctions about his revolt against God whereas Weber sometimes allows sentiment to interfere with the serious business of the ideological revolt. Although, as we shall see, Weber has rejected what is sometimes called 'moralistic liberalism', there remain certain arbitrary elements of 'moralism' which are foreign to the system which he inherits from Nietzsche. In so far as Weber does not entirely reject all considerations drawn from what he calls 'ethics of ultimate ends', he admits certain elements of 'moralism' — deriving from Tolstoy, from Eastern religious ethics and from Kant (whose own system is vulnerable to a disintegration in the direction of Nietzsche) — which he erroneously supposes to belong to the same type as 'authentic' Christian ethics. Finally, one can say that although both Weber and Nietzsche are somewhat under the indirect influence of the post-Aristotelian philosophies of conduct, Nietzsche leans more to the epicureans whereas Weber turns more habitually, at least in the earlier part of his professional life, to the mentality of stoicism.

When we return to the analyses of Marianne Weber, we find that she does not go so far as to deny that her husband's position is incompatible with the Christianities. However, she seems reluctant to say, in so many words, that his doctrine is *against* the Christianities. She prefers to say that his position is *above* them. Yet the apparent implication of this formulation — that Weber's approach was an objective one based upon a true perspective — is simply misleading. Since Weber rejected the Christianities but *not* on the basis of any philosophical (or theological) truth supposedly opposed to them, it is false to claim that he was 'above it all'. If we interpret rightly that part of Weber's thought which underlies his wife's misleading claim that he was above the Christianities, we shall discover, as we have seen, that it implies a certain commitment to go 'beyond' the Christianities (and beyond good and evil) in a sense which owes much to Nietzsche.

Against this background, it is perhaps sufficiently evident that Marianne Weber was not justified in going so far as to say that her husband approached Catholicism and Protestantism with an 'equal love'. What she was adverting to was in reality not a true love of religious truth but, as we have suggested, a strange amalgam of nostalgia, respect and contempt. To characterise such a strange combination as 'love' would involve the use of an illegitimately transvalued concept of 'love'. The fact that Weber had Protestant friends and that he had an affection for his Protestant mother, whom he supported against his unbelieving father, does not mean that he loved Protestantism. If he did not love Protestantism, still less can he be said to have loved Catholicism. Furthermore, it is not simply that Weber did not have an equal *love* for these Christianities, it is also that he did not have for them an *equal* nostalgia. In fact, his reactions to the various forms of Christianity were so varied, complex and idiosyncratic that it would be erroneous to characterise Weber's perspective as a truly objective one. Moreover, the whole idea of seeking to achieve a neutral judgement about the respective merits and demerits of the various forms of Christianity is a mistaken one. The reason for this is evident enough: fundamental truth is not neutral! Of course, a man who is genuinely seeking fundamental truth about the validity of Christian revelation may well be neutral in so far as he is willing to accept the truth wherever it may eventually be found to be. Weber is not neutral in this sense because he presupposes that there is no fundamental revealed truth to be found.

It ought not to be overlooked that Weber professed a certain kind of sympathy for both Protestantism and Catholicism which he did not extend to what he called the 'private prophet'. We discuss more fully in chapter 8 the vexed question as to what Weber had in mind in condemning 'private prophets'. It is sufficient to observe, in the present context, that any preference Weber may be supposed to have had for the 'old churches' over against 'private prophets' is substantially a sociological and ideological preference. This is evident in so far as Weber denies that *any* prophecy is true and is therefore committed to thinking that *every* 'prophecy' (whether it is believed by one man or by hundreds of millions of people) is necessarily a subjective value-choice. Indeed, Weber's doctrine necessarily commits him to the view that everyone, including Weber, is in some sense a kind of 'prophet': a 'private prophet' in so far as each individual is responsible for whatever value-choice he makes and a *false prophet* in so far as none of the pretended 'prophecies' is objectively true.

We have already seen that Weber is an unbeliever who has departed from the Protestant tradition. Like Stephen Daedalus (the apostate Catholic in James Joyce's novel *The Portrait of the Artist as a Young Man*), Weber 'had no compunction in saying that every belief in revelation is ultimately belief in the absurd'.[3] Yet, in their estimations of the various Christian 'absurdities', Daedalus and Weber have mutually incompatible preferences. Daedalus indicates that he prefers Catholicism because Catholicism (unlike Protestantism) is 'an absurdity which is logical and coherent'.[4] Unlike Joyce's Daedalus, Weber is prevented, by lack of understanding and by prejudice, from recognising the logicality and coherence of the Catholicism that he has implicitly rejected. Voegelin observes that:

> His [Weber's] studies on sociology of religion have always aroused admiration as a tour de force, if not for other reasons. The amount of materials which he mastered in these voluminous studies on Protestantism, Confucianism, Taoism, Hinduism, Buddhism, Jainism, Israel, and Judaism, to be completed by a study of Islam, is indeed awe-inspiring. In the face of such impressive performance it has perhaps not been sufficiently observed that the series of these studies receives its general tone through a significant omission, that is, pre-Reformation Christianity.[5]

Voegelin then suggests that the obvious reason for this omission is the fact that 'One can hardly engage in a serious study of mediaeval Christianity without discovering among its "values" the belief in a rational science of human and social order and especially of natural law'. Voegelin is thinking in particular of the fact that 'this science was not simply a belief, but it was actually elaborated as a work of reason'. Weber never seriously weighed the claims of such a science and Voegelin rightly observes that 'In order to degrade the politics of Plato, Aristotle or St Thomas to the rank of "values" among others, a conscientious scholar would have to show that their claim to be a science was unfounded'. Weber's withdrawal from crucial intellectual problems of this kind manifests itself in an habitual unwillingness to grapple with irreducible moderate realist philosophy. Corresponding to this non-acceptance of moderate realism in philosophy, Weber displays a marked unwillingness to grapple with the Christian revelation as this is authoritatively taught by the Catholic Church.

Accordingly, when Weber thinks of Christian revelation, he thinks of Protestant doctrines of revelation; when he thinks of the Church or the churches, he thinks of Protestant doctrines of ecclesiology; when he thinks of natural law, he thinks of Protestant and modern secularised doctrines of natural law. Despite these evident preferences, Weber seems to labour under the misconception that his approach is, in some sense, an objective one. In reality, Weber's mistaken reactions to the Christianities are connected with the ambivalency of his whole ideological vision of the worlds of fact and value. So far as 'science' (as Weber understands it) is concerned, he holds that there is no such thing as authentic Christianity. He supposes that 'authentic Christianity' can be defined only in terms of the preferences (supposedly purely subjective) 'of some theologian or other'.[6] Outside of 'science', Weber's positions (his personal value-choices) are apparently self-contradictory. On the one hand, he evidently holds that there can be no one specific 'authentic Christianity' because he supposes that each of the Christianities embraces its own internal contradictions. On the other hand, Weber evidently holds rather strong views about what Christianity would have to be if, *per impossibilia*, it were to be tenable!

We are not unduly surprised when we discover that there is a close correspondence between what Weber holds to be the most useful 'ideal type' — at one extreme — for the sociological analysis of ethics and the type of Christian ethics which he himself — purely hypothetically — prefers. It is true that Weber tries to rationalise his hypothetical preference by arguing that it relates to the [supposedly] most nearly internally consistent of the whole range of [supposedly] always internally inconsistent types of Christian ethics. Certainly, Weber has no good reason for singling out the ethics of Tolstoy, the ethics of pure pacifism and a certain element of Kantianism as the most nearly consistent of those types of ethics which are sometimes supposed to be quasi-Christian. Although all types of ethics are supposed by Weber to be internally inconsistent, those kinds of ethics which he regards as the most nearly consistent species of 'absolute ethics' seem to have certain functions in his thought.

We have already mentioned in chapter 4 above that Weber is especially interested in the sociology of that 'carnal Calvinism' (to use the phrase of Leo Strauss) which is supposed to have certain interesting social, economic and political effects. Yet Weber is not so insensitive that he fails to see that this 'carnal Calvinism' is not the religion of Jesus Christ. Weber's preoccupation with his preferred kinds of ethics of the 'absolutist' type constitutes a distorted reflection of his awareness that the ethics of Jesus is not the 'carnal Calvinist' ethic. However, there is not in Weber a persevering longing for truth in this sphere of religion and of religious ethics. What we encounter instead is a strain of romanticism and it is this romanticism which is satisfied by the appeal of his preferred kinds of 'ethics of ultimate ends'. This romanticism, which is not absent even from his inordinate nationalism and so-called political realism, is an important general characteristic of Weber's doctrine of subjective value-choice.

Another function of the ideal type of 'absolutist' ethics in Weber's thought is its service as an Aunt Sally which Weber can demolish as unrealistic in order to have recourse to his preferred 'ethics of responsibility'. The prejudiced interpretation of the life of Jesus — derived from Machiavelli and from Nietzsche — supports the ill-founded distinction made in the Machiavellian tradition between a political 'idealism' which is sentimental and a political 'realism' which is unscrupulous. Jacques Maritain's criticism of this distinction — in his critique of Machiavellianism[7] — is equally applicable to the same distinction in the thought of Weber. Finally, Weber's ideal type of 'absolutist' ethics serves as an ideological weapon against any teaching on natural law and Christian ethics — incompatible with both 'absolutist' and 'responsible' ethics in Weber's schema — which claims to be true. Indeed, with such a weapon and such a perspective, Weber is committed to the denial of consistency precisely to that doctrine, namely, the teaching of the Catholic Church, which pre-eminently (and, in effect, uniquely) claims to uphold a consistent Christian ethic. Hence the paradoxical reaction whereby Weber finds himself in the position of purporting to use an admittedly unsatisfactory type as the critical norm for the rejection of every other type including the one which especially claims to be satisfactory.

Accordingly, Weber is implicitly committed to regarding Catholicism unfavourably from two points of view: first, it is not as 'serviceable' and ideologically interesting as 'carnal Calvinism' and, secondly, it is not as romantic as Tolstoy. Hence Catholic ethics are dubbed by Weber as more inconsistent than the religious ethics of India and the East. This leaves Weber free — or, at least, that is what he seems to suppose — to reject the search for a life free from contradictions and to embrace the life of contradictions in the Nietzschean sense. Like Machiavelli and Nietzsche, Weber regards pagan polytheism and its modern secularised ideological equivalents — as more serviceable than Christian ethics in any form. And, in embracing a multitude of incompatible 'gods' — which, in the modern world, are transvalued into explicitly ideological values — he misunderstands the true Christian doctrine of the 'one thing necessary' and misunderstands it in a characteristically lapsed Protestant way.

Weber writes favourably of polytheism by contrasting it with a supposed pursuit of the 'one thing necessary' which is deemed to take away the value of subordinate goods. This seems to be connected with a certain stoic mentality, which is found in Protestant natural law theories, which also devalues human goods other than that human good which is characterised as specifically moral. Weber's perspective is unsatisfactory in so far as he does not properly understand that Catholic teaching on the 'one thing necessary' does not take away the value of subordinate goods but merely insists that any human good whatsoever must be properly ordered to the final good, the last end of human life. Certainly, part of the explanation of Weber's misunderstanding is to be found in the minimising of Christian social teaching in Lutheranism and in certain aberrant manifestations of Catholicism which had been distorted by bourgeois individualism.[8]

The heterogeneity of ethics which Weber opposes to Christian ethics goes far deeper than that which is found in some kinds of pagan polytheism. We must first recall that, having quoted Mill's remark that 'If one proceeds from pure experience, one arrives at polytheism', Weber suggests that 'different gods struggle with one another, now and for all time to come', and then goes on to say that 'every religious prophecy has dethroned polytheism in favour of the "one thing that is needful"'.[9] He envisages this religious preoccupation with monotheism primarily in terms of his ideal type of the 'ethic of ultimate ends' and not in terms of an ordered hierarchy of goods leading to — and consistent with — the highest good. Indeed, whenever he discusses this factor of hierarchy — which he does not properly understand — he is disposed to deride it as 'compromise'. Accordingly, it is significant that the Weberian ideological equivalent of polytheism is more deeply opposed to the truth about the divine unity than some forms of pre-Christian polytheism. As St Thomas Aquinas recognised, there were some heathens who affirmed the existence of one supreme god by whom they asserted that the others whom they called gods were caused. St Thomas concluded from this that the Manichees appeared to be more opposed to the truth concerning the divine unity since they asserted two first principles neither of which is the cause of the other.[10] It would appear that Weber shares one error with the polytheists and a more serious error with the Manichees concerning the fundamental heterogeneity of first principles or values.

In a passage in which Weber attacks philosophy from his own ideological standpoint, he argues that a hierarchical ordering of values cannot be attained *without* appeal to *ecclesiastical* dogmas.[11] Does this mean that a hierarchical ordering of values *with* the aid of ecclesiastical dogmas (and, therefore, Christianity itself) is accepted as a logically possible position within the Weberian realm of values? It might be imagined that this is the implication of Weber's statement and yet the supposition is inadequately founded. Given his own ideology, Weber is committed to relegate everything which has a significance which is not exhausted by investigations within the field of (and conducted by the methods of) scientific sociology to the ambiguous realm which is, for Weber, the realm of mutually incompatible values. In other words, whatever is not exhausted in its significance by science must fall into the realm of values *as Weber conceives this realm*.[12] If Christianity were content to be an *ideology* — a subjective meaning imposed upon a meaningless universe — it would be awarded a place. Given that Christianity — or at least authentic Christianity — is not an ideology, there is in a sense no room for it in Weber's realm of values. Every atheistic or potentially atheistic ideological system (Weberian or otherwise) will seek to neutralise the divine revelation by 'assimilating' it in some way. No such ideological system is competent to do so.

Even the non-ideological doctrine of true philosophy is incompetent to confine the divine revelation to the sphere of natural human reasoning. True philosophy is 'open' to the God who reveals Himself but even true philosophy is incompetent to pass judgement upon the content of divine revelation. Atheistic ideology is 'closed' to God and thereby passes an unfounded adverse judgement against divine revelation.

We have already seen how, in his sociological analyses, Weber reacts towards Protestantism as if its content were simply and exclusively ideological in character. Similarly, Weber is implicitly committed to suppose that even Catholicism itself is an ideology which imposes a subjective meaning — in the form of a merely postulated divine commission — upon the institution of the Catholic Church which Weber is implicitly committed to identify not as a divine society but as a merely human organisation defined in exclusively secular terms. Thus Weber is committed to an exclusively ideological position and perspective which prevents him from accepting as properly conceivable, as a logically possible position, that non-ideological doctrine which the Catholic Church holds about itself. One is reminded of Henri de Lubac's observation that anyone who does not have the faith can hardly help forming a very misleading idea of the Catholic Church whether he or she condemns it or admires it. The reason is that the claims of the Church would be absurd if it were a merely human institution.[13] However, Weber is not unaware that Catholics — and many Protestants — would not accept his view of the nature of their religious beliefs. Indeed, there is a paradox in Weber's perspective which would lead him to transvalue Catholicism as something both somehow within and yet somehow outwith the Weberian realm of 'possible' value-choices. This paradox is loosely analogous to a paradox in the attitude of Hobbes towards Catholicism.

It would appear that Weber envisages a range of logically possible value-choices available to the individual somewhat analogous to the range of logically possible choices of religious legislation which Hobbes envisages as available to the absolute sovereign legislative power. So far as choice among the Christianities is concerned, we know that Hobbes did not personally profess any traditional form of Protestantism and that he specifically rejected Catholicism. Moreover, Hobbes rightly considered that the claims of the Catholic Church were fundamentally incompatible with his absolutist doctrine of sovereignty. However, he found himself driven by this teaching of his on sovereignty and on the supremacy of the 'public conscience' to concede that, *if* the civil sovereign were to choose to promulgate Catholicism, the citizens of the Leviathan would be obliged to receive Catholicism. This means that Hobbes was conditionally committed to accept the suppression not only of his own particular 'value-judgement' against Catholicism but even of certain opinions and arguments in his published works on sovereignty in the case in which these would be incompatible with the public doctrine of a hypothetical Catholic sovereign of his own country. However, Hobbes seems to have found it difficult to confront squarely the final paradox of his doctrine of the supremacy of the 'public conscience'. For it is obvious that Hobbes's positions lead to the dilemma that he can neither accept nor reject the public doctrine of the Catholic sovereign in so far as that doctrine holds that Catholicism is valid in virtue of *true divine law*. Of course, we know which horn of his own dilemma Hobbes actually chose. He held that Catholicism could be received as valid teaching of the public conscience *not* in virtue of true divine law but only in virtue of the civil law of the commonwealth.[14] Yet it is evident that to 'receive' Catholic teaching merely on the authority of the civil sovereign — and not in virtue of true divine law — is not to receive Catholic teaching at all. Consequently, to receive an Erastian transvaluation of Catholicism would not even be to receive the doctrine actually promulgated by the Catholic civil sovereign himself. Hence there is an insoluble paradox built into the erroneous Hobbesian doctrine of the 'logically possible' legislative choices open to the sovereign.

Weber's doctrine of the range of logically possible value-choices available to the individual contains an inescapable dilemma with regard to the choice of the Catholic faith: a dilemma which is analogous to the dilemma built into the Hobbesian doctrine of the possible legislative choices of the sovereign. Certainly, Weber, like Hobbes, personally rejects Catholicism. Moreover, like Hobbes, he considers that the claims of the Catholic Church are incompatible with his modernist perspective upon all the facts and values that are or can be in the world. This would lead him to exclude Catholic doctrine from the scope of the supposed entire realm of logically possible incompatible values. At the same time, Weber is driven by his own doctrine of the autonomy of individual value-choice to concede that, *if* the individual chooses Catholicism, then, that is the individual's choice against which, in a sense, no other individual can really prescribe. Accordingly, the Weber who is committed to accepting that the Catholic is, in a sense, just as entitled to his private value-judgements as Weber is entitled to his, will purport to make room for the value-choice of the Catholic although it is against other implications of his vision of the whole realm of incompatible values. However, Weber seems to find it difficult to cope with the final paradox of his doctrine of the autonomy of individual value-choice. For it is obvious that his positions lead to the dilemma that Weber can neither accept nor reject the propriety of the value-choice of Catholicism. He seems to evade this paradox by finding a place for the value-choice of the Catholic upon the hypothesis — which he knows to be incompatible with Catholicism — that such a choice can be deemed to be subject to the ideological jurisdiction of the Weberian realm of ideological values. That is to say that Catholicism is admitted to Weber's world on the assumption that it will concede something which Catholicism could not concede without ceasing to be what it is and must be.

Of course, if Weber had chosen the other horn of his dilemma *vis-à-vis* Catholicism, he would have found himself trying to accept Catholicism as a logically possible, legitimate value-choice not subject to the condition of its acceptance of Weber's conception of it (as an ideology) but on the Catholic's own terms. In that case, Weber would immediately have been driven to adopt a questioning approach to the whole theory of a value-realm comprising varied incompatible subjective meanings available for imposition upon a supposedly meaningless universe. This questioning of the ideological foundation of the Weberian theory of logically possible values would have led him on to question his own particular ideological judgements about religion, philosophy and morality. He would have found himself in a position in which it would no longer have been possible to avoid addressing himself seriously and persistently to the question of the fundamental truth of the Christian revelation.

Weber and the Kulturkampf

Any general assessment of Weber's attitude towards Catholicism must include an attempt at the interpretation of his attitude towards Bismarck's *Kulturkampf* against the German Catholics. The evil of the *Kulturkampf* was firmly denounced by Cardinal Manning who proclaimed that 'the aberrations of a false philosophy, the inflation of a false science, the pride of unbelief and the contemptuous scorn of those who believe are preparing Germany for an overthrow or for suicide.[15] Where does Max Weber stand in relation to this intellectual, moral, spiritual and political conflict between those who agreed with Bismarck and those who agreed with Manning?

It is well known that Weber was in various ways dissatisfied with Bismarck's policies towards the German Catholics and both Marianne Weber and Karl Jaspers have praised his attitude towards the *Kulturkampf*. Nevertheless, there seems to be an element of ambivalency in Max Weber's own attitude towards the German Catholics. It is important to notice that Weber was opposed to Bismarck's policy in *revoking* the *Kulturkampf* as well as being opposed to the policy under which it was originally imposed. Marianne Weber's gloss on Weber's statement would seem to imply that Weber wished to relieve the pressure exerted by the *Kulturkampf* upon the German Catholics. She admits, however, that her husband did not approve of the sudden and complete revocation of the policy because this was 'tantamount to a confession that an injustice had been done to the Catholics'.[16] This statement, taken together with the relevant passage from Max Weber himself, would seem to suggest that Weber agreed that an injustice had been perpetrated against the Catholics but that — for reasons of expediency — he would not have wanted Bismarck to retreat (as he did) in a way which could be interpreted as a confession that his original policy had been unjust.

Unfortunately, there is some difficulty in interpreting Weber's views on the substantive question about the treatment of the German Catholics because he continually writes of what 'we' thought and did in a way which does not facilitate the making of careful distinctions between the thought of Bismarck, the thought of Weber, and the common opinion of the non-Catholic Germans. Nevertheless, we have on record the important passage in which Weber observed 'We have acted without conscience, then, and are the losers morally as well. This is the worst part of our defeat, for it prevents us from ever resuming the struggle the way it must be resumed if it is to lead to victory'. Accordingly, one reason why Weber disapproved of Bismarck's policy on the revocation of the *Kulturkampf* was precisely because it made it difficult for a future German government to pursue the struggle against the German Catholics. Evidently, Weber would not have wanted to renew the struggle against the German Catholics by the way of the *Kulturkampf* but he would seem to have wanted to be able to pursue such a struggle by some other means.

Since Weber argues that mere reasons of expediency do not suffice to justify the persecution of the German Catholics, it is not unreasonable to conclude that, in propitious circumstances, Weber would have wished to pursue some sort of struggle against the German Catholics which he would be disposed to characterise as 'a struggle of conscience against conscience'. Bearing this in mind, the question could be raised as to what Karl Jaspers meant by the expression 'freedom of conscience' when he suggested that Weber 'rejected every form of violation of the freedom of conscience'.[17] After all, consciences are sometimes so variously formed that the possibility of a more or less *direct* conflict between two men's consciences cannot be regarded as absolutely impossible. In other words, it could conceivably happen that one man, in following his conscience, would undertake some more or less coercive act which would tend to do violence to the differently formed conscience of another. Indeed, Weber himself seems to envisage such a struggle of 'conscience against conscience' and, since Jaspers himself quotes this relevant passage from Weber, it would appear that Jaspers's statement about Weber's supposed rejection of *every form* of violation of the freedom of conscience of another to follow his conscience is somewhat inaccurate.

Like Jaspers, Marianne Weber also refers — in prefatory remarks to her comments on Weber's attitude to the *Kulturkampf* — to her husband's concern with intellectual freedom. Indeed, she goes further and refers to Weber's concern for *truth*. This last reference does not seem to be really apposite because the Catholic faith is concerned with *fundamental* truth whereas Weber holds that there is no such thing as fundamental truth; he is concerned only with truth in the field of the natural and social sciences and the factual analysis of power politics and so on. From the fact that Weber desired that he and others should be free to publish analyses of the political situation which Treitschke and others might have considered 'inopportune', it is not possible to deduce that Weber was opposed in principle to *every kind* of pressurisation of the

German Catholics.

T.S. Simey sums up Marianne Weber's evaluation of her husband's attitude to the *Kulturkampf* in suggesting that Weber's reaction was formed by a desire to preserve 'the dignity of individual choice'.[18] In so far as this expression embodies a liberal conception which is unsecured against the trend to nihilism and ideology, Simey's characterisation of Weber's position is not wrong. It is important to emphasise, however, that there is a difference between this liberal conception of 'the dignity of individual choice' and a true perspective upon the dignity of the human person. We cannot know what the dignity of the human person can be properly thought to require unless we have some fundamental understanding of that human nature which forms the human person. We shall investigate further the basic philosophical weaknesses of Weber's quasi-liberal approach to the human person in chapter 7. Considering here the specific question of religious freedom, it is evident enough that we cannot have a definitive basis upon which to develop a prudent judgement about the scope and limits of religious freedom unless we know the truth about man's natural inclination to know God and to be open to the acceptance of the truth of any divine revelation. Needless to say, this does not mean that it is unreasonable for civil toleration to be granted to anything other than true knowledge and true belief.

In order to view these various considerations in a true light, we must distinguish between the respect of the erroneous conscience which is envisaged in the Declaration on Religious Freedom of the Second Council of the Vatican[19] and that confused doctrine of 'freedom of conscience' which secular liberalism came to develop in the wake of the Protestant principle of 'private judgement'. Inheriting this lapsed Protestant/liberal doctrine of 'conscience', Weber denies that any objective moral, philosophical or theological knowledge is available to man and he is consequently committed to denying that the expressions 'the *proper* formation of conscience' and 'the *true* dignity of the human person' have any meaning which is objectively valid. Accordingly, the nature of the dignity of the human person — and its possible requirements — is, in terms of Weber's ideology, inherently indeterminable.

At this point in the argument, the following question arises: Could a statesman formed upon the ideology of Max Weber advance within that system any intelligible distinction between political action based on expediency and political action prompted by conscience? Since Weber is bound by his ideology to hold that the so-called 'values' of conscience (like the so-called 'values' of expediency) are all equally subjective 'values' imposed upon a meaningless universe, it would seem to follow that 'expedient' action and 'conscientious' action, understood within the terms of Weber's basic ideology, are *not fundamentally different in status.* Of course Weber *qua* sociologist knows that various people do think that there is a fundamental distinction between action based upon an evil kind of expediency and truly conscientious action but this sociological awareness does not mean that Weber's own 'value-system' provides for any such fundamental distinction.

In reality, it would appear that Weber's aspiration towards a supposedly 'conscientious' struggle against Catholicism was no more fundamentally justified, even in terms of Weber's own theory of values, than the admittedly merely 'expedient' policy of Bismarck. Like Bismarck, Weber was formed by an inordinate nationalism which took its ideological sustenance from a rationalised and secularised Protestant culture and from the strategic 'values' of Machiavelli.[20] Indeed, since Bismarck (unlike Weber) had not entirely abandoned his Protestant belief, he could have tried to argue more plausibly than Weber that his attitude on the *Kulturkampf* was a case of a Protestant conscience necessarily violating a Catholic conscience. Such a pretext was not available to Weber and nor could Weber argue in favour of the struggle against Catholicism in terms of an atheistic conscience. To struggle against Catholicism on the basis of an atheistic conscience would involve a similar struggle against Protestantism. The fact that Weber did not have in mind a struggle against Protestantism is sufficient to dispose of this last possible defence of Weber's position.

Accordingly, we arrive at this crucial question: Was Max Weber a more virtuous man than Bismarck (as Marianne Weber and others have suggested) or was he a morally worse man than Bismarck (as Eugène Fleischmann seems to imply)? Certainly, when Fleischmann compares Weber with Bismarck with regard to the general questions of world politics, he suggests that the political thought of Weber is crystallised around the doctrine of domination (*Herrschaft*) and thus around 'a *Fuhrer* who must be at the same time more resolute and more capable than Bismarck or Wilhelm II'.[21] In defence of this judgement, Fleischmann points to the consequences of Weber's assimilation of Nietzschean themes. In doing so, he argues that Marianne Weber erroneously minimised the Nietzschean influence as the result of misunderstanding Weber's reservations about the particular brand of Nietzschean culture which manifests itself in Stefan George. We must therefore go on to ask what consequences the Nietzschean element in Weber's thought may have had for his attitude towards Catholicism. Certainly, the Nietzschean motif seems to be crucial in the fabrication of Weber's ideological distinction between expedient and conscientious action. Evidently, Weber's distinction can no longer mean what it had meant to men who accepted that conscience should be formed on the basis of true morality. It would seem that Weber's ideological distinction can be understood only as belonging to a post-Nietzschean perspective which envisages the notion of a 'heightening of consciousness'. If this is so, then Weber's so-called 'conscientious struggle' would appear to involve a 'heightening of consciousness' whereby a tragic and consciously ideological value-choice generates a supposedly conscientious action. Thus the rationale of 'conscientious action' is, for Weber, neither vulgar expediency nor true morality but the energy of an arbitrary will.

A critical examination of the structure of Weber's thought suggests that Fleischmann's adverse judgement upon Marianne Weber's 'tendentious biography' is in various respects justified. However, she was not simply lying or entirely deceiving herself about Weber's positions *vis-à-vis* Christianity. In so far as she implies that Weber's views on sexual ethics were partially in accord with Christian teaching, she is not wrong. Certainly, in the earlier part of his professional life, Weber held views on sexual morality which, despite elements of scrupulosity (and elements of laxity increasing in later life), were to some significant extent in accord with Christian morality. Marianne Weber does not say that Weber's evaluation of suicide was consonant with stoicism and atheistic humanism rather than with Christianity but her account of his views allows us to make this inference. On private morality, then, Weber's views were eclectic. Moreover, we should recognise that, in spite of his various interventions in politics, Weber did not have the vocation of a statesman. No doubt, in his private life, he was sometimes and in some respects humanly better than his ideology would logically permit him to be. If he had seriously undertaken the role of a statesman, the outcome of the interior conflicts which would have been occasioned by this would have been difficult to predict. Nevertheless, with all these reservations, it remains true that an element of quasi-Nietzschean dynamism is an essential part of Weber's ideology and, consequently, this is a fundamental factor in Weber's stance *vis-à-vis* Catholicism.

Ambiguity of the secularism of the sociological methodology of Weber

In one of his papers, Weber endeavours theoretically to enlist the participation of the Catholic in his sociological discussions. Weber suggests that, while a Catholic may be permitted (by Weber) to doubt whether a sociologist has explained certain things adequately in terms of science, the Catholic is expected (by Weber) to admit that, if they can be explained without recourse to revelation, then, in general, Weber's method of seeking an explanation is a sound one. Weber says:

> science 'free from presuppositions' expects from him [i.e. the devout Catholic] no less — and no more — than acknowledge-

ment that if the process can be explained without those super-natural interventions, which an empirical explanation has to eliminate as causal factors, the process has to be explained the way science attempts to do. And the believer can do this without being disloyal to his faith.[22]

Elsewhere Weber suggests: 'That science today is irreligious no one will doubt in his innermost being, even if he will not admit it to himself'.[23] It is not entirely clear from these two passages whether Weber is pur-porting to suggest that his approach to social science ought to concern itself exclusively with non-supernatural facts or whether he is pur-porting to suggest that it is (and should be) in its very method some-how formally agnostic or somehow formally atheistic in character or tendency.

What is Weber really trying to do in this purported dialogue with the Catholic when he says that science is irreligious and that empirical explanation 'has to eliminate' supernatural factors as causal factors? It would be one thing not to advert to matters in the supernatural order; it would be quite another thing positively to reject supernatural causes as impossible or as necessarily irrelevant in the search for the truth. Obviously, the truth or falsity of the Christian claims has a major bearing upon the kind of sociological investigation of Christianity which can yield important results. If the Christian claims in general are true, a sociologist who seeks to explain the rise of Christianity *as such* purely in terms of non-supernatural facts is wasting his time. If the specific claims of the Catholic Church are true, a sociologist who seeks to explain the Catholic Church *as such* purely in terms of non-supernatural facts is wasting his time.

If Weber's sociology of religion is prevented — by reason of the very method which he imposes upon it — from even considering the possi-bility of according an appropriate place for the Christianities in the Weberian realm of values, are there statements outside his sociology which might afford a satisfactory basis for dialogue? Certainly, as we have seen, Weber regards the religious return to 'the old churches' as something which 'stands higher than the academic prophecy'.[24] Yet before we suppose that Weber has abated his scepticism about even the conceivable consistency of Catholicism or of traditional Protestantism, we must be careful to note that Weber explicitly asserts — without proof — that the acceptance of revelation involves an 'intellectual sacrifice'.[25] This statement is then qualified by Weber when he puts in a plea in mitigation for the man who makes such an intellectual sacri-fice. Weber says that this sacrifice is 'ethically quite a different matter than the evasion of the plain duty of intellectual integrity'. In sum, these observations of Weber are both puzzling and unsatisfactory. Certainly, it is the case that an 'intellectual sacrifice' is built into the very notion of heterogeneous ethics and mutually conflicting values which is essential to the Weberian realm of ideological values. Since Weber supposes that all men are necessarily ideological sinners against logic, how can he purport to point an accusing finger at the Christians in particular? Weber himself does not have an adequate understanding of the demands of intellectual integrity with regard to fundamental truth.

Even if we were to confine our attention to the historical consequences of Christianity for socio-political morality, it could be argued that Weber underestimates the importance of Christianity. Indeed, this criticism of Weber has been advanced with good reason by Werner Stark.[26] Stark has pointed out that without Christ the world would have been morally worse than it is and that a shrewd sociologist ought to be able to judge that this is the case. However, Stark's criticism of Weber's deficiencies in this regard is confined to the sociological plane. The criticism does not live up to the claim which would seem to be implicit in the title of his article that it will deal with the problem of moral philosophy. Certainly, Weber does not have a moral philosophy in the true sense: he has only an ideological substitute for a moral philosophy. In order to criticise this substitute in relation to Christian ethics, it is necessary to observe the failure of Weber to confront adequately the challenge of Christ's advent.

We have seen that Weber stands in the shadow of Nietzsche's atheistic revolt against God and religion as Marx stood in the shadow of Feuerbach's revolt. Weber implicitly presupposes the Nietzschean perspective as Marx presupposes that Feuerbach has asserted whatever positive atheism is capable of saying 'from the intellectual standpoint'. Weber and Marx inherit the atheism of their respective predecessors. They both seem to imagine that the work which has already been done in the conversion to atheism is inevitable and irrevocable. Accordingly, although Weber sometimes attempts to read his own ideology into the Bible, this is not very serious.[27] Certainly, Weber, like Marx, failed precisely to address himself seriously and persistently to the task of investigating the truth of the authentic Christian revelation. Indeed, it is possible to apply to Weber to some extent the following observations of Henri de Lubac about the work of Marx:

> There is every reason to think ... that the Marxist analysis, applied conscientiously and as intelligently as possible twenty centuries ago, in Palestine, would have overlooked the humble fact summed up in a name: Jesus of Nazareth — as in fact the Jewish and Roman historians overlooked it. That almost imperceptible fact slipped through their nets, and, if it happens to be caught in the mesh of learned explanations, it is emptied of its explosive force.[28]

Certainly, if Weber fails as a sociologist to register adequately the beneficial effects of Christianity upon human morality, he is even more defective in his failure to advert properly to the special, unique, humble, yet divine, fact of which de Lubac writes.

Consequently, Weber does not squarely confront the questions raised by the Christian claims: Was Jesus Christ the God-man? Was He crucified? Did He rise from the dead and ascend into heaven? Did He institute a Church? Is that Church such that the ecclesiology of Catholicism, or of Eastern Orthodoxy or of Protestantism gives an authentic account of it? These serious questions are not allowed to arise in Weber's sociology in consequence of the method which he has imposed upon it. These serious questions are not properly considered by Weber in writings outside of sociology. These lacunae correspond in Weber's thought with his significant failure to consider the problems raised for his ideology by moderate realist philosophy and in particular by Thomism.

Weber's systematic avoidance of these crucial problems is related, as we have seen, to his assimilation of Nietzsche's view that reason and revelation are necessarily opposed to each other. It is also relevant to observe that this tendency to identify that which is above human reason with the irrational is a tendency which Weber also shares with Troeltsch. It is particularly important to explain what is wrong with Weber's positions on this matter since even serious critics of Weber such as Leo Strauss and Eric Voegelin have not been able to provide any adequate solution to the problem of the relation of reason to revelation. We shall therefore expound the fundamental differences between the Thomist teaching on the relation between the natural order and the supernatural order and the teachings of the modern ideologies of the superman.

What distinctions, then, are required in order to explain the fundamental difference between the Thomist doctrine of the supernatural order and the ideological concept of the superman? First, it must be emphasised that the ideologies of the superman teach that man's nature is, as it were, ontologically unstable and that it can be — and, in some sense, should be — transmuted, by human endeavour, into another nature: the nature of the superman. Secondly, these ideologies hold that this ontological transmutation is of such a sort that it necessarily involves the destruction, elimination or displacement of the original human nature. Indeed, in so far as some of the ideologies conceive of a continuous transmutation of man's nature, human nature may come to be envisaged as totally historical and the term 'human nature' would then have no determinate meaning at all. For, according to an evolutionary ideology of continuous human transformation, no condition of man contains human nature as such; every condition of man is, at once, *sub*-human in comparison with some other condition of man and also *super*-human in comparison with yet another condition of man. In so far as the nature of man and the state or condition of man are identified, the concept of human nature distinguishable in the various states of man becomes (so these ideologies suppose) meaningless and redundant.

Whilst Catholic doctrine envisages many actual or possible states or conditions of human nature, it denies that human nature as such can either be simply destroyed — or be destroyed in any supposed process of transmutation — by any actual or conceivable human endeavour.[29] Catholic doctrine does not deny that God, in His absolute power, could (if He chose) annihilate the human species and create in its place some other species of creature with a different (and therefore not human) nature. Not even God, however, can create a being with a nature which is both specifically human and specifically not-human. The reason is that such a being is impossible absolutely and because whatever implies an inherent contradiction does not come within the scope of even the divine omnipotence.[30] Accordingly, not even God can effect a transmutation of man in the ideological sense of the development of a superman. The ideological concept of a superman is not the concept of a creature with a nature higher than human nature (as, for example, an angelic nature is higher than human nature); it is the concept of a pseudo-being supposedly the production of man himself: an impossible attempt at ontological transmutation undertaken in despite of God who has created human nature such as it is.[31]

Consequently, when St Thomas Aquinas discerns, in man, natural tendencies[32] which are shared with the lower beings and a natural tendency towards God, he is not to be misunderstood as saying that man is an inherently contradictory pastiche of natural inclinations, some belonging to a sub-human nature and some belonging to the nature of a superman. On the contrary, those operations of the natural powers of man (such as the growth of the human body) which are not human acts (since they are not subject to the control of reason) do not participate in any interior struggle with human reason and do not introduce any inherent contradiction into human nature. Similarly, those supernatural gifts which God infuses into man entirely free from outside him do not involve the transmutation of man's natural being into another grade of being. Whether man comes to be elevated by the light of glory or finally deprived of any beatitude, human nature itself is not thereby destroyed. Man's nature is not *destructively* exalted in the one case nor *destructively* cast down in the other case. In other words, unless man were to be annihilated by God, he could not cease to possess human nature and a destructive ontological transmutation of human nature is impossible.[33]

Perhaps what has been written here — though too brief for the subject — will suffice to correct the perspectives of both the atheistic ideologists and those of their Christian critics who seem erroneously to suppose that it is necessary to diminish the traditional Christian teaching in order to secure their intellectual positions in the face of the objections of atheistic ideology. Certainly, however, the misunderstandings of Catholic doctrine on the part of the ideologists themselves and their modernist or neo-modernist Christian opponents have evidently served largely to insulate Weber and his disciples from authentic contact with the Christian mind in its coherence, its incisiveness and its plenitude.

Historically, the modernist and atheist ideological misperceptions of the Catholic doctrine derive ultimately from the abandonment of the Thomist teaching on the eternal law as the ultimate standard and source of every valid law,[34] from the rejection of the Thomist doctrine of the relation of the natural and the supernatural and from the increasingly radical distortion and transvaluation of the very idea of divine revelation in consequence of the Protestant revolt. Accordingly, there was a tendency in Protestant and Rationalist thought to confuse human nature as such with one or other of the states of human nature and to misconceive the natural law as such (pertaining to human nature as such) as if it were peculiarly tied to some supposed state of nature.[35] Hence there was a failure to understand the Thomist doctrine of the 'openness'[36] of the natural law to completion by divine positive law and the fecundity of the natural law in prompting man to establish human positive laws in accord with natural law. These various and complex deviations in Protestant and Rationalist thought practically inevitably engendered the erroneous supposition that the Christian mind cannot envisage even the possibility of a natural law or Christian morality without inherent and irresolvable dilemmas and contradictions.

Against this background, we shall not underestimate the difficulties which stood between Weber and the arduous path towards an intellectual life which shuns ideology and which seeks to follow right reason and right faith. Nevertheless, we must conclude by summing up what is, objectively speaking, unacceptable in Weber's reluctant and largely implicit 'envelopment' of Christianity in his ideology. Obviously the Catholic mind will object specifically to Weber's teaching because it fails to accept the Christian revelation, because it fails to recognise the natural and divine order and because it fails to accept that there is a Church, divinely instituted by Jesus Christ, which is Holy, Catholic and Roman. However, the basic Catholic objections to Weber's 'ideology of ideologies' go even further since these failures of Weber, taken together, provide the context in which he will fabricate an 'ideology of ideologies' which will not properly allow even for the *real possibility* that certain *facts* (including supernatural facts) and an ordered hierarchy of *values* could have a real and objectively justified connection with each other. This might be the point to recall Jean Guitton's criticism of those, including Loisy and Bultmann, who 'take it for granted that the more religious significance a story has the less historical it is ....'. Weber is willing to respect, in a certain way, the positions of Christians but he takes these positions to be ideologies chosen in abstraction from the facts. Our reply to Weber must be in the terms of J. Guitton's reply to the Modernists: 'How can they fail to see that the essence of the religion of the Word incarnate is just this — never to dissociate the historical reality of the event from its mystical and theological significance?'[37]

With regard to the Church, it is accepted that the divine treasure is borne in earthly vessels. These earthly vessels, since they are human, will not be immune from human failings. These failings will sometimes be individual failings but, since the force of evil custom can be found among the faithful as well as elsewhere, these failings will sometimes manifest a social pattern and so constitute a datum of which some kind of sociological account might be given even without reference to the fact that the Church is the body of Christ. But, if there can be (within limits) a legitimate sociological analysis of certain historical ecclesiastical facts of a somewhat profane character, the sociologist who knows the Church for what she is will exercise caution. For he will remember that 'the union between the human and the divine is a subtle one; so delicate that if we push ahead without critique without due caution, we very often run the grave risk of behaving like the son who insults his mother'.[38]

Notes and references

1   *From Max Weber*, p.119.
2   See Eugène Fleischmann, 'De Weber à Nietzsche', *Archives Européenes de Sociologie*, vol.5, no.2, 1964, pp.190—238 commenting on Marianne Weber's *Max Weber: A Biography*, New York, 1975 (especially p.337).
3   See Leo Strauss, *Natural Right and History*, Chicago, 1953, p.71.
4   See James Joyce, *The Portrait of the Artist as a Young Man*, Penguin Modern Classic edn, London, 1960, p.243.
5   See E. Voegelin, *The New Science of Politics*, Chicago, 1952, pp.19—20.
6   See discussion in R. Aron, *German Sociology*, New York, 1964, p.72.

7   J. Maritain, 'The End of Machiavellianism', *Review of Politics*, January 1942.

8   Against such individualism, see J. Folliet, *Man in Society*, London, 1963, pp.79—80.

9   *From Max Weber*, pp.147—9.

10 St Thomas Aquinas, *Summa contra Gentiles*, book I, chap. 42.

11 M. Weber, *The Methodology of the Social Sciences*, p.19.

12 Weber's 'ideology of the ideologies' is considered further in chapters 7 and 8.

13 See H. de Lubac, *The Splendour of the Church*, London, 1956, p.192.

14 Hobbes, *Leviathan*, ch.42.

15 See S. Leslie, *Henry Edward Manning: His Life and Labours*, 2nd rev. edn, London, 1921, pp.242—4.

16 Marianne Weber, *Max Weber*.

17 K. Jaspers, *Leonardo, Descartes, Max Weber: Three Essays*, London, 1965, p.269.

18 See T.S. Simey, 'Weber's Sociological Theory of Values: An Appraisal in Mid-Century', *Sociological Review*, vol.13, 1965, pp.51, 62 footnote 16.

19 *Dignitatis humanae*, Rome, 7 December 1965.

20 See J.P. Mayer, *Max Weber and German Politics*, 2nd rev. edn, London, 1956, especially pp.26, 117.

21 See Fleischmann, 'De Weber à Nietzsche', p.215.

22 See *From Max Weber*, p.147.

23 Ibid., p.142.

24 Ibid., p.155.

25 Ibid., pp.154—5.

26 Werner Stark, 'The Agony of Righteousness: Max Weber's Moral Philosophy', *Thought*, 1968, pp.380—92.

27 Weber's attempt to identify his ideological aspirations and lamentations with the voices of the Jewish prophets was misconceived. See Mayer, *Max Weber and German Politics*, pp.86—7.

28 H. de Lubac, *The Discovery of God*, London, 1960, p.29.

29 This subject is discussed at greater length in my *The Natural Law Tradition and the Theory of International Relations*, London/New York, 1975.

30 St Thomas Aquinas, *Summa theologiae*, I, q.25, art.3.

31 An interesting survey of the ideology of the superman is given in J. Chaix-Ruy, *The Superman from Nietzsche to Teilhard de Chardin*, Notre Dame, Indiana, 1968.

32 St Thomas Aquinas, *Summa theologiae*, Ia IIae, q.94, art.2.

33 See Midgley, *Natural Law Traditions*, especially p.33.

34 Ibid., pp.459 n.100, 479—80 nn.42 and 43, and other relevant

references indexed under 'eternal law' and 'law natural'.

35   Ibid., especially pp.80—2 and 143—6.
36   Ibid., and also J. Fuchs, *Natural Law: A Theological Investigation*, Dublin, 1965.
37   J. Guitton, 'Born of the Virgin Mary', *L'Osservatore Romano*, weekly edn in English, 26 March 1970.
38   H. de Lubac, *The Splendour of the Church*, London, 1966, pp.67—9.

7 Weber's attitude to liberal and atheist ideology

Weber, the decline of liberalism and the rise of sociological ideology

Although Weber's thought is profoundly influenced by sociological ideologies which were both atheistic and post-liberal in character, it cannot be seriously doubted that there are in Weber certain elements of a kind of liberal ideology. Friedrich suggests that 'Weber in many spheres conducts an allegedly value-free discussion with value-concepts which now seem to us liberal'.[1] Bahrdt observes that 'Weber finds himself in a complicated situation ... impelled by liberal motives ... but having outgrown ... the thought of classical liberalism'.[2] In order to proceed a little further with our consideration of the antecedents of the various components of Weber's ideology, let us recall that, despite their differences, various types of liberal ideology and various types of sociological ideology can both be shown to have a common ancestry. Even when one or other of these ideologies reacts against its intellectual ancestry, the common ancestry provides the setting and the conditions within which the intellectual revolt proceeds.

In the pre-history of liberalism, the teaching on natural law, on its proper relation to divine positive law and on the eternal law as the ultimate source of every kind of valid law, was variously undermined under the influence of Protestantism, rationalism, voluntarism and empiricism. In England, John Locke was the writer among others whose work was ambiguously but characteristically designed to promote this undermining process prior to the explicit and general rejection of every teaching on natural law, Christianity and the existence of God, by modern atheism. Leo Strauss has rightly pointed out that there is a sense in which one may hold that Machiavelli's revolt against political morality is somewhat mitigated by Hobbes and further mitigated in Locke.[3] Yet, as Strauss himself explains, these mitigations are ambiguous and the mitigation is more apparent than real. Indeed, there is another sense in which it may be argued that Hobbes and Locke are responsible for the aggravation of certain trends in the work of Machiavelli. It is accepted that, in spite of his preoccupation with paganism and his inadequate understanding of Christian teaching, Machiavelli does not seriously undertake the invention of a new morality. Hobbes's manipulation of Christianity is a new undertaking but it remains an eccentricity in the literature of Erastianism. It is Locke's simplified and rationalistic 'Christianity'[4] which is the more significant precursor of the secularised pseudo-mysticism and, consequently, the modernist new morality which emerges in Rousseau and eventually in Hegel. Given Strauss's teaching that Machiavelli and Hobbes lead the first wave of modernity and that Rousseau leads the second wave of a more radical modernity,[5] Locke is at once an apparent mitigation of the first and a real precursor of the second. It is a corollary of this analysis that the modernist principles of individualism and absolutism are to be found together even in Locke's later work on toleration.[6]

In chapter 2, we have already considered the intimate connection between the modernist principles of individualism and totalitarianism in Hobbes and Rousseau.[7] For both, there can be no truly rational means of achieving political order without resort to a kind of absolutist or totalitarian principle of sovereignty. Any attempt to undertake Rousseau's pseudo-mystical eliciting of a supposed 'social contract' and 'general will' could lead only to a socio-political state founded upon a totalitarian sovereignty which is, in truth, arbitrary and unfounded. Therefore, it has been said rightly that Rousseau is 'a declared libertarian and a disguised despot'.[8] Certainly, Rousseau's inadequate modernist concept of man, once accepted, would render nugatory every attempt to develop an adequate theory of socio-political reality.

The atheistic sociological ideologies of Comte, Durkheim and Lévy-Bruhl seemed to be seeking to emancipate themselves from the elements of rationalism in ethics and of individualism in socio-political thought which they had inherited indirectly from Rousseau. Deploige has rightly indicated that Comte was not wrong to see, in the proliferation of Utopias and universal panaceas, a rationalistic mentality among the successors of Rousseau which in the name of the absolute in theory provided the arbitrary in practice. Durkheim complained of Rousseau's individualism in observing that 'While ... social life for Rousseau is not contrary to nature, it has so little in common with nature that one wonders how it is possible'.[9] Yet, in seeking to remedy the defects of certain kinds of ethical rationalism and socio-political individualism, the sociological ideologists did not fully appreciate the depth of the problem with which they were confronted. Instead of reversing Rousseau's modernist rejection of true moral and socio-political philosophy, they complicated the scene by undertaking a partial revolt against the heritage of Rousseau in a way which led to the aggravation of some of the errors which were endemic in that heritage itself.

The rebellion of the sociological ideologists took the form not simply of a revolt against ethical rationalism and socio-political individualism but of a generalised attack upon moral philosophy as such. This attack is most explicitly and pointedly stated by Lévy-Bruhl who peremptorily announced that 'There is not and cannot be any theoretical ethics'.[10] Since, in the course of rejecting bad philosophy, the sociologists found themselves committed to rejecting philosophy itself, their controversial commitments to moral or socio-political values are properly designated as ideological commitments.

Although the sociological ideologies and the ideologically distorted teachings of a so-called philosophical liberalism were in some ways opposed to each other, both types were modernist ideologies developed against the remote background of modernist thinking including the thought of Rousseau. Whether they 'transvalued' or simply rejected the authentic teaching on natural law in moral philosophy and in the socio-political philosophy of the common good, these ideologists were faced by a fundamental common dilemma. The dilemma was simply this: that neither knew how to save, at the same time, the good of the human person and the good of socio-political life. Henri de Lubac makes a similar point when he insists that atheistic humanism in particular has never known how to save both the meaning of history and the meaning of the person.[11] We shall find that liberal and sociological ideologists will sometimes seek to save the supposed meaning of history and of socio-political life at the price of admitting some violation of the right and dignity of the human person. Alternatively, they will sometimes seek to save the supposed meaning of the human person at the expense of the justice and order of socio-political life. Raymond Aron rightly observes that, in the case of Comte, the attempt 'to establish a new morality on the basis of sociology' was 'not only dangerous for scientific truth and moral honesty' but that 'it also endangered the dignity of the human person'.[12]

Various commentators will claim, not without reason, that Weber sought and purported to advance a perspective on values which would be answerable both for the human person and also for the socio-political life of the people judged from the standpoint of history. We cannot agree, however, that this enterprise of Weber's succeeded in overcoming the antinomies of his predecessors. He merely repeated, in another form, the previous pastiche of the two erroneous but inter-dependent principles of individualism and totalitarianism with no real attempt at even a rationalisation of their supposed joint validity.

The philosophical problem of the relationship between the right of the human person and the right of socio-political life cannot be satis-factorily considered without reference to a true and adequate under-standing of human nature. The liberal and sociological ideologies had failed to solve the problem precisely because their perspectives on the autonomy of the individual and the autonomy of socio-political life were not reconcilable with a doctrine of human nature which was true or even sufficiently intelligible. Certainly, neither the autonomy of the person in individualism[13] nor the autonomy of society in 'sociol-ogism'[14] could be reconciled with the natural law which truly pertains to human nature properly understood. Weber's teaching can contribute nothing towards the restoration of an authentic understanding of the true norms of human nature in socio-political life or in the human person himself.[15]

In order to evaluate the specifically Weberian form of liberalism we need to consider further the real significance of the historical trans-formations of liberal ideology. Certainly, Weber inherits elements of thought derived from more than one of the various progressive (yet mutually incompatible) stages in the liberal and modernist revolt against philosophical and theological truth. The historical transform-ation of liberalism may be generally characterised as a transition from a liberalism diversely understood as integral or 'moralistic'[16] to a liberalism variously assessed as formal and positivistic. Weber's liberal-ism certainly belongs in a general sense to the liberalism of the last category. Consequently, if the historical transformation of liberalism must be judged to be a progressive subversion, Weber's liberalism is one of those liberalisms which have succumbed to that subversion. However, it is necessary to do justice to the positions at both ends of the liberal spectrum. For, if the integral or moralistic liberals can rightly complain that formal, positivistic or decadent liberalism is without a substantive doctrine, it is a fact that this outcome was, in a sense, implicit in the positions of integral liberalism itself. J.H. Hallowell has pointed out that, latent in integral liberalism, there are to be found, conjoined by historical accident, two logically independent philosophies of law: one supposes a substantive criterion of the validity of law, the other a merely formal criterion.[17] Since the substantive criterion was always somewhat elusive and because the formal principle was evidently incompatible with a truly substantive teaching on the validity of law, liberalism was always an unstable 'synthesis' of mutually incompatible elements. This state of affairs was the eventual outcome of the earlier abandonment of the fundamental principle of intellectual unity in moral and political philosophy, namely, the natural law understood as deriving from the eternal law, the ultimate source of all orders of valid law.

The basic defence of the disciples of Weber against their more traditional liberal opponents must therefore take the form of a counter-attack. The Weberians can argue that, if integral liberalism itself is not founded upon a consistent doctrine of fundamental philosophical truth, it would be more straightforward for all those who are committed to liberalism to concede and to emphasise this important point quite explicitly from the start. However, it must be recognised that the eventual outcome of a sceptical liberalism must be some kind of doctrine which can no longer call itself in any sense liberal. To retain the title 'liberal', even by courtesy, a modernist ideology cannot be *totally* post-Nietzschean. Yet again, if the ideologies reasonably described as liberal have variously remote historical sources which are pre-Nietzschean, this does not mean that liberalism in its decadence has not been profoundly contaminated by the radical modernism of Nietzsche. Indeed, Leo Strauss has astutely observed that the problem raised by the Nietzschean criticism of modern rationalistic thought is perhaps the deepest reason for the intellectual crisis of modern liberal thought.[18]

If we consider the historical transformation of German liberalism in the field of jurisprudence, we find that it comes to be reduced to an insubstantial formal system in the work of Weber's friend Jellinek. Although Jellinek's work does not appear to have entirely satisfied Weber, it is not surprising to find that Weber himself rejects integral liberalism in the sociological field in somewhat the same way in which Jellinek rejects it in the field of jurisprudence. Although Jellinek's jurisprudence has the practical effect of removing substantive limitations from the more or less arbitrary exercise of absolute State sovereignty, it can be argued that it was only after the progressive influences of neo-Kantian and neo-Hegelian thought that German jurisprudence reached the term of its decadence.[19] So far as the neo-Kantian 'pure' theory of law was concerned, the eventual development of the theory of Kelsen was prepared, in effect, by Stammler. Some of Stammler's work provoked the hostility of Weber[20] despite the fact that both Stammler and Weber were at one in rejecting every substantive kind of liberalism. The main reason for Weber's animosity was probably the fact that Stammler did not make it consistently clear whether or not or how his formalistic philosophical idealism could have anything whatever to do with actual legal systems. In spite of the spurious ideological character of the unreal concepts of Stammler, Weber's somewhat abrasive treatment of Stammler seems rather unreasonable even in terms of Weber's own position. For, despite the acceptance of Nietzschean perspectives (which logically involve superseding even the neo-Kantian and neo-Hegelian perspectives), Weber always clung to certain pre-Nietzschean positions. Hence Weber's own view was no less eclectic than that of Stammler himself.

In the modernist tradition which originates in Machiavelli and which is progressively formulated from Rousseau to Nietzsche, Weber adopts a principle of individualism which leads to the acceptance — even for the sake of any kind of socio-political order — of a kind of totalitarian principle. Unlike Rousseau, Weber did not trouble to undertake the false 'rationalisation' of this commitment by any appeal to a social contract theory. He merely asserts, with a kind of Nietzschean dynamism, his endorsement of a paradoxical modernist politics based on two mutually incompatible principles jointly engendered by nihilism, namely, the arbitrary will to power of the nation State and the arbitrary value-choice of the individual man. Mommsen suggests that Weber's attitude could be summed up in the following paradox: 'The utmost possible freedom through the utmost possible dominance'.[21]

This Weberian teaching, which is evidently untenable, is the teaching which Aron and Jaspers have sought to defend. Aron implies that Weber, unlike Comte, upholds the dignity of the human person. Jaspers seeks to excuse Weber by saying that 'Human dignity and Germany's position in world affairs were what he was concerned with, not one without the other'.[22] Jaspers's defence does not suffice because it is obvious that Weber's ideology of inevitable value-conflict — which Jaspers discusses in other passages — cannot provide a basis for the harmonious pursuit of both his aims.

Furthermore, it is not simply that Weber's doctrine about the task of saving political society in the midst of historical change is a threat to the morality of the person in his private concerns. It is also the case that Weber's doctrine of the primacy of the will to power of the nation State does not properly respect man's true sociality which has its foundation in the natural socio-political inclination in man. It is very evident that Weber's teaching does not properly respect the common good of international political society (or the universal Church) or the legitimate roles of subordinate groups within the State whenever these conflict with the demands of the totalitarian element in Weber's eclectic but inordinate nationalism. Although Weber's principle of individualism is intimately connected with his totalitarian principle, he can find no valid reconciliation of the two norms. In case of conflict between them, Weber rather generally prefers the nationalistic norm to the individualistic norm but the two norms are not harmonised; when they conflict, they merely alternate. J.P. Mayer indicated that he was not unaware of Weber's problem when he observed that, in seeking to reconcile *Realpolitik* and moral individualism, Weber proceeded in such a way that 'both phenomena have been falsified'.[23] It would be better to say that *Realpolitik* and moral individualism are teachings which are incompatible with the truth and also incompatible with each other.

Many commentators have considered that Weber's teaching is manifestly less harmful than the totalitarian ideologies of Nazism and atheistic Communism. J.P. Mayer suggests that if Weber had experienced Hitler's régime, he 'would have died in a concentration camp'. In regard to the 'tracing of ideological lineages', G. Roth seeks to defend Weber by 'the rule of the lesser evil'.[24] Yet this defence fails because we are obliged to reject not merely the more spectacularly evil ideologies but every kind of ideology since every ideology is evil. Roth argues more specifically, however, that Weber is not only opposed to 'ideological absolutism' but that he is 'anti-ideological'.[25] It would appear that these judgements of Roth involve a misunderstanding of the nature of ideology and that this misunderstanding derives from a more or less nihilistic liberal perspective which Roth seems to share with Weber himself. Certainly, a more or less nihilistic liberalism will itself engender some kind of ideology even though such ideology is distinguishable from (say) the Nazi and the Communist ideologies. Roth seems to envisage a struggle against ideology conducted in terms of a teaching which is, in reality, ideological although Roth represents it as anti-ideological. We are reminded of an astute observation of Voegelin in this connection. Voegelin, who considered that the ideological teachings deriving from such thinkers as Marx and Nietzsche were modern versions of gnosticism, went on to observe that, in the confused situation of our time, 'the struggle against the consequences of gnosticism is being conducted in the very language of gnosticism'.[26] Voegelin does not make application of this statement in order to explain the inadequacy of Weber's critique of the revolutionary ideologies of the extreme left and the extreme right but such an application would appear to be justified.

We can begin to understand the paradox of an ideological criticism of ideology if we recall that just as there are degrees and types of modernism, there are corresponding degrees and types of ideological thinking[27] and of totalitarianism. Just as the stages of progressively more radical modernism are not wholly compatible with each other — since the later stages are more radical than the earlier ones — so are the stages of totalitarianism and of ideology not fully compatible with each other. The intellectual situation resulting from these currents of modernism, totalitarianism and ideology is further complicated by the mutual contamination of the various historical currents in the context of modern thought. In particular, we find in Weber, in Roth and in

Jaspers, the coexistence of pre-Nietzschean and post-Nietzschean types of ideological thinking. Accordingly, such thinkers as these may resist one or other of the exigencies of the Nietzschean stage of ideology in the name of an ideological pastiche which owes much to Nietzsche but which owes something to an incompatible pre-Nietzschean ideology. What has been said of this confused ideological criticism of ideology can be applied *mutatis mutandis* in the analysis of the modernist criticism of modernism, the nihilist criticism of nihilism and to the totalitarian criticism of totalitarianism.

Against this background, we are driven to recognise that the opposition of writers such as Roth[28] and Jaspers[29] to all intellectual 'absolutisms' is fundamentally ambiguous. The very notion of intellectual 'absolutism', as they variously employ it, presupposes a decadent liberal perspective. In other words, the supposedly 'moderate' ideologist's rejection of intellectual 'absolutisms' involves the rejection, at one and the same time, of 'radical' ideological errors and permanent truth! Without seeking to identify the position of Weber with either the position of Roth or that of Jaspers, it can be said that Weber's own 'moderate' ideological thinking has this same consequence. This kind of rejection of permanent truth engenders in the thought of Weber a degree and type of nihilism and even a degree and type of totalitarianism as well as a degree and type of ideology. Although Weber would have rejected the degrees and types of these things which came to be manifested in certain totalitarian régimes, this does not mean that there is no connection between these and the degrees and types which Weber did accept.

Hallowell suggests that since German liberalism itself declined to the point at which it had 'no doctrine, no way of life to defend', the suspicion will arise that 'liberalism was not murdered, as is often said, but that it committed suicide'.[30] When academic ideologists, like Weber, found their eclectic systems upon a nihilism which is envisaged as being susceptible of being overcome, if it can be overcome at all, only by admitting some kind of arbitrary and potentially totalitarian principle, they do not necessarily desire to see the achievement of political power by any specific contemporary type of totalitarian régime. Nevertheless, such academic ideologists do bear some intellectual responsibility for promoting an intellectual climate which is not unfavourable to anyone seeking to establish some sort of totalitarian régime.

In order to clarify the complex relationships between the acceptance of a kind of totalitarian principle and the promotion of some specifically totalitarian régime, it is necessary to bear in mind what Maritain has said about the possibility, in favourable circumstances, of a kind of practical agreement about human rights between men holding diverse philosophical positions. Accordingly, even those who are committed to an eclectic value-system which does not exclude an ideological and totalitarian principle, may still, in fortunate cases, collaborate with those who uphold a valid philosophical foundation for human rights, in the practical task of defending those rights in a pluralistic society. Yet this does not mean that the practical co-operation of the ideologist is anything other than precarious. Certainly, for example, the totalitarian principle implicit in a so-called 'piece-meal social engineering' is likely to be considerably less harmful in practice — especially in a pluralistic society committed to a democratic régime — because the political pressures exerted by those who hold to the truth may operate (with the acquiescence of the 'democratic social engineer') to nullify the potentially totalitarian effects in many cases. Of course, there is always the dangerous possibility that the majority of people in a democratic society may become converted to a more explicitly totalitarian principle of thought and action. Hence the erosion of the practical agreement about even fundamental rights is always possible even under a régime with a democratic electoral process.

Recent liberal ideologies are showing themselves increasingly incapable of upholding certain crucial human rights under pressure from materialistic attitudes and atheistic theories which embody a more developed kind of totalitarian principle. A crucial instance is the current failure of the liberal ideologies to uphold the fundamental right to life of the human foetus in the face of atheistic ideologies which seek to promote abortion on demand. The true remedy for this state of affairs is to defend fundamental rights on the basis of objective natural law.[31] Certainly, the quasi-liberal atheistic ideology of Weber is theoretically unserviceable for the purpose. Indeed, no liberal theory, either integral or formal, can provide a satisfactory philosophical foundation for human rights.

Weber, positive atheism and the revolutionary atheistic ideology of Marx

Henri de Lubac has suggested very generally that, when two different kinds of thought confront one another, each tends spontaneously to 'comprehend' or 'envelop' the other. It will be supposed that one will have satisfactorily refuted the other only when it has in some way annexed it and gone beyond it. The other will not have been effectually conquered until it has been assimilated. In particular, de Lubac observes that this is the natural 'strategy' of contemporary atheism which — in one form or another — has been in use for more than a century.[32] This strategy, used by Hegel and developed by Feuerbach, Marx and Nietzsche, depends upon the joint deployment of modern rationalism and modern irrationalism. Modern rationalism had attacked religion; modern irrationalism claimed to be able to comprehend it and to transmute it into something else. We shall need to consider whether and to what extent Weber participates in this strategy which manifests itself specifically in the revolutionary ideologies of positive atheism and especially in Marx and Nietzsche.

We have already presented some of the evidence for that important fact concerning the intellectual history of modernity: namely, that the unbalanced rationalism of modern times is both an opponent of right reason and a preparation of irrationalism. Accordingly, it is a common characteristic of those positive atheists — such as Marx, Comte and Nietzsche — who undertake a radical attack on religion and morality, that they forbid the intellectual analysis of their own ideological presuppositions.

The typical obstruction presented to reason by the ideologists of positive atheism is a rationalistic misrepresentation of the theistic arguments and a refusal, on purely ideological grounds, seriously to examine the argument from contingency in its authentic formulation. Indeed, we find that some positive atheists seek to make a virtue of the rejection without argument of the theistic position.

Marx will proceed by the method of rationalism up to a certain point but only in order to reach a point of departure from which the supposedly supra-intellectual volitions of 'practical-critical activity' can supersede 'the intellectual standpoint'. Feuerbach will help him to establish that universal 'country of reason' where (we are assured) God ceases to exist.[33] The young Marx gives us one of the keys to his attempt to envelop Christian theism — so far as he thinks that this can be done from 'the intellectual standpoint' — in his early note on the proofs for the existence of God.[34] Marx criticises the so-called ontological proof and he seems to suppose that all the arguments purporting to prove the existence of God are alike invalid. He thinks that they would have to be drafted in such a form as the following: 'Because nature is badly organised, God must exist'. It is here that Marx's error is fully apparent.

Certainly, it should be sufficiently well known that the fundamental proof, advanced by orthodox Christian theists, for the existence of God, is the argument from contingency. If we apply the Marxist criticism to this argument, it becomes perfectly clear what Marx is doing. He is asserting that the proposition: 'The beings known by the senses are contingent' is equivalent to 'The beings known by the senses are badly organised'. In other words, there is an inherent connection between Marx's denial of the existence of God and his denial of an intrinsic order in the universe or in man himself. Indeed, the mere fact that man is a contingent being — quite apart from any actual inconvenience in his historical condition — is sufficient to lead Marx to suppose that there are no intrinsic principles of order in human nature. If man is not God Himself but only a contingent creature, he has not made his own being and, for Marx, the mere idea of such a status is considered to be a symptom of human alienation. This emerges from the following passage in Marx's *Economic and Philosophic Manuscripts of 1844*:

> A being can consider itself independent only when it is its own master, and it is its own master only when it is to itself that it owes its existence.

Of course, whatever Marx may have supposed, it remains true that there is no evidence that there is anything intrinsically absurd or unreasonable or alienating in man's contingent being as such. There are many sources of man's actual miseries and it is in consequence of human pride that men succumb to the temptation to ascribe their sufferings or the sufferings of others, without good reason, to some alleged intrinsic absurdity in the very nature of man or in the very nature of the universe, for which — if there is a God — God would be responsible.

Accordingly, amongst the positive atheists, the rejection of theism is intimately connected with their view of the absurdity of man and the universe. When Hegel announces the death of God, he does not use good logic. He invents an erroneous dialectical substitute for logic and purports to envisage the death of God by surpassing the human consciousness which knows Him and substituting a new mode of consciousness invented by Hegel himself. Feuerbach ingeniously misunderstands and misrepresents the philosophy of universals and the relation of existence and essence in man. Feuerbach eliminates God by replacing Him with the human essence conceived in a contradictory fashion as embracing the infinite attributes of God.[35]

For Marx and for Nietzsche, positive atheism is not, in any really significant sense, an intellectual argument: it is primarily and fundamentally a non-intellectual decision. Nietzsche states that 'it is our preference that decides against Christianity — not arguments'. For Nietzsche, the death of God is not simply a terrible fact but something willed by him.[36] Marx himself admits that the idea that nature should be through itself, as well as the idea that man should exist through himself, is inconceivable to people because it contradicts all the evidences of practical life.[37] Accordingly, as Voegelin[38] has pointed out, Marx can reject these evidences only by suppressing the very *question* about man's origin which arises in our human life. Marx simply insists that socialist man is the man who does not even raise the question about the ultimate origin of man. It is only against the background of this ideological suppression of the evidences about man's ultimate origin that Marx can formulate his doctrine that the 'whole so-called history of the world' is nothing but the production of man by human work.

Hegel tells us that God has died because the Absolute had to encompass His death. Nietzsche regards Nietzsche as one of the principal participants in the conspiracy which has supposedly accomplished the assassination of God. Marx admits that, like Prometheus, he hates all the gods (including the true God) and he tells us that God will finally perish at the hands of the revolutionary proletariat. Weber also holds, as these others do, that God is dead but Weber is less confident in attributing responsibility for what he apparently considers to be a strange and tragic event fated to happen in our modern world. Sometimes, one feels that it is as if Weber merely acquiesces, as it were, in what he might suppose to be the suicide of God. At other times, he seems to imply that God has died at the hands of the whole rationalistic generation which formed the culture of Weber's own time. However this might be, Weber, no less than the others, takes his ideological decision against the existence of God.

Since there is, in Weber, a certain ambiguity manifested in his appraisal of the question about who is really responsible for the death of God, it is not surprising that there is a corresponding ambiguity in Weber's evaluation of the consequences of this mysterious fatality which no detective has been able to explain satisfactorily in spite of the fact that everyone can see (so Weber supposes) that it was an inevitable side-effect of the rise of scientific rationality. No doubt, Weber is committed to the position adopted by the positive atheists: that, if God is dead, man must take His place. However, Weber does not really imagine that, when man ceases to accept the existence of God, he will be able to undertake the tasks of a substitute for God with hope of definitive success. Indeed, the peculiar flavour of Weber's thought manifests itself when he shows himself continually aware — in the midst of the ideological dynamism of his thought — that he has failed to advance an adequate solution for the predicament of modern man.

Like Marx, Weber finds himself committed to the view that modern man is in some way alienated. Like Marx, Weber is committed to some kind of modern struggle which is occasioned by the alienated condition in which modern man is supposed to find himself. But here the comparison ends. Weber, unlike Marx, cannot give any sufficient characterisation of what he thinks is the real significance of alienation. Although Weber is committed to struggle, apparently in vain, for an atheistic solution of the problem of human alienation, he seems to admit (unlike Marx) that one of the main factors operative in the specifically modern type of alienation is precisely the rejection of God and religious values. If Weber, unlike Marx, cannot offer a sufficiently definite diagnosis of the alienation of modern man, it is not surprising that he cannot commend to us any sufficiently definite way of deliverance.

Marx, unlike Weber, grasps that, in order to purport to take the place of God, it is not plausible merely to deny the divine order of the existing world, it is also 'necessary' to make out the claim that modern man can impose a new system which, in truth, could be only an ideological system. Such a system will purport to remedy current inconveniences by serving as a substitute for that divine order in which men formerly believed but which is supposed not to exist merely because it did not 'succeed' in preventing the incidence of current inconveniences. It is in this context that we need to recall that Marx was not completely satisfied with the work of Feuerbach because (so Marx tells us) Feuerbach did not give an adequate account of the process whereby 'the mundane basis set itself against itself, and fixes for itself an independent realm in the clouds'.[39] Marx understands more completely than Feuerbach the subversive consequences of modern atheism and, not content simply to 'reduce' theology to the human essence, Marx goes on to promulgate his fundamental doctrine which means, in effect, that there is something radically wrong with the human essence.

Of course it is impossible for there to be anything *radically* wrong with the human essence in an ontological sense because, if there were any inherent contradiction in the human essence, human beings could not actually exist. Certainly, in his own way, Marx half accepts this consequence in so far as he does indeed deny that there is any such thing as the human essence. But, in doing so, his characterisation of man as a purely historical being without an essence makes it impossible for him to give an account of man's current existence. Logically, on Marx's premises, man does not yet exist. Moreover, given the obscurity of Marx's characterisation of the final state of humanity, we cannot even say that man would exist at the end any more than he can be conceived as existing now. Nevertheless, in the midst of these paradoxes of the Marxian ideology, it is not unfair for a Thomist to insist that the effect of Marx's thought is to attribute the historical proliferation of religion and philosophy to certain supposed radical contradictions in the essence of man in the historical periods prior to the advent of socialised humanity. Finally, those writers are not mistaken who have envisaged Marxism as a kind of modern atheistic gnosticism which claims to deliver man from an alienation supposed to be ontologically radical by an historical process effected by purely human means. Accordingly, Marx's fundamental rebellion against God, against the order of the universe, and against the nature of man, involves not only the ideological 'envelopment' of Christianity and philosophy but also a *unique* ideological doctrine for the deliverance of man. Marx cannot make his positive atheism plausible without fabricating an ideological caricature of the Christian redemption.

Having characterised the specifically Marxian rejection of Christian theism and the truth of human nature and having identified the specifically Marxian neo-Gnostic substitute for redemption, we must consider further how Weber's own ideology stands in relation to these Marxian positions. We shall begin this part of our discussion by first considering a very general difficulty with which every ideological doctrine is confronted. The difficulty arises from the tension between the content of an ideology and the philosophical scepticism which is the first principle of both the life and the death of ideological thinking. In rejecting both philosophical and theological thinking, every ideologist commits himself to choosing a 'value-position' (with a view to practical action) which cannot be intellectually justified? At the same time, the ideologist is committed to the assumption that any-one else who chooses any 'value-position' whatsoever is *eo ipso* also an ideologist. Yet, although the ideologist (so long as he remains an ideo-logist) can hardly avoid committing himself to these two misguided positions, he cannot remain always and in every way content with them. The reason for this unease is obvious to the non-ideological thinker who realises that the implication of the two assumptions of the ideologists is simply that all human thought is simply the continuous proliferation of intellectual error.

The ideologist himself, *qua* ideologist, cannot avoid adopting an ambiguous attitude towards the assumptions which are at the very basis (such as it is) of all ideological thinking. For, certainly, the radical scepticism (which the ideologist claims is subversive of the philo-sophical quest) would (if it were valid) be certainly subversive of the ideological 'quest'. The conclusion would follow that there is no reason for choosing any ideology and no reason for preferring one ideology rather than another. In other words, on the assumption of radical philo-sophical scepticism, search for a justified ideology is just as futile as the search for a justified philosophy is supposed (by the ideologist) to be. It might happen that an ideologist will be found to choose irrationally one particular ideology and simply to ignore the others. He might have the thought in mind that he has nothing to say about subjective ideo-logical meanings except to enunciate the subjective ideological meanings which he has himself chosen irrationally to impose upon the supposedly meaningless universe. In other words, he might deem that, outside his own ideology, nothing can be said by him. However, such a position cannot be perfected in its kind: neither Marx nor Weber will manifest a total indifference to the problems arising from the presence of other ideologies besides his own. But, Marx and Weber react differently towards the fact of the existence of other ideologies.

In Marx we find a sweeping rejection of all preceding thought which is considered by him to be always ideological in character. Yet, in undertaking this sweeping 'reduction' of all preceding thought, Marx does not — and, given his ideological premises, cannot — employ a true canon of criticism. It is merely that his analysis will tend, in some cases, to undermine the claims of historical religions, philosophies and moralities in so far as Marx seeks to relate them in a special way to the historical development of the economic and material order. Maritain has aptly summed up Marx's position by pointing out that although the 'superstructures' are not regarded by Marx simply as an epiphenomenon of economics, they nevertheless lose their proper autonomy in the Marxist account of the matter. Accordingly, for Marx, the superstructures 'are not only conditioned by the economic and social, but from these they have their primary determination, and it is from them that they get their meaning, their real significance for human life'.[40]

Of course, there are many facts which make the Marxist analysis plausible. Despite the fact that false moralities, false philosophies and false religions do point, in a certain way, to true morality, true philosophy, and true religion, the falsity of what is false will inevitably have its illicit origin in some disorder which may well be found in the material order. As de Lubac observes:

> The fakes and illusions of the mind, its habitually lazy or
> bastard forms, its repeated failures, its standardised products,
> like its sudden unforeseen errors, are all plainly visible, and
> the observer cannot fail to see them. The area they cover is
> vast; they encumber the scene.[41]

From the observation of these disordered products that encumber the scene, it is, nevertheless, not reasonable for Marx to conclude that all preceding thought is ideological in character. Yet, given Marx's conclusion, it only remained for Lenin to draw the corollary that Marxist doctrine is itself ideological. Henri Chambre suggests that when Lenin uses the expression 'revolutionary ideology', he gives the lie to Marx's criticism of pre-Marxist thought as ideological mystification.[42] Without disagreeing with Chambre's analysis of one of the two horns of Lenin's dilemma, it is necessary to refer to the other. For, if Lenin is to *retain* the Marxian critique of preceding thought as ideological, he can only do this plausibly by admitting that Marxist-Leninist revolutionary thought is also ideological. Yet, at the same time, this admission is itself self-defeating.

Marxist-Leninism is therefore, in a sense, a closed world: a world in which its own doctrine and all other doctrines are implicitly or explicitly deemed to be ideological. However, Marxist-Leninism is not simply a scepticism: for, if all ideologies are all, equally, ideologies there is one unique ideology (Marxist-Leninism) which is deemed to be on the side of history. It follows that the Marxist-Leninist will tend to be unhappy about the intellectual foundations of ideological thinking because these foundations simply point to scepticism. In other words, Marxist-Leninist ideology can neither simply reject nor simply accept the intellectual foundations of all ideologies including the Marxist-Leninist variety. Perhaps this partly accounts for the fact — noted by Gilson[43] — that Lenin attacks Hume and his progeny more than forty times in *Materialism and Empirio-Criticism*. Hume must be attacked by Lenin because Marxist-Leninism must resist scepticism; Marxist-Leninism nevertheless presupposes Hume as one of the founding fathers of all ideological thinking.

Although we shall finally conclude that Weber has invented a closed ideological world, this ideological invention of Weber's can be seen to be specifically different from that of Marx. In order to investigate this difference further, we shall ask whether Max Weber seeks to 'envelop' Christianity and pre-Weberian philosophy by some strategy analogous to that of Marx. Of course, we have already seen that, in Weber, the denial of the existence of God and the related denial of intrinsic principles of order in man and in the universe lead to a supposed necessity to go beyond rationality in such a way that practical activity becomes inevitably irrational in one way or another. Yet, despite the ideological stance which Weber, in his own way, holds in common with Marx, the Weberian atheism differs markedly from that of Marx. Although Weber shares the position which Marx in effect holds — namely, that the human essence is alienated in the sense that it is subject to absolutely radical internal contradictions — Weber does not see how there can be any radical or adequate solution to this predicament.

Accordingly, since Weber seems to regard man's self-alienation as something ineradicable from which man cannot really expect to emancipate himself, he does not envisage the same kind of revolt against the so-called alienation of man which is crucial in Marx's revolutionary ideology. Consequently, Weber does not crudely express in Marxist terms the Promethean hatred of all the gods. Indeed, in spite of Weber's 'preference' (among religions which are all supposedly erroneous) for polytheism, he does not express hatred specifically against the one true God.

Do these differences between Weber and so many other positive atheists such as Marx indicate that Weber's thought includes no revolt of any kind against God and the divine order? Is it possible to regard Weber's thought as merely a kind of departure into an illusory private 'world'? (Certainly, Weber thinks that, in the end, every ideology is a kind of private 'world' neither constituted by nor containing objective public truth.) Unfortunately, it does not seem possible to sustain this convenient distinction which might be supposed — if it were valid — to enable us to treat Weber's ideology as a private fantasy.

We can approach the same point from a somewhat different angle by considering an observation by Raymond Aron about the element of Nietzschean nihilism in Weber's thought. Aron says that this element was not so much the object of resolute choice as it was the partially involuntary consequence of Weber's fundamental position that value-judgements do not belong to scientific knowledge.[44] Yet, this is not a justification of Weber's reluctant but voluntary choice of nihilism; it can be accepted only as a plea in mitigation from an advocate acting in Weber's defence.

Perhaps Weber would choose to defend himself by reference to his own remark that he was 'religiously unmusical'. In order to avoid nihilism, Weber might argue, faith is required but faith is a divine gift which has not been given to Weber. Certainly, Weber would be right in saying that faith is a divine gift but, unlike a good ear for music, it is a gift which is offered, in one way or another, to everyone who reaches the age of reason.[45] Moreover, even without faith, there can be no good reason for choosing nihilism; right reason itself is fundamentally opposed to nihilism.

We know that Weber has been praised for his 'stoicism' in 'persevering' with certain enterprises against the background of his nihilism. Yet the mark of the virtue of perseverance is not found in 'perseverance' — even 'reluctant perseverance' — in nihilism but rather in the persevering search for fundamental truth. Accordingly, Weber's 'stoical' persistence in nihilism involves a negligence which disregards — and a misintelligence which rejects — the fundamental order of the universe. Given that God exists, there is implicit in Weber's 'stoical' nihilism, an aspersion contrary to the divine honour. However much one might want to extenuate this (by saying that perhaps he did not fully realise what he was doing), Weber's reluctant but persistent nihilism involves denying the God against Whose honour he would otherwise find himself maintaining a defamatory stance. Weber's habitual nihilism leads him to adopt the assumption that each person — each in his own private way — is choosing his heterogeneous values in a world which owes neither being nor order to God. Therefore, despite a certain relative 'modesty', Weber cannot ultimately deny that he is doing what Marx, Comte and Nietzsche each did in his own way: he purports to remove from every religion, philosophy and morality — whether true or false — the very possibility that it might contain an objective public truth. This means that there is built into Weber's ideology an omniverous appetite to swallow every other 'value-system' whether it be truly religious, truly philosophical or partially or substantively ideological.

If Weber is reluctantly disposed to envelop or to swallow up the 'value-systems' of mankind, we must go on to ask whether he is able to retain, digest and assimilate them within his ideological system. We shall evaluate in the next chapter Weber's attempt to envisage and to undertake the ideological re-enchantment of the disenchanted world which modern atheistic nihilism has invented. We shall consider further the method of transvaluation which leads Weber to envisage the fabrication of explicitly ideological equivalents of the various religious, philosophical and moral traditions of mankind. In some cases, the distortion involved in this transvaluation will be limited since many of the traditions subjected to this process will be already in reality ideological even when they do not admit it. Certainly, such more or less ideological traditions lend a certain plausibility to Weber's assumption that his ideological system can swallow up previous doctrines and assimilate them into the Weberian realm of ideological values. Nevertheless, as we discuss elsewhere, Weber's system cannot assimilate natural law morality or true divine revelation.

Like the Marxist-Leninist, Weber envisages a closed world — or a closed 'realm of values' — in so far as Weber's own 'value-position' and all other possible 'value-positions' are deemed to be really ideological. Certainly, Weber did not say what was in his mind in these terms because he did not define the word 'ideology' in the sense in which it is used in this book. Nevertheless, given the definition of ideology which we are using, this is the import of Weber's thought. Moreover, Weber shares with the Marxist-Leninist a certain unhappiness about the closed world which he has constructed. Unlike the Marxist-Leninist, Weber is in a position to alleviate his unease to some extent by means of a rationalisation which might serve to convince himself and others that his ideological world is not really closed. Certainly, Weber does not seek to secure effectively the aggregate of his own particular personal value-judgements against sceptical reduction by giving them some uniquely privileged status among the other possible value-positions. However, Weber does wish to attribute a certain significance to the human debate or human conflict about values: he wishes to say that this debate of conflict is really important and, at the same time, that it is merely ideological. Of course, it is in truth impossible for Weber to have it both ways at once. In truth, it is only possible to claim that debate about values is really important if philosophical scepticism is false. In so far as Weber is committed to philosophical scepticism, he cannot logically avoid the conclusion that all debate about values is purely ideological.

Of course, it may be argued that Weber's ideology is, in a sense, more 'liberal' and less 'dogmatic' than the position of the Marxist-Leninist. Yet, Weber's ideology manifests the fatal flaw which always leads to the decline of a secular liberal ideology. For, if Weber is, in a sense, not 'dogmatic' — since he does not attribute to the aggregate of his particular value-judgements the kind of uniquely privileged status which the Marxist-Leninist attributes to his — he is nevertheless caught upon the horns of the 'liberal dilemma' when he seeks to defend the significance of human debate or human conflict about values. For Weber, who does not insist that we are bound to agree with his every value-judgement, does wish to extract from us the admission that judgements about values are always subjective ideological judgements which are not, objectively, either true or false. Thus Weber seems to insist, by implication, that the importance of the debate about values consists in the supposed importance of a debate that is ideological in character. The corollary of Weber's dogmatic insistence that the significance of the debate about values is its ideological significance is simply this: that any philosophical debate, to the extent that it denies that it is ideological, is deemed to be not tenable. Indeed, this corollary was implicit in Weber's first resort to ideology.

It follows that Weber's vision of a closed realm of heterogeneous ideological values — a vision which we have already designated as his 'ideology of the ideologies' — is closed to a philosophy *qua* philosophy in a specific sense in which it is not closed to the ideologies. To the extent that the philosopher's thought intends to free itself — and eventually succeeds in freeing itself — from contamination with ideology, it will not only be incompatible with Weber's particular personal value-judgements, it will also find itself outside the whole Weberian realm of incompatible values. In other words, although Weber intends his doctrine of the realm of values to be open to every type of position, that doctrine is inherently incapable of properly admitting the truth about values. In a sense, it is true that Weber does not claim that we must embrace his own ideological value-judgements. Nevertheless, he certainly holds that we cannot logically avoid choosing some ideological value-position from the whole realm of *ideological* values *as he conceives this realm*. If Weber permits us to reject his own particular ideology, he implicitly requires us to accept his 'ideology of the ideologies'. Of course, such a position is untenable because Weber's 'ideology of the ideologies' is itself an important element in the sum total of Weber's personal ideological commitments. Dorothy Emmet makes a pertinent remark relevant to our discussion when she says that 'a completely neutral and morally aseptic meta-ethics is not practicable'.[46] Accordingly, the distinction which can be drawn between Weber's particular value-judgements and his general value-judgement about the scope and status of the whole realm of 'logically possible values' is not a fundamental one. Although Weber's ideological meta-value-judgement can be distinguished from his ideological 'particular value-judgement', these value-judgements are both fundamentally alike in being ill-founded since they are alike the products not of philosophical reasoning but of ideology.

Given that the ideological character of Weber's quasi-liberal moral epistemology is generally alien to true moral philosophy, we may go on to enquire whether this moral epistemology is also generally alien to the revolutionary ideologies of positive atheism. Certainly, Weber does not seem to intend to exclude the value-choices of the revolutionary ideologies from the range of 'logically-possible' ideological value-choices. *In a sense*, he must concede that any ideological value-choice is 'possible' — in the last resort — because, even if it seems to be related to irrational or unscientific assumptions, it is, in one sense, in no worse case than any other ideological value-choice, since all ideological value-choices admittedly begin with an irrational choice. Nevertheless, from another point of view, Weber is not in a position to accept the validity of the sociological presuppositions of a revolutionary ideology such as Marxism since he holds that these presuppositions are, in important respects, unscientific and erroneous. Voegelin sets out the problem which these two viewpoints present in Weber's thought, in the following terms:

> if critical objectivity made it impossible for a scholar to be a Marxist, could then any man be a Marxist without surrendering the standard of a critical objectivity that he would be obliged to observe as a responsible human being? There are no answers to such questions in Weber's work.[47]

All these considerations will lead us to examine, in the next chapter, the ultimate significance of the relationship of Weber's ideology of the ideologies to the revolutionary ideologies of positive atheism. For the moment, it may suffice to observe that — given the complexities of Weber's own position — he cannot *insist* upon the exclusion of those ideologies which reject the Weberian characterisation of the realm of mutually contradictory possible values from that realm. Nevertheless, although Weber does not positively exclude these ideologies, he is so driven by the exigencies of his own ideological doctrine of the realm of possible values that the inclusion (say) of Marxism in that realm can only be effected by 'relativising' the exclusive dogmatic stance which the Marxist ideology characteristically claims for itself. Accordingly, in so far as Weber's doctrine of the entire realm of values is in truth fundamentally incompatible with Marxism, this incompatibility will not be insisted upon by Weber. The incompatibility will be insisted upon by those who uphold philosophical truth and, in another way, by the Marxists themselves who will reject Weber's quasi-liberal moral epistemology not on the basis of fundamental truth but on the basis of an ideology which claims to be superseding the liberal ideologies including the ideology of Weber. Weber himself is ambivalent about the relation of his own ideology to the revolutionary ideologies of positive atheism because he is entangled in the paradoxes inherent in ideological liberalism.

Notes and references

1   See Friedrich's contribution to *Max Weber and Sociology Today*, O. Stammer (ed.), Oxford, 1971.
2   See H.P. Bahrdt's contribution to *Max Weber and Sociology Today*.
3   L. Strauss, *What is Political Philosophy?*, New York, 1959, pp.47–9.
4   See discussion of this in R.S. Devane, *The Failure of Individualism*, Dublin, 1948, pp.113–20.
5   L. Strauss, 'The Three Waves of Modernity' in *Political Philosophy: Six Essays by Leo Strauss*, H. Gildin (ed.), Indianapolis, 1975, pp.81–98.
6   The absolutism in Locke's teaching on toleration manifests itself in the unjustified exclusion of Catholics from citizenship.
7   See E.J. Roesch, *The Totalitarian Threat: The Fruition of Modern Individualism as seen in Hobbes and Rousseau*, New York, 1963.
8   S. Deploige, *The Conflict between Ethics and Sociology*, St Louis, Mo., 1938, p.206.
9   E. Durkheim, *Montesquieu and Rousseau: Forerunners of Sociology*, Ann Arbor, Michigan, 1960, pp.135–8.
10   See discussion of this teaching in Deploige, *Conflict between Ethics and Sociology*, p.2ff.
11   H. de Lubac, *Athéisme et Sens de l'Homme*, Paris, 1968, p.63.
12   R. Aron, *German Sociology*, New York, 1964, p.83.
13   See criticism of individualism in J. Maritain, *The Person and the Common Good*, London, 1948.
14   See criticism of Comte's 'sociologism' in E. Gilson, *The Unity of Philosophical Experience*, New York, 1950, ch.10.
15   On human nature in the person, see O. Lottin, *Morale Fondamentale*, Tournai, 1954, p.127.
16   Roth so describes traditional as opposed to Weberian liberalism in R. Bendix and G. Roth, *Scholarship and Partisanship*, London, 1971.
17   J.H. Hallowell, *The Decline of Liberalism as an Ideology with Particular Reference to German Politico-Legal Thought*, London,

1946, pp.9–10, 77, 108–10.

18   L. Strauss, 'The Three Waves of Modernity', p.98. See also E.B.F. Midgley, 'Concerning the Modernist Subversion of Political Philosophy', *New Scholasticism*, Spring 1979, pp.168–90.

19   See Hallowell, *Decline of Liberalism*, ch.5, 'Beyond Good and Evil'.

20   See Weber's review of a work by Stammler, translated by M. Albrow, 'R. Stammler's "Surmounting" of the Materialist Conception of History (Max Weber)', *British Journal of Law and Society*, vol.2, 1975, pp.129–52 and vol.3, 1976, pp.17–43.

21   W.J. Mommsen, 'Max Weber's Political Sociology and his Philosophy of World History', *International Social Science Journal*, vol.17, 1965, p.41.

22   K. Jaspers, *Leonardo, Descartes, Max Weber: Three Essays*, London, 1965, p.220.

23   J.P. Mayer, *Max Weber and German Politics*, 2nd rev. edn, London, 1956, p.28.

24   G. Roth in Bendix and Roth, *Scholarship*, p.67.

25   Ibid., p.57.

26   E. Voegelin's Forward to his *Science, Politics and Gnosticism*, Chicago, 1968, p.vi.

27   Various aspects and types of ideology are discussed in Midgley: 'On "Substitute Intelligences" in the Formation of Atheistic Ideology', *Laval théologique et philosophique*, October 1980, pp.239–53.

28   G. Roth in Bendix and Roth, *Scholarship*, p.57.

29   Jaspers, *Three Essays*, p.267.

30   Hallowell, *Decline of Liberalism*, Preface, p.ix, see also a similar diagnosis in T.P. Neill, *The Rise and Decline of Liberalism*, Milwaukee, 1953.

31   See my article 'Natural Law and Fundamental Rights', *American Journal of Jurisprudence*, vol.21, 1976, pp.144–55.

32   H. de Lubac, *Athéisme et Sens de l'Homme*, Paris, 1968, p.23.

33   K. Marx, Note on the existence of God associated with his doctoral dissertation.

34   See E.B.F. Midgley, 'Authority, Alienation and Revolt' in *Aberdeen University Review*, Autumn 1976, pp.372–83.

35   See C.N.R. McCoy, *The Structure of Political Thought*, New York, 1963, pp.269–90.

36   See discussion in H. de Lubac, *The Drama of Atheist Humanism*, London, 1950, pp.18–27.

37   K. Marx, *Economic and Philosophical Manuscripts of 1844*.

38   E. Voegelin, *Science, Politics and Gnosticism*, Chicago, 1968, pp.23–8; see also his 'The Formation of the Marxian Revolutionary Idea' in *Review of Politics*, 1950, pp.275–302.

39   K. Marx, *Theses on Feuerbach*.

40   J. Maritain, *Humanisme Intégral*, Paris, 1968, p.54.

41   H. de Lubac, *The Discovery of God*, London, 1960, p.28.

42   H. Chambre, *Christianity and Communism*, London, 1960, p.109.

43   E. Gilson, *The Unity of Philosophical Experience*, New York, 1950, p.290.

44   R. Aron's Introduction to Max Weber, *Le Savant et le Politique*, Paris, 1959, p.43.

45   See R. Lombardi, *The Salvation of the Unbeliever*, London, 1956.

46   D. Emmet, *Rules, Roles and Relations*, London, 1966, p.84.

47   E. Voegelin, *The New Science of Politics*, pp.18–19.

8 Weber and the ideological re-enchantment of the world

Weber's rationalistic 'disenchantment' of the world

When Weber seeks to explain the character of modern man in the modern world, he attempts to do this by making comparisons between modernity and pre-modernity. Yet such comparisons can lead to definitive conclusions only if they are conducted on the basis of a substantive general doctrine which can give us a true understanding of the relations between modernity and pre-modernity. Commentators on Weber are generally agreed that no such substantive general doctrine — either a philosophy of man or a philosophy of history — is extant in Weber's writings.

If someone who despairs of philosophy nevertheless undertakes an intellectual enterprise which, in truth, requires a philosophy of man or of history for its solution, that person will inevitably presuppose some ideological substitute for the philosophy of whose very possibility he despairs. We shall endeavour in this chapter to complete our analysis of Weber's ideological substitute for philosophy. The first characteristic of Weber's perspectives upon modernity will certainly be their radical ambivalency. Weber will give a partial explanation of modernity in terms of pre-modernity and he will give a partial explanation of pre-modernity in terms of modernity. These two partial explanations — which certainly stray beyond the bounds of a supposedly value-free sociology — will, in effect, contradict each other. The problem of Weber's ideology can be expounded in terms of his reactions in the face of this contradiction.

When Weber surveys the modern world in the light of pre-modernity, he concludes that the fate of men's historical claims to hold any objective philosophy or morality is linked inescapably with the fate of men's historical claims to possess religious truth. In other words, he holds that the fate of objective values depends upon the fate of the gods. If a claim that God or gods exist could be well-founded, there could then be a foundation for human values. If all claims concerning the one God or the many gods are spurious, then there is no foundation for human values. In this perspective, Weber is in a position to derive certain consequences from his analysis of the process of 'rationalisation' which (he tells us) has resulted in the 'disenchantment' or 'de-divinisation' of the world in modern times. This modern denial of all religious truth leads not only to the conclusion that neither the one God nor any of the gods exist but also to the logical conclusion that there are no true or valid human values. In this perspective, whether or not there are such things as objective human values, rationalistic modern atheism cannot know them.

When Weber surveys pre-modernity in the light of modernity, he accepts the inevitability of the supposed process of 'rationalisation' which leads to an atheism which entails nihilism. One might suppose that, in so far as Weber concludes to nihilism, there can be no foundation left in his teaching for the upholding of values. In fact, however, Weber — like Nietzsche — proceeds to carry on 'choosing' or 'imposing' human 'values' as if this could fill the void. He decides to choose subjective 'values' as if they could be valid and to choose which substitute 'gods' to serve even though he had denied both the objective validity of every value and the real existence of every god.

It is not easy to formulate the self-contradictory ideology which Weber fabricates out of the two incompatible perspectives which have been outlined here. D. Henrich endeavours to characterise it as follows:

> The process of rationalisation ... has, according to Weber, reached a stage in modern times where the old possibilities of explanation fail. Science itself cannot create such possibilities. And thus mankind experiences the conflict of gods, who have all lost their power over the world ....'.[1]

We must notice, however, that this last sentence of Henrich's (which is, in a certain way, faithful to Weber's own characteristic style of discussion) is systematically misleading. In a sense, we need not complain about this because the sentence is systematically misleading in precisely the manner in which Weber's own formulations are systematically misleading. Nevertheless, if we are to expose the crucial point at issue, we must penetrate Weber's formulations and analyse them in language which is free from ambiguity.

Weber's commitment to the process of 'rationalisation' (as he understands this) does not permit him to suppose that the gods (or the one God) once possessed real power and that they (or He) lost their (or His) power when the process of 'rationalisation' reached a certain point in the modern period. Weber recognises that a human belief that the gods or God possessed real power had had certain observable effects in the past. He does not recognise that any gods or God had ever possessed real power themselves. Indeed, Weber's commitment does not recognise that any gods or God had ever existed. Consequently, the process which Weber calls 'disenchantment' or 'de-divinisation' cannot be seen in terms of his commitment to rationalisation as involving any objective change either in the reality or in the power of the gods (or God). Weber is merely describing, in a rather poetical way, a process which, according to him, takes place merely in the consciousnesses of men. We shall come to surmise that Weber's poetical way of writing about the disenchantment or de-divinisation of the world plays a certain role both in half-disguising the avoidance of crucial questions about his resort to ideology and in manifesting his sense of the tragic novelty of the ideological thinking of modernity. Weber's sense of being subject to a tragic fate is summed up by Strauss who attributes to Weber the view that 'We are irreligious because fate forces us to be irreligious and for no other reason'.[2] Consequently, Strauss is right in suggesting that Weber 'despaired of the modern this-worldly irreligious experiment, and yet he remained attached to it because he was [that is, imagined he was] fated to believe in science as he understood it'.[3]

Certainly, the Weber who employed the unfortunate formula, credo ... quia absurdum ..., against the believers[4] would not have been able to give any good reason for denying the application to himself of the inverted form of the maxim, namely, 'I do not believe although that is absurd'.[5] Indeed, Weber sometimes seems prepared to concede implicitly that pseudo-religious atheistic ideology is more evidently absurd than the 'pre-modern' religious beliefs. Mommsen has rightly drawn attention to the fact that Weber is willing to condemn as pseudo-religious in character the (atheistic) 'historico-philosophical constructions' of Comte and Bentham.[6] Yet Weber does not seem fully to grasp all the implications of the fact that he himself, in his own way, is equally implicated in the atheistic enterprise of propagating groundless ideological substitutes for religious, philosophical and moral values.

Weber's ideological re-enchantment of the World

Weber knows, as everybody else does, that as a matter of historical fact, Christianity has dealt a death-blow to the pagan polytheism which prevailed in antiquity.[7] Certainly, Weber does not suppose that modern man (who is fated, according to Weber, to abandon even Christianity) is really able to make a plausible return to religious polytheism. Yet, when Weber comes to undertake the ideological 're-enchantment' of the world, he seeks to 'save' what he holds to be still significant and ultimate in polytheism, namely, the heterogeneous multiplicity of values which corresponds, in Weber's ideology, with the heterogeneous multiplicity of the pagan gods. Accordingly, Weber swallows up polytheism by participating in it whilst withdrawing from it the element of religious belief. For belief in gods, we must henceforth read 'commitment to values' concerning which the very question of the truth or falsity of the commitments is simply excluded.

It is evident that this Weberian transvaluation of polytheism is, in a sense, an aggravation of the evils of polytheism. When primitive peoples, in their ignorance, believed or half-believed in their false gods, or in magic, their ignorance might not exonerate but it might partially mitigate their culpability. Yet, when Weber and his followers choose their arbitrary ideological 'values', they choose them knowing well that they are devoid of objective validity. When the Weberian indulges in the ideological re-enchantment of the world — whilst knowing that his 'gods' and his 'magic' are false — he will seek to defend his action by appeal to the supposed 'necessity' of subjective value-choice. We shall see in a later section of this chapter how Weber and his followers will claim, in effect, that modern man has to be prepared to play his role in the ideological drama whether he likes it or not.

Thus it is in terms of a teaching devoid of objective justification that Weber advances ideological themes which are derived from the transvaluation of Manicheanism, Gnosticism and Protestantism. Weber 'saves' the Manichean heterogeneity whilst abandoning the Manichean belief. He agrees with the Gnostics that the world is structurally incoherent and he does not disagree with their view that some sort of 'liberation' is apparently required but he does not believe in the Gnostic or any other 'liberation'. Denying natural theology and the motives of credibility of divine revelation, Weber transvalues fideistic Protestantism as a value-choice whilst not accepting the content of the 'faith' of Protestant fideism. Even with regard to the 'private judgement' or 'private conscience' of liberal Protestantism and traditional secular liberalism, we cannot say that Weber has assimilated these concepts without reducing them further.

Because Weber knows that his resort to ideology is an irrational choice, he lacks, as we have observed, the kinds of partial extenuation available to those who maintained pre-modernist traditional errors. However, there will be an attempt, in modern times, to advance reasons why a rational value-judgement is supposedly not possible. Whilst Hume is wrong to think that there is no objective intellectual basis for metaphysics and natural law morality, he is right to think that metaphysics and natural law morality cannot be logically defended on the basis of modernist philosophies of rationalism and empiricism. This latter consideration constitutes a pretext, though not an authentic justification, for a supposedly 'necessary' resort to the ideological use of reason as the slave of inordinate passions. The dilemma for the post-Humean ideologist is that philosophical reasoning which purports to indicate that objective metaphysics and natural law are not available also indicates that the resort to ideology will be philosophically indefensible. As W.O. Martin expresses it 'Chaos can only be known in relation to order. Hence ... there can be no ideological foundation of ideology. Herein lies the element of tragedy, for the ideologist can be what he is only so long as he is aware of the non-ideological truth against which, by his own admission, he must fight'.[8]

The ideologist is therefore in a dilemma. In so far as he cannot truly deny that his ideology is founded upon an irrational choice, he stands self-condemned. Yet, if he does deny this, he only deceives himself and others. Martin suggests that 'Of necessity he [the ideologist] must prefer deception to condemnation. By the same necessity, he must try to make this deception universal'. Martin's conclusion is largely justified. Certainly, the Marxist and Nazi ideologists and other modern ideologists of 'progressive' atheistic humanism have proceeded in this way. Martin rightly argues that, when men are indifferent to the truth or falsity of their ideas and are concerned only with their instrumental value for the organisation of 'energies' and the satisfaction of arbitrarily postulated 'needs', they will find these ideas eternally in conflict: thus they will postulate 'perpetual [ideological] war under the guise of progressive humanism'.

It is necessary to ask, however, whether Martin's analysis, which is widely applicable to modern ideologies, is wholly applicable to the ideology of Max Weber. In order to deal with this question, we must first consider a preliminary question, namely: Is Weber a 'progressive' atheistic humanist? To this question, it does not seem possible to give either an affirmative reply or a negative reply without making important reservations. Certainly, Weber *assumes* that the development of science — and the development of scientific sociology as he understands this — is a progress. Yet, even in relation to science itself (as Weber understands it) Weber will suggest that the 'progress' involved is problematical in so far as it seems to have no end. He therefore indicates that it is not self-evident that something subject to a 'progress' of the kind which he finds in sociology is sensible and meaningful in itself. He asks: Why does one engage in something that in reality never comes, and never can come, to an end?[9]

It is perfectly understandable that Weber should regard his commitment to the 'progress of science' as really dubious because the 'science' which he has in mind is really a pastiche of rational thought, scientism and ideology. Nevertheless, despite his hesitancy in committing himself to the 'progress of science', that commitment seems to lead Weber into acquiescence in what he takes to be the implications of this development. If science is supposed to lead to the disenchantment of the world, then Weber's commitment to science will lead him to some kind of commitment to the disenchantment of the world as if that were a progress.[10] However, Weber is less satisfied that the disenchantment of the world is a genuine progress than he is that Weberian sociology represents a progress. Indeed, as we have seen, he seems to envisage his commitment, and the whole 'disenchantment' of the world which he associates with it, as merely the historical 'fate' of his own time: 'the inescapable datum of our historical situation'.

We have seen in earlier chapters that the Weber who complains that he is religiously unmusical combines in himself a rejection of the objective obligation to accept any belief which was promulgated in premodern times with a nostalgia for those beliefs which he thinks himself fated to reject. Accordingly, unlike the militant atheistic ideologist, Weber is not wholeheartedly committed to the task of ignoring (and encouraging his followers to ignore) the irrational beginning and the irrational status of his own ideology. Unlike the average ideologist (as characterised by Martin) Weber does not seem consistently to prefer self-deception to self-condemnation. We shall find that Weber will sometimes succeed in deceiving himself but that he will sometimes prefer to involve himself in, at least, an implicit self-condemnation in order to avoid the somewhat crude form of self-deception of the average ideologist. However, since any man committed to an ideology would presumably fall into apathy or despair if his every ideological thought were to be accompanied by an explicit self-condemnation, Weber cannot and does not sustain constantly the stark contemplation of the irrationality of his ideological starting point and of his ideology as such.

Weber *vis-à-vis* the other prophets of the re-enchantment

Weber sometimes seems to suggest that value-judgements ought not to be propagated in academic work or, at least, if they are so propagated, they should be made perfectly explicit. Since we have seen that Weber's academic writings are full of implicit presuppositions (not made explicit) which — in Weber's own nomenclature — can only be called value-judgements, one wonders to what extent Weber is deceiving himself and to what extent he is simply deceiving his readers. Certainly, Weber himself is one of the pseudo-prophets of the 're-enchantment' of the world. He is not in a position to denounce the others as false prophets. Indeed, there is no basis in his teaching from which he could plausibly advance a radical critique of the various modern ideologies which he does not happen to share. Nevertheless, we find that, in spite of these facts, Weber will sometimes utter reproaches against 'private prophets', 'academic prophets' and 'pseudo-religious' secular ideologists.

Gouldner has given reasons for his view that Weber's attitudes and statements in relation to 'private or academic prophecy' can be explained largely as a complex endeavour directed to the realisation of a curious kind of *modus vivendi* in contemporary German university circles.[11] Certainly, given Weber's erroneous assumption that he is not a private or academic prophet, his statements on the subject taken together seem to promote very conveniently — by accident or design — the ideology of Max Weber himself over against the positions of his intellectual opponents. At least, we have reason to suspect that, in some cases, Weber's abstract argumentation against 'private or academic prophecy' functioned as a camouflaged attack upon those who held specific ideologies or teachings which Weber himself deemed to be objectionable. It would be interesting to know to what extent the main thrust of Weber's opposition to Treitschke was really directed against Treitschke's thoroughgoing commitment to Bismarck's policies, despite the fact that Weber formulated his criticism of Treitschke as an abstract argument against the indoctrination of students with professorial value-judgements.

Furthermore, we must observe that the ideological thrust of Weber's statements on 'private and academic prophecy' tends to apply pressure not only to those who wholeheartedly supported Bismarck's policies but also to those who wholeheartedly rejected the inordinate German nationalisms of Bismarck and Max Weber himself. To see that this is so, we need simply to bring together two positions of Weber: first, his position that professors are not entitled to freedom from State control in the matter of the expression of values and, secondly, his statement that, if value-judgements are to be proclaimed by academics, they should be made absolutely explicit. Since Weber denies the existence of any objective political morality, it is the logical consequence of his first position that the Bismarckian State (whatever personal reservations Weber might have had about it) is being given the 'right' at least to suppress, if 'necessary', any teaching which (unlike Weber's teaching) is opposed to all forms of inordinate German nationalism. Weber's second position (that academic value-judgements should be made absolutely explicit) would naturally ensure that a German academic opposed to all inordinate German nationalisms would be clearly vulnerable to persecution by the Bismarckian tyranny. Consequently, the application of these two principles of Weber would bring no security to any potential academic victim of Bismarck's *Kulturkampf* who was radically opposed to it and to the inordinate nationalisms which had engendered it. It seems reasonable to conclude that Weber's nostalgic preference for the 'old churches' over against the 'private or academic prophecy' could afford no effectual basis for the true defence of the fundamental rights and dignity of the human person.

Further evidence of the intellectually indefensible character of some of Weber's appeals against 'private or academic prophecy' is provided in the analyses of T.S. Simey.[12] Simey's studies seem to imply that Weber's invocation of the principle of value-free analysis in the course of his quarrels with other members of the *Association for Social Policy* was sometimes purely tactical and, on occasion, even hypocritical. Accordingly, when Weber condemns those who manifest 'spurious "ethically neutral" tendentiousness', it would appear that he is denouncing in others a kind of fault which he himself has also committed.

Nevertheless, despite all the evidence which indicates that Weber's objections to 'private or academic prophecy' are generally self-contradictory and commonly opportunistic, the problem remains: Is there some general characteristic of the other pseudo-prophets of the re-enchantment to which Weber has taken exception? Certainly, Weber looks for 'charismatic' leadership and considers, with some perhaps slender hope, the possibility that 'entirely new prophets' may arise in the modern world. Weber's ambiguous attitude to new ideological 'prophecies' seems to spring from the fact that, although he is not opposed to ideological 'prophecy' as such, he is apparently opposed to any recourse to ideology which seems to him to be fanciful, crude, frivolous or unnecessary. Indeed, Weber sometimes gives us the impression that he does not want anyone to indulge in ideology without necessity because (he seems to suppose) the resort to ideological values is a necessary evil. When Weber encounters complacent, naive, crude, fanciful or frivolous ideologists who undertake 'private and academic prophecies' which conflict with his own, he holds, in a sense, that such 'prophecies' are 'logically possible' but he seems to ask: Are they really necessary?

Weber on ideological necessity

When Weber envisages the supposed necessity of the resort to ideological value-judgements, he does not concern himself with the truth. He is not adverting to that necessity to accept the truth to which the canonists referred when they designated the act of true divine faith as the 'one necessary vow'. We have seen, in chapter 4, how Weber's notions of necessary ideological commitments (presupposing necessary intellectual sacrifice) could be derived by the intellectual transform- ation of certain Protestant concepts. Karl Jaspers has assured us that Weber stood his ground 'against the faithlessness of nihilism ...'.[13] Certainly, this statement is not satisfactory as it stands. Weber is not in a position to refute nihilism since his own system presupposes it. Against the background of nihilism, Weber does not have recourse to faith but to ideological value-choice which is incompatible with faith. Hence Weber's system — comprising a pastiche of science, scientism and ideology — purports to enable modern man (despite his nihilism) to pursue a 'vocation' by the imposition of ideological value- judgements under the spur of the 'necessity' of modernity.

It will be asked whether this 'vocation' which Weber envisages for modern man is, in truth, misguided. One might recall some forthright observations of Charles Péguy on the evils of modernity. Péguy records that the modern world debases and that this debasement is its special- ity. Péguy goes on to say that he would almost call it the *métier* of the modern world to debase if the beautiful word *'métier'* were not above all to be respected.[14] We cannot state with certainty how Weber would have reacted to such a criticism but it is possible that he would have accepted a Scottish verdict of non-proven. One element of Weber's thought might have inclined him to respond to the debasement of modernity as Machiavelli responded to the crimes of princes: such things are admittedly base but they are also necessary. Another element of Weber's thought might have inclined him to react (as Nietzsche might have reacted) by arguing that the vocation to go beyond good and evil — sustained by a heightening of consciousness whereby the 'necessity' of the resort to ideology would be [suppos- edly] transmuted in the absolute autonomy of the Nietzschean super- man — is beyond the debasement of vulgar Machiavellianism. In actuality, Weber could not coherently react in either of these two ways because he was always divided in mind and could have accurately expressed his standpoint only in terms of his own paradoxes.

Admittedly, some of Weber's opinions about private morality could be said to overlap to some extent with natural and Christian morality. Moreover, not everything that Weber said about specific questions of political morality was entirely false. In concrete cases, Weber was no doubt occasionally right. Unfortunately, even when there existed an objective justification for his opinion in a concrete case, Weber did not rest upon that justification but sought to 'justify' every opinion as a subjective value-choice. Accordingly, whether — on this point or that point — his opinion happens to be objectively right or wrong, Weber is permanently threatened by the anguish of that nihilism which underlies his ideological value-choice.

What then can assuage Weber's ideological anguish or blur the brutal clarity with which he sometimes sees the irrationality of his commitment to ideology? Surely, his only defence against all this, and his only plea in mitigation, is the plea of an alleged habitual and general necessity to have recourse to ideology in order to formulate, attempt and accomplish any practical policy whatsoever. Once this 'necessity' has been pleaded, Weber will elicit a certain kind of tragic fortitude in the face of his existential distress. G. Roth, observing Weber's acceptance of ideological conflict and of the discrepancies between 'any Is and any Ought', points out that Weber 'advocated moral stamina in the face of these "iron" facts'.[15] Nevertheless, the Weberian 'tragic fortitude' is not the true virtue of fortitude; Weber's 'moral stamina' — in this connection — is not true patience; for, these alleged virtues find no vindication in authentic moral philosophy.

To understand Weber's ideological 'necessity' in its context, it is relevant to refer to his sociological exposition of certain necessities which supposedly pertain to the life of modern man. When he observes that the spirit of a certain kind of Protestantism (supposedly favourable to the development of capitalism) no longer really animates the modern economic order, Weber suggests that: 'The puritan wanted to have a calling: we have to have one'.[16] No doubt this necessity is conceived by Weber in terms of the increased pressures exerted by some of the structures which govern the economic life of a modern industrial society. Nevertheless, there is a more fundamental sense in which Weber regards modern man's 'vocation' to ideology as a matter of hard necessity.

Weber's modernist notion of the necessity of ideological value-choice is apparently connected with a view of the greater self-consciousness of secularised modern man. We have seen that Weber supposes that the achievements of science have chained modern man to the idea of progress. The disquieting reflection of this progress in the sphere of value-choice involves the total absence of gods — and the objective invalidity of modern secular value-replacements for the gods — and this makes human action, on an objective basis, impossible. Hence there is no real meaning in the 'progress' to which Weber finds himself chained.[17] He accepts the consequent resort to the false magic of arbitrary ideological values reluctantly as if he were under some kind of intellectual duress. Certainly, this duress derives not from true science but from positive atheism. Weber is not entirely happy in wearing the yoke of atheism but he feels unable to shake it off.

Although an essential element of Weber's ideology implies that preceding religion, philosophy and morality cannot be objectively based, there is an aspect of his view of man's fate, developed under the influence of historicism, which appears to have different and incompatible implications. The element of historicism in Weber might be taken to involve the postulate that the 'necessity' to impose ideological illusions upon ourselves — in order to replace the religious philosophical and moral 'delusions' of the past which fate has forced us to abandon — is a necessity for our age but not perhaps for other ages either in the past or in the future. Hence we might be led to suppose that Weber's system could envisage at least the *possibility* of an advent of genuine, objectively true (say, Christian) faith and morals *in the future*. Yet this position — which would be incompatible with Weber's own ideological commitment to unbelief — is not properly held by Weber. The reason is evident. For, if, as Weber supposes, there were even one period — namely, Weber's own age — in which objective faith and morals could be legitimately excluded or forgotten in terms of some kind of human necessity, then objective faith and morals would not be possessed of universal validity, which is only another way of saying that they would not be true.

Accordingly, Weber is committed to holding that an habitual or general necessity to resort to ideology has always really characterised the human condition but that this necessity is, in modern times, rather generally *recognised* as an inescapable feature of life. Accordingly, in the secularised world of modern man, it is supposed that there are virtually no witnesses prepared to give evidence against the commission of the supposedly 'necessary evil' of resorting to ideology. All secularised men are involved in a practice which threatens to become general and (given the atheist's denial of the existence of a divine Judge) the 'necessary evil' can no longer be indicted. Yet, despite this modern sociological reinforcement for an impenitent resort to ideology, Weber cannot really succeed in concealing from himself the tragedy of his condition. His nostalgia for Christianity is a symptom of his intellectual disorder but such nostalgia is without efficacy in the right ordering of the intellect. Weber allows himself, as we have seen, to be dragged along behind the chariot wheels of an advancing atheistic humanism.

Strauss recognises the existence in Weber of a principle of ideological necessity when he suggests that 'The final formulation of Weber's ethical principle would ... be "Thou shalt have preferences" an Ought whose fulfilment is fully guaranteed by the Is'.[18] Weber seems to suggest by implication that we cannot be criticised for resorting to ideology as such because the resort to ideology as such is not voluntary but necessary. In reply to Weber, one might recall the observation of St Augustine that sin is so voluntary that, if it were not voluntary, it would not be sin. Similarly, the resort to ideology as such is — in truth — so voluntary that, if it were not voluntary, it would not be ideology.

Weber's erroneous teaching on necessity may be formulated as follows: 'Ideology is to be generated under necessity and not to be generated without necessity'. Weber supposes, in effect, that there is an habitual and general necessity to have recourse to ideology as such and this 'necessity' presides as an irrational 'first principle', as an underlying erroneous 'value' or as a false 'god' whose false 'prophet' is Weber himself. Yet this 'principle', 'value' or 'god' does not and cannot preside over an ordered hierarchy of other 'principles', 'values' or 'gods'. On the contrary, Weber's assumption concerning the habitual or general necessity of ideology as such presides over the disorderly incidence of cases of a supposed actual and specific necessity to choose *this* ideological value rather than *that* one in order to ensure that *some* value-choice is actually made for the purposes of action here and now. One might designate these two types of ideological necessity in Weber as *necessitas in habitu* and *necessitas in actu*.

This twofold ideological 'necessity' comprises a 'strong' necessity to have resort to ideology as such and a 'weak' necessity to choose *some* specific ideological value and this twofold necessity corresponds, in a certain way, with Weber's doctrine of the heterogeneity of 'logically possible' ideological value-choices. Hence we shall not be surprised to find paradoxes in Weber's 'ideological necessity' just as there are paradoxes in his 'ideology of the ideologies'.

It is the teaching of St Thomas Aquinas and of the Council of Trent that, in consequence of original sin, human nature is wounded and weakened but is not put fundamentally out of order. In assuming that man is inherently subject to 'ideological necessity', Weber is attributing to man a condition of 'ideological bondage' in so far as Weber misinterprets the ontological status of the actual bondage of the human condition. In so far as he implicitly presupposes a fundamental ontological disorder in man, Weber does not really deny the tragedy of his doctrine of the condition of man in general and modern man in particular. Moreover, from the standpoint of atheism, Weber does not very seriously expect to 'overcome' the 'ideological bondage' which he has envisaged. In this respect, Weber's ideological perspective differs from those of Nietzsche and Marx who entertain a vain expectation to 'overcome' decisively the supposed 'ideological bondage' by resort to a radical ideological dynamism. In truth, if *per impossibilia* this 'bondage', supposedly intrinsic in the historical actuality of man, were found to be present, it could never be overcome either by resort to ideology, however radical or dynamic, or by any other means.

Despite their general incompatibility with Weberian ideology, the ideologies of Nietzsche and Marx imply two different criticisms of

Weber's twofold 'necessity' and his ideological heterogeneity. Nietzsche upholds one ideology of the future envisaged by the superman who purports to overcome both the hesitations and the necessities of modern man. Marx seeks to promote a so-called 'practical-critical activity' — which is, in fact, an ideological conception — which he commends as both necessary and efficacious. Weber is in difficulties in relation to Nietzsche because Weber is himself both a Nietzschean and a pre-Nietzschean at the same time. Weber is in difficulties in relation to Marx because he is driven to accept Marxism as a 'legitimate' value-choice whilst, at the same time, his system also necessarily involves the rejection of Marxism.

Nietzsche advanced an ideology pertaining to the 'substitute intelligence' of the superman which is elicited when all preceding truth and morality accepted by human intelligence has been repudiated and surpassed. There is a pale reflection of this Nietzschean 'substitute intelligence' in the actual and specific necessity in Weber's perspective. For Weber, as for Nietzsche, ideological choice was a 'creative' act and, consequently, although Weberian ideological choice takes place under the sign of necessity, the actual specific ideological choice is nevertheless a creative choice which supposes that man has usurped the creativity of God. Like Nietzsche, Weber presupposes that man's conjectures should not go beyond his creative will[19] and that this is what is meant by limiting one's conjectures to what is 'conceivable'. Despite these similarities, however, Nietzsche would have regarded Weber's pale imitation of his doctrine as quite inadequate because an actual and specific ideological choice in Weber's perspective does not even claim really to 'overcome' nihilism and really to 'transcend' the necessities of human bondage.

Marx bases his teaching on a scientism which comprehends 'practical-critical activity' in terms of an emergent 'substitute-intelligence of nature'.[20] In the centuries before Marx, modern political thought had already abandoned, in progressive steps, the right use of human intelligence and this process was concluding with the substitution for right reason of what Aristotle designates as the 'substitute intelligence of nature' not found in man but in sub-rational creatures lower than man. In establishing the content of this sub-rational 'norm' for man, there is an implicit reference to actual or average or debased practice rather than to a practice which is truly reasonable. There is a pale reflection of this Marxian 'substitute intelligence' in the human condition of habitual and general necessity which Weber envisages as characterising the 'natural' sub-rational condition of man in respect of 'values' generally. Again, Marx, like Nietzsche, would have regarded this pale reflection of his doctrine as quite inadequate because Weber's characterisation of man's 'natural' sub-rational condition does not even claim really to achieve the 'naturalisation of man' and thereby definitively eliminate or surpass the varieties of preceding ideological choices.

Of course, it might be argued, on behalf of Weber, that Nietzsche cannot simply rest his doctrine upon the 'substitute intelligence of the superman' because the natural world will still exist if and when the superman emerges. Similarly, Marx cannot simply rest his doctrine upon the 'substitute intelligence of nature' because Marx envisages not merely the 'naturalisation of man' but a 'socialised humanity' — acting as if it had usurped the divine prerogatives — establishing the 'humanisation of nature'. Accordingly, the Nietzschean and Marxian criticism of Weber's twofold ideological necessity must presuppose some kind of synthesis — not found in Weber — of the two types of 'substitute intelligence'. Certainly, nature 'has become a problem for Nietzsche'[21] but he seeks to cope with it by characterising the natural sciences as fictions and by assuming 'nature' in some way to the invented activity of the superman. Marx purports to solve the problem by postulating the achievement of an 'identification' or 'coincidence' of the two substitute intelligences whereby the supermen who constitute 'socialised humanity' will exercise the 'substitute intelligence of the superman' whilst achieving a complete consubstantiality with sub-rational nature.

Accordingly, Nietzsche and Marx each chose his own ideology — and rejected all religions, philosophies, moralities, *and all ideologies other than his own* — in his one (irrational) ideological choice. In each case, the choice of ideology as such and the choice of the preferred ideology (Nietzschean or Marxian as the case may be) is deemed to be one single choice. For the Nietzschean, the ideological choice of the superman is not considered in terms of the habitual or general necessity arising from modern nihilism but as 'overcoming' that necessity. For the Marxian, the twofold ideological necessity of Weber is fused — as it were — into one single ideological necessity to become a Marxian. Accordingly, the radical or revolutionary ideologist — such as Nietzsche or Marx — will purport to 'overcome' by one unique ideological choice the tragic condition of bondage which would otherwise be simply admitted, as it is postulated by Weber, in terms of an habitual and general necessity. Consequently, from the standpoint of the radical or revolutionary ideologist, Weber's first, supposedly necessary, choice of ideology as such must appear ineffectual and, in a sense, *opposed in principle to ideological effectiveness as such*. This 'ideological ineffectiveness' is recognised — within a perspective which is not Thomistic — by T.B. Bottomore who observes that:

> Weber, notwithstanding his own injunctions, showed himself
> to be incapable of choosing, in a coherent and consistent way,
> the political god he would serve; and ... the wavering god which

can be elicited from his writings is at least as 'unrealistic' as those he rejected.[22]

If there is a correlation, and a kind of mutual implication, between the two types of 'substitute intelligence' employed in atheistic ideology generally and the two levels of 'ideological necessity' in the doctrine of Max Weber, there appears to be a further correlation between the two types of 'substitute intelligence' and Weber's two types of ideological ethics, namely, the ethics of responsibility and the ethics of absolute ends. The ideological ethics of responsibility involve a quasi-sociological responsibility to 'history' in a way which is somehow concomitant with the quasi-biological 'responsibility' for the process of (sub-rational) nature involved in the 'substitute intelligence of nature'. Correspondingly, the ideological ethics of absolute ends — involving consciously 'value-creating' acts intended to determine a new course (whether for the individual, for 'history' or for 'nature') — is correlated with the 'substitute intelligence of the superman'.

Although there would appear to be an inferred correlation, in Weber's system, between the two levels of ideological necessity and the two types of ideological ethics, such a correlation is, nonetheless, logically untenable. In so far as the typology of ideological ethics ('responsible' and 'absolutist') pertains to Weber's actual and specific ideology, it would be internally inconsistent for Weber to characterise his habitual and general necessity (even partially) in terms of conceptual 'types' drawn from value-choices made under his actual and specific necessity. This internal inconsistency appears to be simply a particular illustration of the impaired generality of Weber's concept of the general necessity of resort to arbitrary value-choice. For even if Weber's position were to be evaluated simply in its own terms, it would not be possible to conceal its inherent structural defect. The defect is this: Weber's doctrine of the general necessity of resort to ideology is formulated *as if* it possessed some general validity anterior to the actual imposition of specific value-choices, whereas, in fact, the general doctrine is really advanced as a function of, and in terms of, some of Weber's own actual and specific value-choices. In other words, Weber is faced with the dilemma that his system requires him to accept and to reject, at the same time, the distinction between meta-ideology (for example the doctrine of habitual and general ideological necessity) and actual and specific ideology.

Given the structure of Weber's thought, his first order value-choice purports to provide the context for all second order value-choices. At the same time, it is inevitable that some of Weber's second order value-choices will help to frame a vision of the world of values in which his first order choice of ideology as such must find its place. In other words, certain second order choices necessarily involve interpretations which reflect back, in a logically illegitimate way, upon the first order choice of ideology as such and its significance in Weber's whole ideological vision of the world. Evidently, however, any such reflexive application of second order value-choices upon the underlying first order choice cannot have the character of a foundation or a justification.

It is one of our conclusions, then, that the inter-relationship between first order and second order ideological value-choice is, in Weber's system, inherently self-contradictory. Another of our conclusions is that the interrelationship between Weber's two levels of ideological necessity is inherently self-contradictory. The arguments in support of these specific conclusions about the structure of Weber's system constitute particular applications of the general principle that ideology cannot provide an intellectual justification for ideology.[23] More fundamental than the internal inconsistencies in Weber's system is the fact that his entire ideology is falsified in so far as it is subject to the inherent defect of all substantively ideological thinking, namely, that it does not even claim to be ordered ultimately to the truth.

Notes and references

1   See D. Henrich's contribution in *Max Weber and Sociology Today*, O. Stammer (ed.), Oxford, 1971, p.70.
2   L. Strauss, *Natural Right and History*, p.73.
3   Ibid., p.74.
4   *From Max Weber*, p.154. (Weber fails to recognise the distinction between what is *above* human reason and what is *contrary* to it.)
5   See the fatal formulations of the atheist V. Gardavsky in *God is not yet Dead*, Harmondsworth, 1973.
6   See W.J. Mommsen, 'Max Weber's Political Sociology and his Philosophy of World History', *International Social Science Journal*, vol.17, 1965, p.26.
7   See discussion of differing types of ideology in paganism, Christian heresy and modern atheism, in E.B.F. Midgley, 'On "Substitute Intelligences" in the Formation of Atheistic Ideology', *Laval théologique et philosophique*, October 1980, pp.239–53.
8   W.O. Martin, *Metaphysics and Ideology*, Milwaukee, 1959, p.73.
9   See discussion in R. Bendix and G. Roth, *Scholarship and Partisanship*, London, 1971, p.92.
10   Ibid., p.93.
11   A.W. Gouldner, 'Anti-Minotaur: The Myth of a Value-free Sociology' in I.L. Horowitz (ed.), *The New Sociology*, New York, 1964, pp.196–217.

12 T.S. Simey, 'Max Weber: Man of Affairs or Theoretical Sociologist?', *Sociological Review*, vol.14, 1966, pp.303—27.

13 K. Jaspers, *Leonardo, Descartes, Max Weber, Three Essays*, London, 1965, p.267.

14 C. Péguy, *Cahiers de la Quinzaine*, IX, 1, Paris, 1907.

15 Bendix and Roth, *Scholarship and Partisanship*, pp.56—7.

16 See E. Topitsch's analysis in *Max Weber and Sociology Today*, O. Stammer (ed.), p.10.

17 See Bendix and Roth, *Scholarship and Partisanship*, p.92.

18 Strauss, *Natural Right and History*, p.47.

19 See discussion of Nietzsche's position in E. Voegelin, *Science, Politics and Gnosticism*, Chicago, 1968, pp.54—5.

20 See C.N.R. McCoy, *The Structure of Political Thought*, New York, 1963, chapters IX and X and earlier on p.197.

21 See L. Strauss, 'Note on the Plan of Nietzsche's *Beyond Good and Evil*', *Interpretation: A Journal of Political Philosophy*, vol.III, Winter 1973, p.105.

22 T.B. Bottomore in *New Society*, 13 April 1972.

23 W.O. Martin, *Metaphysics and Ideology*, p.73.

Conclusion

In conclusion, some main points in the evaluation of Weber's ideology will be recapitulated very briefly in order to place this critique even more firmly in the context of the Thomistic critique of ideology in general.

Contrary to many superficial appearances, the most fundamental debate of our times (however much it may be obscured by contemporary diversions and anachronisms) arises from the confrontation between the theistic wisdom of Thomism and the atheistic ideologies.[1] The philosophical/theological synthesis of Thomism envisages two harmonies or 'economies': one concerning the immutability of true natural moral law and the fundamental homogeneity of its applications and developments in the varied states or conditions of humanity; the other pertaining to the fundamental unity of true divine revelation promulgated at the various stages of sacred history. Modern atheistic ideology in general rejects these two true economies and it seeks to replace them, or to fabricate substitutes for them, by means of a radical ideological transvaluation of values already understood or misunderstood in other phases of the intellectual history of humanity. Consequently, in so far as Thomism teaches that the two true economies derive from their ultimate source in the eternal law, atheistic ideology will be driven, consciously or unconsciously, to seek in vain some kind of non-eternal ideological substitute for the ultimate eternal source of intellectual unity.

Given that the human intellect is capable *per se* of knowing the natural moral law, and since there is, in this life, sufficient promulgation of at least indispensable faith, ideological distortion of either of these kinds of truth will never be objectively justified. The modern atheistic phase in the ideological rejection and transvaluation of the economies of the eternal law represents a kind of ambiguous consummation of other phases of ideological error. In consequence of actual human ignorance concerning the two economies (and especially of the economy of revelation), the ideological rejection and transvaluation of fundamental truth proceeds always, to some degree, in the dark: it is a kind of anticipation of some possible deeper or more irrevocable revolt. Even in the case of men who receive no human promulgation of either the specific revelations received by Abraham and by the prophets or the revelation transmitted through Christ to the Church, ideological error concerning fundamental truth will always involve a distortion of revealed truth which is a kind of heresy. Finally, the ideological distortion of divine truth (whether naturally knowable or divinely revealed) involves a kind of rejection of God which proceeds somehow as if God does not exist. Hence the ideological rejection and transvaluation of fundamental truth is not only anticipatory and at least implicitly heretical; it is also at least potentially atheistic.

All these three aspects are always present, either explicitly or implicitly, in every phase of man's ideological enterprises. However, in pagan antiquity, the polytheistic ideologies are predominantly anticipatory. Ideological thinking immediately parasitic upon the Judaeo-Christian revelation is primarily heretical. The modernist phases of ideological transvaluation comprise a series of intellectual transit camps leading to the emergence of ideologies which, despite their inescapable eclecticism, are primarily characterised by a specific and explicit atheism.

The deliberate introduction of fictions into the philosophical sciences in recent centuries has sometimes encouraged the illusion that the changes introduced by the modernist intellectual enterprise were merely methodological and not substantive in character. In truth, however, when Grotius sought to revise the theory of natural law on the basis of a fictional hypothesis about the non-existence either of God or of providence, he promoted a change which was not only methodological[2] but also ideological in character. Accordingly, modern individualism is not found to be a merely methodological individualism but rather an individualism which includes substantive errors both in social philosophy and even in metaphysics. In the course of an exploration of Weber's teaching, J. Rex does not deny that the teaching of the Enlightenment is ideological and he also admits that the teaching of revolutionary Marxism is ideological.[3] However, he seeks mistakenly to maintain that Weber's sociological nihilism is not a source of ideology. In truth, Weber conjoins an individualism and a political absolutism or collectivism, neither of which are merely methodological in character. Indeed, the conjunction of these two doctrines in Weber is an apt illustration of E.J. Roesch's thesis that individualism necessarily leads — in the mind of anyone who rejects political anarchy — to some kind of absolutism or collectivism which is, in a broad sense, totalitarian in tendency.[4] It is because modern liberalism has failed to understand the factor of continuity in modern ideology that it has failed to recognise that the various forms of irrationalist totalitarianism have been occasioned by the nihilism of positivistic liberalism itself. For the same reason, modern liberalism has failed to identify properly the tendency towards, and the element of, absolutism or totalitarianism in even the 'moderate' atheistic ideological 're-enchantment of the world' envisaged in Weber's teaching.

If we correct the error of liberalism and take care to identify the factor of continuity in the modernist intellectual enterprise, we shall recognise that the distinction between the twin aberrations of ideological traditionalism and ideological modernism cannot be profound or absolute.[5] In so far as there is an underlying solidarity in the ideological reaction against fundamental truth in all phases of human history, the ideologies of traditionalism and modernism are always potentially or actually allied against the fundamental truth which they both seek to reject and to transvalue. Consequently, we are not surprised to find that specifically modernist ideologies comprise some kind of pastiche of modernist scepticism or relativism with some content of 'traditionalism' in the form of a modernist transvaluation of pre-modern teachings. The factor of relativism in modern atheistic ideology is anticipated, in a certain sense, in the polytheism of pagan antiquity. Certainly, as we have seen, the heterogeneity of values, postulated in the ideologies of Weber and others, embodies a pattern of value-judgements which bears a kind of structual resemblance to pagan polytheism. The archetypal pagan polytheistic ruler is not a man who desires to know the truth about religion but is rather a man who is anxious to get out of a political difficulty. Consequently, such a pagan ruler runs backwards and forwards in perplexity offering incense first to one god and then to another.[6] This ideological perplexity and reaction to the supposed conflicts among the imaginary gods of pagan antiquity is a remote anticipation of the perplexity and reaction of the Weberian ideologist to the heterogeneity of subjective value-choices envisaged against the background of a modern atheistic nihilism.

The role of Protestantism in the pre-history of atheistic ideology is a commonplace in the history of ideas. We have considered at some length the influence of, and the transvaluation of, specifically Protestant ideology in Weber's atheistic ideology. We have seen that

Weber's reluctant rejection and transvaluation of Christian beliefs and values, already somewhat transvalued by Protestantism, had contributed largely to his complex ideological stance involving the denial of any fundamental truth in ethics, philosophy and theology. We have observed how Weber comes to fabricate or 'create' an 'ideology of the ideologies' which leads him to adopt an approach, both to pre-modern thought and to atheistic ideologies other than his own, which is ambiguous and self-contradictory. Although some commentators have praised the ambiguity and contradictory character of Weber's thought, we have not seen fit to do so.

In purporting to promote or to acquiesce in the supposed 'demystification' of the world, modern atheism has not undertaken a pursuit of values knowable by reason alone. We have seen that, in rejecting the true religion, modern atheism has undertaken a kind of 're-enchantment of the world' with ideological values which are not supernatural and religious but irrational and quasi-magical in character. Within this class of atheistic mystifications, we have encountered Weber's peculiar notion of 'religious and ethical values' which are supposed to be both genuine and not true at the same time. The various positions adopted by Weber evidently lead his successors to contemplate a choice among the differing elements, aspects or phases of his ideological teaching on ethical values.

A. Mitzman has indicated how Weber's approach to private morality became modified so that, beginning with a kind of 'asceticism', he moves towards a kind of 'mysticism'.[7] Mitzman has also indicated the rapports which exist between this process of intellectual change and the changes in Weber's attitudes and his personal behaviour in the field of sexual morality. Although Weber employs a reminiscence of non-modernist norms and beliefs, his successive invocation of a supposed 'asceticism' and a supposed 'mysticism' involves no true recourse to the Judaeo-Christian tradition or even to philosophical theism or the natural moral law. Weber's ethics include, at most, only an essentially modernist invocation of a purely ideological traditionalism. Accordingly, despite the reminiscence of religious values, the change, in Weber, from 'asceticism' to 'mysticism', which Mitzman has described, is a change within the spectrum of values which are basically modernist and atheistic. Thus Mitzman is mistaken when he suggests that the values of 'mysticism' in Weber were in some real sense 'truly Christian'. In fact, Weber's 'mysticism' reminds one of the false autonomous 'mysticism' of Rousseau. Weber's 'asceticism' reminds one of the autonomous secular ethics of Kant. These moments in Weber's thought, which echo the modernisms of Rousseau and Kant, are reasserted, in the context of post-Nietzschean atheism, as a transvalued pseudo-asceticism and pseudo-mysticism which prescribe the false rigour and the false indulgence of a purely ideological system. Against the background of the changes in Weber's successively erroneous attitudes to sexuality, we encounter a kind of inhuman 'asceticism' which is not unconnected with the genesis of the superman and a kind of earthly 'mysticism' which is deprived of its truly religious significance.

In evaluating Weber's teaching, J. Rex seems to suppose that the alternative to the various types of ideological sociology must consist in a sociology which is somehow based upon nihilism.[8] In reality, the nihilism of modern atheistic sociology (including that of Weber) is never a purely methodological nihilism. In so far as modernist nihilism is constitutive of a sociology, that sociology will embody a scientism which is, at least, incipiently ideological in character. We have previously indicated (in chapter 2 and elsewhere) that the valid special sciences and the valid philosophical sciences respectively postulate each other. In so far as nihilism is a grave philosophical error it will engender a basic disorientation of both the intellectual synthesis of, and the intellectual distinction between, philosophy and the special science of sociology. Neither Weber nor Rex nor any other modernist can validly escape from the consequence that 'nihilistic sociology' involves a fundamental error both in philosophy and also in sociology.

It is interesting to note that Rex himself seems to admit, in effect, that Weber's nihilism was not merely a matter of sociological methodology. Rex says that Weber 'seems eventually to have accepted in practice a very radical relativism akin to what we have called moral nihilism'.[9] Although Rex seems to concede that his own and Weber's concept of 'nihilistic sociology' involves the denial of any objective or true morality, he desires, following Weber, to insist that his nihilism is not inconsistent with our having a 'profound moral purpose'. In taking a stance of this kind, both Rex and Weber are committing themselves, in effect, to a quasi-Nietzschean atheistic quest for ideological norms beyond good and evil.

In order to argue at all plausibly that Weber's 'nihilistic sociology' is not ideological, Rex would have needed to show that it was not designed to subserve Weber's substantively ideological theses. Certainly, Rex argues that 'nihilistic sociology' of the Weberian type is a diagnostic technique which does not prescribe remedies for social ills. Yet, in so far as this diagnostic sociology implicitly denies the validity of true wisdom, morality and social philosophy, it is certainly not free from ideological motivation and has therefore already sought to begin to 'overcome' or to 'go beyond' nihilism in some quasi-Nietzschean sense. Certainly, this diagnostic sociology of Weber and Rex, considered in itself, does not provide a sufficiently specific basis for practical decision-making. Indeed, this somewhat scientistic sociology itself implies a supposed requirement for a more specific content of ideological 'values' in order to extend the sociological diagnosis into the explicit study and prescription of social remedies. In the cases of both Weber and Rex, their fundamental doctrine of sociological science and their more ideological value-judgements both presuppose and contradict each other at the same time. These considerations are logically connected with the argument which we have sufficiently expounded to the effect that Weber's 'ideology of the ideologies' is both fundamentally untenable and even internally inconsistent.

Rex recognises that Weber's sociological methodology incorporated elements which might be thought to belong respectively to a phenomenological and to a positivistic approach. Rex appears to commend this eclecticism in suggesting that 'We do not need ... to take a stand either for phenomenology or for the positivistic study of behaviour. Both have their uses ....'.[10] Rex goes on to discuss the later development of Weber's sociological methodology which he considers to be important. It seems sufficiently clear, however, that nihilistic positivism on the one hand and as an eclectic approach to ideology conducted in phenomenological terms constitute quasi-permanent parameters of Weber's doctrine. We have seen that certain basic dilemmas which Weber failed to resolve were built into the very structure of his scientistic and ideological doctrine. The positivistic element in Weber's thought tends to eliminate meaning; the phenomenological element tends to provide for ideological meanings but to eliminate true meaning. Hence the two elements do not collaborate in the search for truth. Rather do they reinforce each other in the work of rejecting and transvaluing true philosophical and theological meaning.

In common with ideologies generally, modern atheistic ideologies will differ from each other in the emphasis placed upon each of two factors, namely, the false relativisation of values and the pseudo-dogmatic imposition of specific false ideological 'values'. Amongst atheists such as Comte, Marx and Nietzsche, there is a great emphasis upon pseudo-dogmatic ideological 'values' advanced against the background of nihilism. Criticising the internal incoherence of modernist rationalism, Nietzsche seeks to 'overcome' the nihilistic tendency of modern rationalism by a means which really involves the aggravation of that tendency. Exulting in man's animal body as if it were sub-human and in acts of irrational will attributable to a supposed super-man, Nietzsche confidently envisages an ideology which is represented at once as the philosophy of the future and the supreme manifestation of the supposed 'eternal return' allegedly prefigured especially in Heraclitus. The French atheist, Michel Foucault,[11] has traced the history of the modernist experiment and has especially considered its culmination in Nietzsche. Foucault identifies Nietzsche's strange drive towards a new atheistic manifestation of 'man' but he concedes that any momentary hope that modern atheism might yield an intellectual synthesis has not been fulfilled. If Foucault has remained an atheist, this does not detract from the fact that he has disclosed, more tortuously and more relentlessly than almost any other writer, the radical non-availability of an atheistic synthesis. Foucault has explored the problematic endemic in the modernist experiment, which attempts to cope with an 'empiricist-positivist' and an [entirely secularised and transvalued] 'eschatological' type of knowledge.[12]

Although positivism is nihilistic and nihilism entails nothing, positivistic thought, in practice, is incipiently ideological in the sense that it tends to envisage the replacement of the true philosophy of human nature and the natural moral law by substituting for them, in man, a 'substitute intelligence of nature' which is properly attributable only to sub-rational nature.[13] To the extent that scientistic sociology is not simply positivistic but also phenomenological in character, it will commonly tend to incorporate a more complex and substantive ideological content which attributes to 'man' not only a substitute intelligence of sub-rational nature but also some elements pertaining to the substitute intelligence of some kind of superman. Certainly, the supplementary atheistic ideologies which are parasitic upon scientistic sociology will specifically seek, consciously or unconsciously, to replace the economy of revelation with the substitute intelligence of the superman.

Foucault was not in a position to identify exactly the atheistic ideological revolt as an erroneous rejection of the economies of the eternal law and a vain attempt to undertake an ideological substitution for them. Nevertheless, in recognising the intellectual failure of the pseudo-dogmatic emphases in atheistic ideologies akin to the teaching of Nietzsche, Foucault reluctantly concedes the failure of the modernist and atheistic enterprise. He admits that modernism has been unable to sustain an intellectually viable theory of morality and that it has failed even to uphold a doctrine of human existence. According to Foucault, the inexorable outcome of modern atheism, which claims to have demolished God, is simply the disappearance of man.[14] Thus the admitted non-humanism of structuralism simply illustrates without prevarication what has been implicit in radical atheistic ideology from the beginning.

But, if Foucault has admitted the paradox of those atheistic ideologies which put the primary emphasis upon pseudo-dogmatic ideological 'values', he also implicitly concedes the paradox in those systems which put the primary emphasis upon the factor of nihilistic relativisation of values. Even amongst such atheists as Lévi-Strauss and Weber, in whom the factor of false relativisation is predominant, there is nevertheless a view of the necessity of some resort to some eclectic

157

assortment of ideological 'values' or pseudo-dogmas of one kind or another. In Weber, as in Lévi-Strauss, there are irrationalist ideological elements derived from Nietzsche, Marx and others, in conjunction with an element of pre-Nietzschean modernist rationalism. In advancing their heterogeneous ideological systems, governed in Lévi-Strauss's case by the so-called 'uncertainty principle', Lévi-Strauss and Weber are driven, no less than Marx and Nietzsche themselves, to undertake some kind of impossible non-eternal traditionalist/modernist substitution for the economies of the eternal law. Marx and Nietzsche, in their differing ways, ask us to abandon fundamental truth (together with many past errors) on the assumption that that truth is merely one among many instances of out of date ideology which is to be rejected, superseded and even consummated in some new atheistic pseudo-dogmatic praxis. Lévi-Strauss and Weber, in their differing ways, ask us to accept that fundamental truth is not what it claims to be but is only, at most, merely one somewhat out of date system among many possible systems of heterogeneous ideological 'values'. The invitation issuing from Marx and Nietzsche is the more abrupt; the request of Lévi-Strauss and Weber is the more insidious. Despite the important difference of emphasis between the Marxian/Nietzschean types and the Weberian/Lévi-Straussian types of atheism, they both fail, in their various ways, to achieve a valid and coherent intellectual synthesis.

The resort to irrationalism may take the form of an ostensibly optimistic ideology — as in Marx and Nietzsche — or an admittedly pessimistic ideology — as in Schopenhauer. We have seen that Weber is a somewhat reluctant ideologist (acting under an imagined 'necessity') and, by the same token, his attitude towards his ideology is characterised by a certain pessimism. By comparison with Marx and Nietzsche, Weber might be represented as a kind of 'ascetic' amongst atheistic ideologists. However, true intellectual moderation is absent from atheistic ideology as such. Weber's 'ideology of the ideologies', in putting the emphasis upon its ideologically 'permissive' character, will admit the propriety of evidently non-moderate ideological choices and will postulate the transvaluation of even the moderate realism of the *philosophia perennis* into a subjective ideological value-choice.

The diverse intimations of Weber's ideology are variously explored, exploited and modified by his successors. Rex apparently shares with Weber a preoccupation with implicit assumptions about social and political life which are ambiguous and malleable. Rex also seems to carry forward some of the elements of Weberian ideology in tentative utopian perspectives which move to some extent in the direction of the more radical ideological thinking of Marx. In doing this, Rex develops in a certain direction Weber's uncertain endeavour to incorporate traditionalist norms or reminiscences in a basically modernist system.[15]

Our analysis has previously shown how, despite the potentially totalitarian element in Weber, the complex structure and ambiguous attenuation of his ideological system has played its part in making his thought more accessible and more palatable to certain Western liberals. T. Parsons and others have sought to eliminate much of the tension from Weber's flawed attempt at a synthesis, by more or less gratuitously excising from the Weberian doctrine the elements of tragedy and pessimism. In promoting a neo-Weberian process of 'relativisation', they have sought to render Weber's teaching more pedestrian and 'serviceable' whilst erroneously imagining that this modified product could achieve the 'end of ideology'.[16]

Those sociologists who seek to 'develop' the inner significance of Weber's ideology to yield either an untroubled evolutionary or a drastic and 'effective' revolutionary ideology have evidently abandoned one of the central and crucial elements of his teaching. We have seen that Weber's commitment to atheistic modernism is characterised by a wavering and ineffectual nostalgia for values already upheld in premodern times. These reactions to modernist and pre-modernist or nonmodernist values give rise to a variable 're-enchantment of the world' in a sense which involves a somewhat pusilanimous groping towards a traditionalist/modernist ideological substitution for the fundamental truth of the eternal law. The element of pessimism, in conjunction with a faltering and somewhat despairing desire for the future emergence of new ideological 'prophets', is endemic in Weber's thought and derives necessarily from his premises.

Whether our modern atheistic ideologists adopt an 'optimism' or a 'pessimism' or something of both, they cannot escape their ideological predicament unless they abandon its modernist and atheistic presuppositions. Therefore, when Weber or any other atheist chooses his modern atheistic ideology and accepts its implications, he enters into a kind of bondage in the moral, intellectual and spiritual domain from which there is no deliverance within the field of ideology itself. In such a case, the only authentic deliverance lies in the rejection of the entire ideological enterprise as such. Indeed, Weber himself sometimes seems to be obscurely aware that there is something profoundly questionable about the entire modernist ideological enterprise despite the fact that he continues to belong to it. Weber seems to have had obscure intimations about what he had done and he apparently understood better than some of his disciples some of the consequences of what he had done.

In responding to the bizarre optimism with which Nietzsche advances his irrational 'values' as if they could 'overcome' his nihilism, Voegelin writes with considerable severity as follows:

Does a man really have to make a virtue out of the misery

of his condition, which he perceives to be the graceless disorder of the soul and set it up as a superhuman ideal? ... Let us, with the brutality that the times compel if we are not to fall victim to them, ask if he is not rather obliged to be silent.[17]

Despite the fact that Voegelin's own intellectual position is not very well founded, his rejection of the irrationalism of Nietzsche, the 'pseudo-John the Baptist to the antichrist',[18] is not without reason. When Weber drifts reluctantly into nihilism, he lacks that degree of sustained relentlessness in irrationality with which Nietzsche exults, without compunction, in his drive to go beyond good and evil. This fact may be pleaded in mitigation of Weber's ideological errors but it remains reasonable to ask: Since Weber knew that he had advanced an ideology which could not even claim to be true, why did he not abandon the enterprise? Weber was not in a position to give a satisfactory answer to this question. Admittedly, Weber, unlike Nietzsche, did not expound his ideology explicitly at any great length. Strauss has suggested that 'Weber, who wrote thousands of pages, devoted hardly more than thirty of them to a thematic discussion of the basis of his whole position.[19] There are more pages in which Weber's ideology is implicit. Nevertheless, what Weber does, he does briefly.

Finally, let us recall that, in a time of persecution of Israel, the ancient scribe Eleazar was urged, by certain old friends, privately to bring meat of his own providing proper for him to use, and pretend that he was eating flesh of the pagan sacrifice. It is a temptation to those who still love fundamental truth, amid the pressures of today, to bring forward that truth as a merely private choice and to speak of it as if it were a product of the intellectual sacrifice of Weberian ideology. Why this temptation ought to be firmly resisted has been indicated in this book.

The task of repelling ideology within our modern cultures is sometimes wearisome. It might be possible to appropriate and redirect some words of Weber's and say that it is 'like digging slowly and steadily into hard ground with both enthusiasm and judgement'. Some of the necessary spadework has been attempted in this book. Despite whatever may be deficient in what has been written here, it is hoped that it may suffice, from the standpoint of logic and rationality, to dispose of the ideology to be found in Weber's writings. Of course, even if the Thomistic philosophy were no longer to be commonly denied, true philosophy alone would not suffice, of itself, effectively to exorcise the ideological mentality. This is because the ideological mentality derives not merely from philosophical error but from human aspirations and passions which are not rightly ordered. To complete the task of overcoming ideology, it would be useless for the philosopher to seek the aid of some pseudo-charismatic leader or some ideological 'hero' whom Weber might have occasionally commended to us. The remedy for what cannot be cured by our human efforts does not lie in the desperate superhuman effort of some tragic ideological superman. It lies in a different gift whose source has not been concealed in this book.

Notes and references

1   See my article 'On "Substitute Intelligences" in the Formation of Atheistic Ideology', *Laval théologique et philosophique*, October 1980, pp.239–53.
2   See C.N.R. McCoy, *The Structure of Political Thought*, New York, 1963, pp.191–4.
3   See J. Rex, *Sociology and the Demystification of the Modern World*, London/Boston, 1974.
4   See E.J. Roesch, *The Totalitarian Threat*, New York, 1963.
5   See my article 'Traditionalism and Modernism in Ecological and Liberationist Ideology', *Catholic Social Review*, VI, no.3, Trinity 1977, pp.13–30 and especially p.18.
6   See Catherine Emmerich's meditations on the case of Pontius Pilate.
7   A. Mitzman, *The Iron Cage: An Historical Interpretation of Max Weber*, New York, 1970, ch.7, 'Asceticism and Mysticism'.
8   See Rex, *Demystification of the Modern World*.
9   Rex, *Demystification of the Modern World*, p.92.
10   See J. Rex, 'Typology and Objectivity: a comment on Weber's four sociological methods' in *Max Weber and Modern Sociology*, Sahay (ed.), London, 1971, p.26.
11   See M. Foucault's works, *The Order of Things*, London, 1970, and *The Archaeology of Knowledge*, London, 1972.
12   Foucault, *The Order of Things*, especially pp.305–43.
13   See discussion of the relevant passage of Aquinas's *Commentary on Aristotle's Physics* in C.N.R. McCoy, *The Structure of Political Thought*, New York, 1963, p.197.
14   See Foucault, *The Order of Things* and also his *The Archaeology of Knowledge*, p.211.
15   See Rex, *Demystification of the Modern World*, ch.16.
16   See T. Parsons, 'Value-freedom and Objectivity: Weber and the Problem of Ideology' in *Max Weber and Sociology Today*, Stammer (ed.), Oxford, 1971.
17   E. Voegelin, *Science, Politics and Gnosticism*, Chicago, 1968, p.32.
18   See C.R. Jette, *The Philosophy of Nietzsche in the Light of*

Thomistic Principles, New York, 1967, p.3.
19   L. Strauss, *Natural Right and History*, p.64.

Index of names

Page references to works cited in this Index under Max Weber's name refer either to bibliographical notes to chapters or to significant quotations in the text.

Manning, H.E., Card., 98, 109
Marin-Sola, F., 84
Maritain, J., 8, 15, 40, 69, 74,
   77, 93, 109, 118, 125, 131, 133
Marsilius of Padua, 3
Martin, W.O., 19, 27, 40,
   138–9, 149–50
Marx (& Marxism), ix, 4–6, 15,
   17–8, 38, 41–2, 53, 76–7, 87,
   104, 117, 119–30, 132,
   138, 145–7, 152, 156, 158
Mayer, J.P., 109, 116–7, 132
Midgley, E.B.F., 16, 40–1, 56,
   109, 131–2, 149
Mill, James, 94
Mitzman, A., 56, 154, 161
Moehler, J.A., 69, 76
Mommsen, W.J., xii, 52–3, 57,
   66, 68, 77, 85, 116
Munz, P., 14

Neill, T.P., 132
Nietzsche (& Nietzscheanism),
   xiv, 4–8, 10–2, 16, 29–30,
   42–4, 53, 56–7, 61–2, 66,
   76–8, 87–90, 93–4, 101–2,
   104–5, 108–9, 115–22, 127,
   135, 142, 145–7, 150, 154–61

Ong, W.J., 23–4, 26, 40

Parent, A.M., 37, 41
Parsons, T., xi, xii, xv, 159, 161
Paul, St., Apostle, 5, 50, 86, 88
Paul VI, Pope, 84–5
Péguy, C., 142, 150
Pilate, Pontius, 161
Pius,IX, Pope, 76, 85
Pius X, Pope, 79–81, 83–4
Plato (& Platonism), 2, 8, 10–2,
   92
Pufendorf, S., 51

Ramus, P., 26, 40

Rex, J., xv, 152, 155–6, 158,
   161
Rheinstein, M., 57
Rickert, H., 30
Roesch, E.J., 10, 16, 41, 131,
   153, 161
Roth, G., xv, 14, 117–8,
   131–2, 143, 149–50
Rousseau, J.J., 6, 8, 33, 41,
   77, 112–3, 116, 131, 154

Sahay, A., xv, 41, 57, 161
Schopenhauer, A., 28–9, 40,
   43–4, 89, 158
Simey, T.S., 100, 109, 141,
   150
Simon, Y.R., 18–9, 40
Smith, A.P., 41
Socrates, 87–8
Spener, P.J., 43
Stammer, O., xv, 131, 149,
   161
Stammler, R., 115–6, 132
Stark, Werner, 104, 109
Strauss, Leo, vii, xii, 1, 6–16,
   43, 60, 64, 68, 71–2, 77,
   93, 105, 108, 112, 115,
   131–2, 136, 149–50, 162

Taparelli d'Azeglio, 29, 41,
   69, 77
Teilhard de Chardin, 109
Thomas Aquinas, St. (&
   Thomism), 2–4, 9, 11–16,
   20–2, 24–5, 27–8, 35–7,
   40–1, 44–5, 47, 51, 55, 57,
   73, 79, 80, 92, 94, 95,
   105–7, 109, 123, 145, 151, 161
Todd, J.M., 77
Tolstoy, L., 90, 92, 94
Topitsch, E., 150
Treitschke, H. von, 99, 140
Troeltsch, E., 64, 73–4, 77,
   79–80, 84, 105